David Ross was brought up in Blairgowrie, Perthshire and North Connel, Argyll. After studying history at Edinburgh University and training to be a teacher, he entered the world of journalism, where he worked for his whole professional life. In February 2017 he won the Barron Trophy in recognition for his lifetime achievement in journalism in the Highlands and Islands. In 1986 he wrote *An Unlikely Anger* (Mainstream), about the Scottish teachers' controversial campaign of industrial action.

# HIGHLAND HERALD

## REPORTING THE NEWS FROM THE NORTH

DAVID ROSS

BIRLINN

*For Mary, Calum and Catherine*

First published in 2018 by
Birlinn Limited
West Newington House
10 Newington Road
Edinburgh
EH9 1QS

*www.birlinn.co.uk*

ISBN: 978 1 78027 550 5

British Library Cataloguing-in-Publication Data
A catalogue record for this book is available from the British Library

Typeset by Initial Typesetting Services, Edinburgh
Printed and bound by Gutenberg Press, Malta

# Contents

# List of Illustrations

# Acknowledgements

THIS BOOK WOULD not have been possible without the support and encouragement of senior editors at *The Herald*, particularly Tom Thomson and Graeme Smith, who allowed me to use articles and photographs under copyright. Multimedia editor Craig Alexander and his colleague Colin Mearns have been particularly helpful. Literary editor Rosemary Goring emboldened me. Peter Jolly (my accomplice on so many missions), Cailean Maclean, Greg Fullarton and Dipesh Gosar also provided photographs. The assistance of John McNaught, studio manager at the Highland Print Studio in Inverness, has simply been immense throughout. He also supplied the photograph for the front cover. John Ross (much more of him later) provided wise counsel. Cailean Maclean has helped and advised me on innumerable projects, including this one.

I am indebted to Chris Tyler for allowing me to reproduce a cartoon of his in the *West Highland Free Press*. *Free Press* editor Ian McCormack also deserves my gratitude for help over many years. Meanwhile, Norman Campbell of BBC Radio nan Gàidheal provided invaluable guidance on many matters, as has Hugh Dan MacLennan.

Ian McCrorie was always so generous with his encyclopaedic knowledge of ferries on the Clyde and Hebrides routes. I would often go to him for information. The Papa Westray-based writer and historian Jim Hewitson was my first news editor in the Edinburgh office of *The Herald*, and has long been a trusted adviser. So many members of the Highland press corps, too many to list, deserve my gratitude for their help over the years, including Pete Bevington and Hans Marter in Shetland, especially Stuart Taylor and Ken Jones in Lochaber, Moira Kerr in Argyll and Bill Lucas on Lewis.

I am also grateful to my cousins Marjorie Kennedy, Janetta Tindal and Mairi MacArthur for information provided and encouragement given for this book. The same applies to my sisters Janet Sirrell and Isabelle Macdonald.

Finally I would like to thank all at Birlinn for their advice, encouragement and patience in the production of this book, in particular Andrew Simmons, editorial manager, whose quiet but steady guidance has been much appreciated.

# Foreword

DAVID ROSS IS a man apart – literally so because for several decades he has been reporting and interpreting the Highlands and Islands of Scotland for an audience that is largely based in the country's Central Belt. He is a man apart in another, more important and more personal sense, for he is an authentic character, a natural optimist and a wonderful friend. I write that with total confidence, as I have known him well for many years. We first met as far back as 1975, when I was education correspondent of *The Scotsman* and David was a student leader. In that controversial role he was, unlike some of his colleagues, always effective, reasonable and friendly. Later, when I was deputy editor and then editor of *The Herald*, I became ever more aware of his merit as a journalist and friend.

The Highlands and Islands is a huge beat, almost impossible for one correspondent to cover effectively if you want old-fashioned reporting but also interpretation. David excelled at both. In a sense he explained the Highlands and Islands to the rest of Scotland.

David is the cheeriest of men, always optimistic and always good company. His job at times placed him under severe stress and strain, not least because of the need to travel long distances often on difficult roads in bad conditions. Never once, over several decades, did he complain.

This fine book gives you a keen sense of the Highlands. It is written by an exceptional journalist and an unusually decent man.

Harry Reid
August 2018

# Introduction

THE MAN LARGELY responsible for persuading me to write this book is a consultant medical psychotherapist, but hopefully his professional expertise has not influenced his enthusiasm for this project. I have known Ian Kerr since we were students at Edinburgh University. We have kept in touch ever since and on a regular basis, with telephone calls normally starting with the comparative fortunes of Stirling Albion and Ross County. Every time we have talked these past five years, however, he has also been badgering me to write a book and not to throw away the memories, professional and personal, of the last 30 years as Highland correspondent of *The Herald*. He thought my position had best been defined by the anthropological notion of 'participant-observer' as opposed to that of a detached or remote reporter. Initially I thought I would want a break from writing, but as my actual retirement approached last year, I started to think maybe Ian was right. Mind you, I am not entirely sure this is the book he really wanted me to write, but for all that I am indebted to him for his relentless but comradely encouragement.

There will be some that might be disappointed that I have not tackled, or have just touched on, other important issues about which I have written in the past, from wind farms to red deer numbers; or from the Crown Estate to the impressive Our Islands Our Future campaign conducted by Shetland, Orkney and Western Isles councils. This book can lay no claim to being an exhaustive modern history of the Highlands and Islands. It simply tries to pull together my reflections on some of the most significant issues which have occupied me. Not least amongst these has been the growth of community land ownership, and as I finished writing this book the island of Ulva off the north-west of Mull and its six inhabitants were set to join the ranks of community landlords.

There are people I deeply regret not writing about in the book, such as the late North Strome crofter Angus MacRae, chairman of the old Scottish Crofters' Union. He was a big man in every way: in physique, intellect and character. It has been one of the great joys of my job to get to know so many fascinating characters and tell their stories. There was another MacRae, Calum Og, a renowned GP on Skye and a man possessed with the most wonderful sense of the ridiculous – he once had my mother-in-law believing that he had got a great bargain on his latest Mercedes, having bought it 'from the Argentinian ambassador to Peru'. Then there was the Danish ceramicist Lotte Glob, who lives on Sutherland's north coast and leaves examples of her work, *Floating Stones*, in lonely lochans for the enjoyment of walkers.

It has been a privilege to work in the Highlands and Islands, which have been described as 'Scotland's lungs'. It can be a dangerous place, often attended by tragedy. Too many news bulletins start with deaths on the road, the mountains and at sea. The loss of four young men in the Sound of Iona in 1998, and that of five members of three generations of one family swept away by a storm on South Uist in 2005, are amongst the saddest I covered. They offended against the Hebridean ideal of the young staying or returning to build their lives in the islands.

In 2013 the Highland press corps lost one of our own when Clive Dennier failed to return from walking on the Knoydart peninsula. The alarm was raised when he did not turn up for work at the *Strathspey and Badenoch Herald*. The Highlands also has one of the highest rates of suicide in the land amongst young men. A cruel statistic, which leaves so many families bereft, but is as yet not properly understood.

### *The Herald*

I joined *The Herald* when Arnold Kemp was editor and Harry Reid his deputy. I had been friendly with Harry ever since my days as a student involved in campaigning, when he was the *Scotsman*'s education correspondent. Harry was to become the *Herald*'s editor, and always supported and encouraged me in my career, as he did others. When I was appointed Highland correspondent, Arnold joked that henceforth every place with the 'CH' sound would be my responsibility. He would come north for a visit once a year, when we would head off on different trips so that he would be better informed on Highland issues.

Highly enjoyable times, but they always meant more work for me on our return. On one occasion on these Johnson-and-Boswell-style tours we were invited up on to the bridge of the Caledonian MacBrayne ferry that was taking us across the Minch from North Uist to Skye. This pleased Arnold, but he told me I had to follow up whatever intelligence the skipper was imparting to us as soon as I was back at my desk.

He believed deeply in the importance of good journalism and would always back his staff. That certainly was my experience when I got into scrapes. He was very hospitable, some would say too hospitable. Newspapers can be tough on staff. Whatever his failings, Arnold's *Herald* was a civilised and enlightened place to work, a legacy that Harry protected when he became editor, as did others. That certainly was my view, albeit from 200 miles away. I don't remember falling out too badly even with my line managers, the procession of those who occupied the news editor's chair. It was a position popularly associated with sharp exchanges, but as far as I can recall the worst meted out to me was Bob Sutter yawning very loudly over the phone when I was trying to explain why I thought some crofting story or the like was vitally important.

When I started working in the Highlands, it was long before mobile phones. I was given a bleeper at one point, but it only worked in Inverness, and at that time all my stories seemed to be elsewhere. It was easy to go off Glasgow's radar, but I like to think I only did so rarely. Working at such a distance also meant that I could know people for years, talking to them almost daily on the phone, without actually meeting them. I went down to Glasgow infrequently. When I did, I used to go into the Press Bar in Albion Street and listen into conversations so I could identify long-standing colleagues.

## The poet

This book is also my own small tribute to my late father-in-law, the poet Somhairle MacGill-Eain/Sorley MacLean. I never wrote about him when he was alive, apart from the odd passing reference. It would have been excruciatingly embarrassing for him, and the rest of the family, had I done otherwise. I certainly don't try to comment on the importance of his writing. I am not qualified and am happy to leave that to the likes of Aonghas Phàdraig Caimbeul and Aonghas MacNeacail,

amongst others. It has, however, been an honour to have been associated with him and to write about our relationship. I call him Sorley in
the book, something I never did when he was alive; it was always Sam.
But somehow that didn't seem appropriate. When I met him first his
fame had begun to grow internationally, and he was invited to speak or
be honoured at different gatherings in England, Wales, Ireland, Canada
and France, as well as at home in Scotland. He and my mother-in-law
loved these trips.

The first I heard about Sorley's family – the Macleans of Raasay
– was from my granny on Iona, who had heard of his academic achievements and those of his siblings. Like so many in the Highlands and
Islands she greatly valued education. The first member of the Maclean
family (Sorley latterly spelt his surname MacLean; I don't know why)
I met was Uisdean, Sorley's nephew. It was in the Captain's Bar in
South College Street in Edinburgh. We were supposed to be studying
in the late-night reading room next door. Our books were there even if
we weren't.

In the interests of candour and in anticipation of allegations of
hidden agendas, I would declare that I am a member of no political
party and have not been since I left Edinburgh three decades ago. I
was then a member of the Labour Party (Leith CLP), and before that
I was in the breakaway Scottish Labour Party led by Jim Sillars. I was
also a member of the Young Liberals as a teenager. I was in favour of
'Devo-Max' but voted Yes in the independence referendum of 2014
and Remain in the one on European Union membership in 2016. I
tried to give fair coverage to all the politicians in the Highlands and
Islands, of whichever party or none. It is up to others to say whether I
was successful in that.

# 1

# First Few Paragraphs

IN LATE AUGUST 2017 I finished writing a story about the SNP MSP Kate Forbes raising concerns over staffing levels in a Ross-shire primary school, sent it to Glasgow, and that was it. After more than 30 years I had transmitted my last copy down to *The Herald* and had officially retired. Much of my working life had been taken up with stories just like the one concerning Kate Forbes, involving communities fighting to safeguard their services, the more so in the most remote outposts of humanity in the UK. As it happened, by the end of the day the Highland Council had taken steps to answer the MSP's concerns.

No longer would I have to check local bulletins on radio or headlines in the weekly papers or work out what ungodly hour I'd have to rise in order to get across the Minch or the Pentland Firth in time for a meeting. It was an end to the constant low-level dread that some huge event had just happened somewhere in the Highlands and Islands, and the only person who didn't know about it was the *Herald*'s man in the north.

After my retirement was announced, good wishes followed from many *Herald* readers, including members of the family of Kevin McLeod. They thanked me for my efforts over the years in keeping their search for the truth about Kevin, whom they believe had been murdered, in the headlines. He was found dead in Wick harbour aged 24 in February 1997 after a night out. Police Scotland made an 'unreserved apology' to them just before Christmas 2017 as the latest review of the case said that failures in the initial investigation, 20 years earlier, meant it was uncertain how he had died. In May 2018 police were 'actively investigating new evidence'.

On a happier note, there was cross-party support for a motion tabled in the Scottish Parliament by the Scottish Green Party MSP for the Highlands and Islands, John Finnie, which stated that 'the Parliament notes the retirement from *The Herald* of the journalist David Ross, who has covered the Highlands for the newspaper since 1988; praises his dedication to the region, covering issues ranging from land reform and the environment to transport and Gaelic; further notes his award earlier in 2017 of the Barron Trophy for lifetime achievement in journalism in the Highlands and Islands, and wishes him well in his retirement'.

Both very flattering and much appreciated. My retirement was reported through local news outlets. There was, however, a different reaction at home in Cromarty, where I had lived and worked since 1988, but where it appeared I had been held to have been pretty indolent. I met a man in the local shop with whom I normally discussed football. He had heard of the Holyrood motion and said, 'I hear you are now retired officially. Well you have had plenty practice.' Others present seemed to agree, clearly still unconvinced by the concept of home working.

Apart from a brief period working in Inverness, my base was our house, which for the most part worked well. Every so often, however, combining work and home life in the same building would become complicated. On one occasion I was on the phone to the Crown Office seeking guidance to avoid a possible contempt of court in an article I was preparing. I was rudely interrupted by my daughter Catherine, who had just returned home from the local primary school. She picked up the extension and asked me to get off the line as her friend Vaila wanted to phone home. Nowhere is far from anywhere in Cromarty, and Vaila's home was all of 25 yards away. The official in the Crown Office, however, agreed that Vaila should indeed take precedence over the Contempt of Court Act.

In truth I was leaving behind a job that had taken me from a cliff top on the Shetland island of Unst looking down on Muckle Flugga Lighthouse to the Mull of Kintyre. My bailiwick had been the size of Belgium but with fewer people than Edinburgh. It had thrown up issues of national, and at times international, significance over the past three decades, from the prospects of a nuclear waste dump in Caithness to a super-quarry that would replace a mountain on Harris; and from the creation of a University of the Highlands and Islands to the first wave of wind farms and opposition to them.

Nothing in my early life had suggested I would join the Fourth Estate, nor that I would devote most of my working life to the Highlands and

Islands. I had gone to Edinburgh University to train as a dentist. The training didn't go well and fairly early I realised I had made a pretty poor career choice, and I often found myself in the university library reading books on history and politics, not teeth. Inevitably this was reflected in examination results. The draw of the arts faculty grew irresistible and I transferred to study history. After that it was a year at Moray House College of Education to train as a teacher, but I never taught. My time at Moray House coincided with students occupying colleges of education up and down the land. This was in protest at the lack of job opportunities due to public spending cuts as Britain tried to haul itself out of recession. History and Modern Studies, the subjects I would be qualified to teach, were particularly oversubscribed. It was during that time I first met Harry Reid, the *Scotsman*'s education correspondent, who was to be my future editor. After Moray House I got work on a Job Creation Programme research project run by the Manpower Services Commission, which employed unemployed teachers in Scotland to survey the employment opportunities for young unemployed teachers being offered by the Job Creation Programme. This ludicrous symmetry wouldn't have been out of place in a satirical sketch. It was, however, to give me my first journalistic opportunity.

Part of my job was to write reports in the community education newspaper *Scan*, published monthly by the Scottish Community Education Centre, which at that time was bringing the youth and community work sector together with that of adult education. It was led by the late Jim McKinney, who had been something of a visionary in this field. He was to give me a full-time job with responsibility for editing *Scan*. While I was working there I started doing some freelance reporting for the *Times Educational Supplement Scotland* (*TESS*), courtesy of an old university friend, Neil Munro. He had returned to Edinburgh to join the staff of *TESS* having spent a year editing the Skye-based *West Highland Free Press*. The *TESS* was to undergo staffing changes itself with the departure of its founding editor Colin MacLean and then its deputy editor, the wonderful Iain Thorburn. Neil was promoted deputy and the new editor was Willis Pickard, formerly features editor and leader writer on *The Scotsman*. He appointed me to the staff in Neil's former position, my first real job in journalism. I was to spend nine happy years learning my trade and, more importantly, how this participative democracy of ours in Scotland actually worked.

## A dentist's hands

When I eventually transferred from dentistry to history, it was after taking a year out in what was not then called a 'gap year'. My abandonment of dental surgery was explained by some on my mother's native island of Iona as being due to my hands not being suitable for the tasks that would lie ahead in patients' mouths. It was a kindly, if inaccurate, spin on academic failure by people who wanted the best for children of the island's diaspora. When I was growing up, the island was like a second home to me and my two sisters. Every summer holiday was spent there on the croft at Clachanach that had been home to our mother. It was worked intensively by her brother Neil. Our grandmother, originally from Mull, and my unmarried aunt, Mary, still stayed in the house they had once run as a guest house, where artists would sometimes stay.

When very young Iona meant playing with cousins. Seven others would arrive from Gourock (Lambs, five) and St Andrews (MacArthurs, two) on holiday and two, Uncle Neil's daughters, lived on the island. Looking back, it seems every day was spent at the beach below the croft; my mother was so often in charge that her favoured spot was called Aunty Eilidh's Bay by my Iona cousins Marjorie and Janetta. There were trips in my uncle's motorboat for picnics in more exciting places such as Balfour's Bay on the island of Erraid. This was where in *Kidnapped* Robert Louis Stevenson imagined David Balfour being washed ashore after having been shipwrecked on the Torran Rocks to the south-west. Uncle Neil would usually be working on the croft, so his elder brother Dugald, chief librarian at St Andrews University and wartime officer in the Royal Navy, would often be at the helm on such expeditions (his daughter Mairi was to write well-received histories of the island and its people – *Iona: The Living Memory of a Crofting Community* and *Columba's Island*, both published by Edinburgh University Press).

There were other forms of recreation, including rolling down a hill inside a rusty old oil drum. For some reason the wearing of goggles and a lady's bathing hat was mandatory for those taking the challenge. As my parents were both teachers, the best part of two months, and the occasional Easter break, would be spent there by the Rosses every year. Admiration grew in me of how the islanders would adapt to whatever nature threw at them. The crofters and boatmen were heroic figures in young eyes as they battled through storms in oilskins and waders.

Teenage years were spent trying to help Uncle Neil on the croft, largely haymaking or working with sheep. The high point would be preparing for the lamb sales in Oban. We would gather on the family's second croft on the north-west of the island before getting the sheep and their lambs back to be marked and taken down to a park behind the Argyll Hotel, where they would be held overnight. In the early hours of the morning one of MacBrayne's cargo ships would slip into the Sound of Iona. There was real excitement seeing the *Loch Carron*, *Loch Ard* or *Loch Broom* lying at anchor in the morning light. The lambs would be ferried out in one of the open motor boats normally used to take tourists off the steamer *King George V* on her daily summertime cruises from Oban. My uncle would board the cargo boat and head to Oban with his lambs and we would head back to Clachanach, often charged with checking the 'slochs' at the back of the island to see if any sheep had got lost. These are amongst the more inhospitable and inaccessible places on Iona. On one occasion while checking them with Janetta, we were greeted by a middle-aged woman emerging from behind a rock. She had been staying at the Iona Community and had come out for a late-night walk, only to get lost. But she was convinced that 'David the shepherd boy and his sister' had been sent to take her back. This we did, only to hear that later that day she had chased a holi-daying doctor with a bread knife and had to be taken off the island in a straitjacket.

My uncle also had the grazing of two tiny islands off the west of Iona, and going out in his motor boat to remove or deposit sheep was enor-mously exciting. On one occasion he left his *cromac* behind on one of them. This shepherd's crook had a shaped wooden handle rather than one of horn, and when he returned a year or so later it had been all but straightened by the weather. There must be a metaphor in that about island life.

Coal used to arrive in a puffer which would sail into Martyrs Bay just to the south of the village on the high tide and wait till the ebb left it resting on the sand. Horses and carts, then tractors and trailers, would come alongside to be filled by large metal buckets, which were swung out over the side of the puffer by a derrick. As one bucket was being emptied another was filled by three men with shovels until there was no coal left. I was in one such team with my cousin's husband, Ken Tindal, himself an islander, along with a man from Mull whose name escapes me. I think we held the record for the amount of coal discharged in one tide. I certainly have been claiming as much ever since.

Such memories of Iona have remained with me and certainly helped in my later role as the *Herald*'s Highland correspondent. I knew the difference between inbye land and common grazings, and that between a ewe and a tup. I also learnt how to moor a motor boat, drive an old grey Ferguson tractor and reverse a trailer, although these skills were rarely called on in my journalistic career. But probably most important of all was that I gained some kind of understanding of life on a small island.

Iona, however, could only ever be claimed as a second home. I grew up in Blairgowrie in Perthshire before we moved back to Argyll, where my parents had met. My father, the son of a Presbyterian minister from Perthshire, was a time-served joiner who retrained to become a technical teacher. My mother had gone to the Dunfermline College of Physical Education to train as a PE or 'gym' teacher, as they used to be called. She had started her training in Dunfermline College when it was still in the Fife town. My parents both taught at Oban High School, but part of my mother's job was to travel up the old Connel to Ballachulish rail line and then onwards to Kinlochleven Junior High School for two days of PE classes. They were to begin their married life there after my father returned from the war. They also lived briefly in Glencoe village before heading east.

Blairgowrie was a good place to grow up. My parents were very involved in the nearby St Andrew's Church of Scotland. My father was an elder and my mother used to take the Sunday School. The other great parental focus in the early years was the local Highland Society, which was really an embryonic branch of An Comunn Gàidhealach. It organised ceilidhs and dances. I remember the excitement when Alasdair Gillies would come to sing. My mother was secretary and some of the other officers were also exiled islanders. She was particularly close to a young primary teacher from Barra, Anne Campbell, who was to marry physiotherapist Tom Kearney. One of their sons is actor/presenter/director Tony Kearney. There were people who came down from Strathardle and Glenshee to these social events in Blairgowrie. These were places from which Gaelic had retreated in the not-too-distant past. The 1901 census had 31.1 per cent of residents in Kirkmichael in Strathardle as Gaelic speakers. My mother taught there for some time and she said local people told her Gaelic could still be heard in the main street till the First World War. The figure in 1901 for Glenshee, where my paternal grandfather James Ross had been minister for a time (there was also a Ross Memorial Church named after him in Dalmuir, since renamed), was almost 20 per cent, but some facility in the language survived. The celebrated folklorist and poet Hamish Henderson was taught his first Gaelic phrases there. He and his unmarried mother moved to a rented cottage at the Spittal of Glenshee to get away from her home in Blairgowrie and her family's shame of illegitimacy. Hamish told me of his connection with Glenshee and Blairgowrie during the many hours – too many – I spent in his company as a student in Sandy Bell's Bar in Forrest Road, Edinburgh. Hamish's biographer Timothy Neat starts the first volume of his work on the man in Glenshee, underlining its importance to his subject.

Children from Strathardle and Glenshee attended Blairgowrie High School, being bussed in daily. We would head up the glen for grouse beating in the late summer. For those of us who liked walking, although we would never admit it, this was always seen as a great way to earn 30 shillings. Especially in the mid to late 1960s, when an underage drinker could buy a pint of light for one shilling and tenpence in a public bar, and a bottle of the considerably stronger Carlsberg Special for three shillings and sixpence. The gamekeepers also used to pass round beer and the occasional dram if they had been happy with our day's work, something I would have to hide from my parents. We were paid the same for a day picking tatties at local farms, but there would be no drink, only back-breaking work. Many of my friends would also work picking raspberries and strawberries in the summer, but I think I only did this for one morning when very young. When the school closed for the summer, we were off to Iona.

It was in Blairgowrie I first met somebody who made a living working in newspapers. This was Robert (R.D.) Low, who along with W.D. Watkins created 'Oor Wullie' and 'The Broons' for the *Sunday Post*. He was the father of my lifelong friend Duncan and lived across the wall from us. He once gave me a mention in 'Oor Wullie': 'David Ross is getting to stay up for New Year and he is younger than me.' And my father had his name above a shop in 'The Broons': 'John Ross – Butcher'.

I had already embarked on my ultimately unsuccessful excursion into dental surgery when the family moved back to Argyll, to North

Connel, where our new home looked eastwards up Loch Etive to Ben Cruachan. My father had retired and my mother had been appointed infants' mistress in Dunbeg Primary School. Many hours were spent on the loch in my 12ft clinker-built boat with Seagull outboard engine, my 21st birthday present, later replaced by a 16ft version with inboard engine. I also bought a chainsaw and joined a team of wood cutters who had a contract to fell and extract conifers from the different woodlands managed by the Forestry Commission in the area.

I returned to the woods every university holiday to subsidise student life in Edinburgh, but in truth I loved the work. It was a welcome distraction from the growth of liberalism and radicalism between the reform acts or Anglo-Irish Relations 1918–22. There was something in it about the nobility of hard labour that appealed, the more so that it was done in the Highland landscape. Despite warnings from some, I was never treated badly or differently by my colleagues because I was a student. Some had endured tough lives, but they never seemed to resent my presence. I did, however, often disappoint them in not doing better in quizzes in newspapers. They expected more from me given I was at university. The length of the human intestine was one question which for some reason I always recall failing to answer.

We worked in forests from Ardnamurchan to Glendaruel, sometimes living in a caravan or digs, more often commuting daily and always to the sounds of country and western music, particularly Johnny Cash and Charley Pride. Some of us would socialise together at weekends. One summer we lived in a Forestry Commission house in the tiny settlement of Polloch near Loch Shiel, having been contracted to fell areas of the conifer plantation on the challengingly steep slopes of Glen Hurich. We had a new recruit in Polloch, another student. Ali MacKinnon was from Appin, where his father was farm manager/shepherd for Brigadier Stewart, one of the last of the Stewarts of Appin to live locally. It was decreed by the others that since Ali and I lived in flats in Glasgow and Edinburgh, we should do the cooking. A decision that was later regretted. Ali was studying physiotherapy at the time, but eventually was to become a successful businessman. We remained friends and I was to be best man at his wedding.

Around this time Donald Gillies moved to the area, with his father James taking up the post of postmaster in Oban. Donald was also studying history at Edinburgh University and was also about to go into his junior honours year. We became very close, as did our respective families. I shared a flat with him and his brother John, then a medical student who was later to chair the Scottish Council of the Royal College of General Practitioners. Donald introduced me to my future wife, Mary Maclean, the artist and the youngest daughter of Sorley MacLean. This was in the romantic setting of the bar of the West End Hotel in Edinburgh. They had both taken a course in oral literature and tradition offered by the university's School of Scottish Studies, which Sorley's brother Calum had helped establish. Donald had passed the course. Mary hadn't, helping her decide to leave university and go to Edinburgh College of Art, where she should have gone in the first place, as her father had advised.

In his final year, just a few weeks before his final honours exams, Donald contracted meningitis. He graduated with an aegrotat, an unclassified degree granted to a student who has fulfilled all requirements for graduation but has been prevented by illness from attending the final examinations. He was to be the best man at my wedding. In November 2001 Donald died of an overwhelming meningococcal infection, the same condition he had already beaten more than 26 years earlier. It was almost unheard of, we learnt, to contract this illness twice. Tragically Donald, not for the first time, was to be an exception.

Like me, he also trained as a teacher at a time of few jobs. He spent a few years as a tourist information officer in Callander, St Andrews and Dundee, where he worked for the local council. He had, however, resolved to become a journalist and completed a Pitman's shorthand course at night classes while in Dundee. He gave up the comparatively attractive conditions of local government to become the editor of the Lochgilphead-based *Argyllshire Advertiser* or 'the Squeak' as it has always been known. At the Squeak he was in charge of a staff of one – himself. He later claimed that it was during the Lochgilphead years that he first noticed leadership qualities in himself, although he did concede that discipline was not all it could be in the office. It was also at this time he met fellow journalist Catherine MacDonald, another Edinburgh graduate who was then working on the *Campbeltown Courier*. They were to marry and head to Orkney, where Donald became first chief reporter on *The Orcadian* and then the recognised National Union of Journalists freelance on the island group. It wasn't long afterwards that he and his family were on the move again, back to Argyll, where he and Catherine established the freelance agency Reporting Argyll, working principally for BBC Radio Scotland and latterly the old Grampian Television. With two children, however, Donald thought perhaps it was time to go back to teaching and started working at Oban High School a few months before he died. We lost a dear friend.

# 2

# The *Herald*'s Man in the North

MY PREDECESSOR AS the *Herald*'s man in the north was Stuart Lindsay, who somehow had managed to buy the *Inverness Courier* from its renowned owner and editor Miss Evelyn Barron in 1988. Numerous newspaper companies had coveted the twice-weekly title, which in 2017 celebrated its 200th anniversary. The paper had been in Miss Barron's family since 1865, and it was her life. She was renowned for her forthright and at times eccentric editorials, which she would write in longhand after hearing the last edition of the BBC world news at 10 p.m. the night before publication. She wrote, for example, against the establishment of a university for the Highlands in Inverness, as she believed that young Highlanders should get away and experience life elsewhere. She did not have to worry, as in the 1960s the government chose Stirling over Inverness as the new seat of higher education, although the idea of a Highland university was to be resurrected and realised later. Miss Barron died aged 77 just two years after she retired. She had resisted attempts to buy the *Courier* building by those constructing the horrible concrete headquarters of the Highlands and Islands Development Board round about it in the 1960s.

The paper didn't carry news or photographs on the front page until 1990, but it was an institution. Stuart had a desk in the *Courier*'s office overlooking the River Ness, which *The Herald* rented. That is where I began my tenure on 1 August 1988 (shortly after that I started to work from home). Stuart soon embarked on a modernisation programme, but before that the charming wood-panelled offices and open fires had the feel of another time. This was reinforced for me just around the corner on my first reporting job in Inverness's fine Town House. Here the *Courier* journalists had covered town council meetings over generations, heading back to the office to write their reports. There are still carvings in the wooden surfaces in the press gallery expressing reporters' boredom over many decades. It overlooks the same room where the first-ever meeting of the British cabinet outside London was held. Prime Minister David Lloyd George had called the senior ministers in his Tory–Liberal coalition cabinet to Inverness to discuss events in Ireland, when he was on holiday in Gairloch. The Cabinet was to agree the 'Inverness Formula', which created the basis for discussions with those hitherto in armed struggle against such as Sinn Fein, leading to the Anglo-Irish Treaty. Still on display at Inverness Town House is a facsimile of a sheet of paper passed around by council officer William Bain on 7 September 1921. It was signed by, among others, the future Prime Ministers Stanley Baldwin and Winston Churchill, as well as long-forgotten figures such as the Liberal Scottish Secretary Robert Munro and Sir Hamar Greenwood, the Chief Secretary for Ireland. It was the only time the cabinet was to meet outside London until Gordon Brown took his Labour cabinet to Birmingham in September 2008. When Alex Salmond had taken his Scottish cabinet to the Highland capital a month earlier, the Highland Council representatives got ministers to sign a paper just as their municipal forebears had done in 1921.

## The *Herald* job

I had long held the Highland reporters' posts on *The Herald* and *The Scotsman* to be the most appealing of any in Scottish print journalism. I had never been attracted to the broadcast media, not that I would have had any facility – with my natural tendency to speak too quickly and at times, I am told, rather unintelligibly I was never really radio or TV material. At any rate it was the written word that excited, as did the prospect of writing about the Highlands and Islands.

During my time as a student in Edinburgh in the early and mid 1970s something important was happening in Scotland, which I tried to examine in an article I wrote in *The Herald* on 28 August 1991 about the achievements and significance of the Gaelic rock band Runrig:

> Runrig is now a force in Scotland, and not just a musical one. Its immediate roots are traceable to the first five or six years of the 1970s, when there was an extraordinary burst of intellectual and creative activity in Scotland that was caught between

the political dynamics of Scottish nationalism and Labour's claims on her heart and political tradition. This against the backcloth of Edward Heath's government with its three-day week, UCS [Upper Clyde Shipbuilders work-in from 1971 to 1972 which thwarted the Tory government's attempts to close the yards] and the miners' strike. An integral part of it all was a new focus on the Highlands and Islands. When setting up the Highlands and Islands Development Board in 1965 Scottish Secretary Willie Ross had declared from Labour's front bench that the man on everybody's conscience, was the Highlander. But five, six, seven years afterwards there were still the burning issues of land ownership; of the Gaelic language; of continued depopulation. Others took up the cause.

One who did was the playwright John McGrath, who was born in Birkenhead into an Irish Catholic family. After national service, in 1955 he went to Oxford. As an undergraduate he made his mark both as playwright and director. He went on to work at the Royal Court Theatre in London and then to write and direct many of the early episodes of BBC TV's *Z Cars*. His *Random Happenings in the Hebrides* of 1970 was the first of many plays he wrote about Scotland's troubled history and struggles. A man of the left, McGrath wanted to go further, and in 1971 he set up the 7:84 Theatre Company. Its title was taken from a figure in an article in a 1966 edition of the *Economist* which reported a mere 7 per cent of the UK population owned 84 per cent of the country's wealth (now it is estimated that the globe's richest 1 per cent own half the world's wealth). The new theatre company's strategy was to deliver the socialist message through popular, political theatre in shows at venues normally shunned by established companies.

Its most famous production was McGrath's brilliantly written *The Cheviot, the Stag and the Black, Black Oil*, which started touring in 1973. It told the story of Scotland's exploitation, from the Highland Clearances to the oil boom, through Gaelic song, fiddle music and comedy: a ceilidh punctuated by satirical sketches. Some of the original cast were to have highly successful careers in Scotland and far beyond: Bill Paterson, Alex Norton, John Bett, Dolina MacLennan (whose native Gaelic singing was much admired), David MacLennan and his sister Elizabeth MacLennan, who was John McGrath's wife. It opened in Aberdeen but went on to play in communities throughout the Highlands and Islands, many where there were still folk memories of the Clearances. My wife Mary saw it in Dornie village, where it was later filmed, but for me it was the more traditional thespian territory of the Royal Lyceum in Edinburgh. It was deemed a huge success artistically, and politically. It stimulated much debate. More than 40 years later Dundee Repertory Theatre Company saw the work as sufficiently relevant to return to it, and Neil Cooper, the *Herald*'s theatre critic wrote: 'In the 42 years since, John McGrath and his 7:84 Theatre Company's melding of music hall and political commentary has become an iconic benchmark of how theatre can fuse radical intent with populist heart in a way that has trickled down to the National Theatre of Scotland's equally seminal production of *Black Watch* and beyond. The show more or less invented Scotland's small-scale touring theatre circuit . . .' His counterpart on *The Scotsman*, Joyce McMillan, described it as a 'glorious revival of what's arguably the single most important show in the whole history of Scottish theatre'.

## The arrival of the *Free Press*

The year before the play opened for the first time, the *West Highland Free Press* was launched on Skye by four young men who had met at Dundee University: Brian Wilson, Jim Innes, Jim Wilkie and Dave Scott. Their mission was summarised in the Gaelic slogan on its masthead: 'An Tir, an Canan 'S na Daoine – The Land, the Language, the People', previously the motto of the 19th-century Highland Land League in its fight against the excesses of Highland landlords' evictions. The new paper lived up to the words. With local councils often under the sway of councillors who were also landowners and saw keeping the rates down as their most solemn duty, there were plenty causes to champion right across the region.

At that time, before the local government re-organisation of 1975, Lewis was part of Ross-shire while the remaining Outer Isles, from Harris south, came under Inverness-shire. One story which was particularly celebrated was the paper's pursuit of Sir Hereward Wake, an English landowner who could trace his family back 1,000 years to the ancestor of the same name who had rebelled against the Normans of William the Conqueror. The 20th-century Hereward owned 64,000

acres of Harris and Amhuinnsuidhe Castle on the north-west of the
island. The winding single-track B887 public road to the township of
Hushinish passes right in front of the castle. The *West Highland Free
Press* uncovered a plan whereby Inverness County Council would build
a bypass round the castle so that Sir Hereward would have greater
privacy when he happened to visit. The public purse and Sir Hereward
would split the projected £80,000 bill. It also established that Sir
Hereward, like the chairman of Inverness County Council roads committee, Lord Burton of Dochfour, was an old Etonian and member of
Brooks's, a club for gentlemen in London. The idea of the two chatting
about their road plan over brandy and cigars at the socially prestigious
St James's Street establishment gained currency. Whether it happened
that way or not, there was such a furore that the road was never built.
That the idea was ever mooted on an island with some of the poorest
roads in the country did little for the image of the many Highland landowners, whether absentees or councillors.

The *Free Press* was decidedly pro-Labour, and of course Brian Wilson
was to become one of the party's MPs and a government minister. But
when the Labour government adopted plans to give crofters the right to
buy their own crofts, becoming owner-occupiers, the paper campaigned
against the move despite many of its readers standing to benefit. The
paper argued it was against the whole spirit and legal basis of crofting
tenure, and that community ownership was the way ahead. The great
fear was that it could have led to significant areas of crofting land being
sold off, not least for holiday houses. The provision was incorporated
in the Crofting Reform (Scotland) Act 1976, but the worst fears were
not realised. The *Free Press* can claim some of the credit for that. At
the time of writing this book, out of a total of 20,566 crofts, only 5,668
were owner-occupied.

### Dancing through history

In the same year as the Crofting Reform Act, James Hunter's book *The
Making of the Crofting Community* was first published by John Donald.
Based on Hunter's PhD thesis, it was a conscious attempt to present,
in an academically reputable way, the history of his people, which he
had first begun to learn from his maternal grandfather from Strontian.
His work directly challenged those established historians who variously

argued that the Highland Clearances never happened; that they had been grossly overstated in oral tradition; or that they were an economic necessity. My father-in-law, Sorley MacLean, reviewed it for the *Times Literary Supplement*, hailing it as 'magnificent, marvellously comprehensive, just and profound'. Hunter had also seen *The Cheviot, the Stag and the Black, Black Oil* when he was working on his original thesis and said it strengthened his belief he was on the right line. It is a book I still refer to frequently, as I do its author's other works. We will return to Hunter later, but one of his subsequent books on the Gaelic diaspora was to take as its title *A Dance Called America*. It was best known as the title of a song by Runrig, who had referenced it from James Boswell's *The Journal of a Tour to the Hebrides* about his trip in 1773 with the celebrated man of letters Samuel Johnson. On 2 October of that year, Boswell, staying at the minister's house at Ostaig, recorded: 'In the evening the company danced as usual. We performed with much activity, a dance which, I suppose, the emigration from Sky [*sic*] has occasioned. They call it "America".' That such a journal entry on the subject of emigration was written at Ostaig on the Sleat peninusla on Skye is perhaps fitting because this was where, a year short of two centuries later, one of the most important modern developments was launched which has given a reason for so many not to leave, but to live and work in Sleat, along with those who have arrived from elsewhere.

### Gaelic's big barn

Merchant banker the late Sir Iain Noble arrived to live on Skye in 1972. He was the nephew of the former Tory Secretary of State Michael Noble. Their family owned the Ardkinglas Estate on the shores of Loch Fyne across from Inveraray. It had been home to Sir Colin Campbell, Sheriff of Argyll, to whom MacIain, chief of the Glencoe MacDonalds, tried to make his oath of allegiance to William III in the last days of 1691 and first few of 1692. Sir Colin was at home and didn't return to Inveraray till 5 January, when he finally received MacIain's oath. The government decided, however, that the old MacDonald had missed the deadline and his people would have to pay a price, which they did in the following month's massacre in Glencoe. Two hundred and eighty years later the man from Ardkinglas had a different mission on Skye.

Sir Iain was a Gaelic enthusiast and he embarked on a fund-raising campaign to convert a farm steading at Ostaig, which was amongst the properties and land he had acquired. He wanted to build 'the first Gaelic establishment of further education in Scotland since the Vikings burned down Columba's abbey on Iona'. The Norsemen no longer posed a threat, but there were others who presented a problem. One of the first people Sir Iain wrote to was the chairman of a distilling company he had dealt with at the bank, but the proposal was not well received: 'He turned down our request for financial support on the grounds that his board believed no advantage would come to the people of Skye from a project designed to resuscitate the Gaelic tongue. He said it was well known that the education of the people of Ireland was greatly held back by a similar policy there.'

Sir Iain loved retelling that story down the years as Skye's Gaelic college, Sabhal Mòr Ostaig (literally 'the big barn of Ostaig'), progressed on its remarkable journey from farm buildings to becoming an integral degree-awarding part of the University of the Highlands and Islands. I recall attending an early conference there, when the estimable Gaelic poet Aonghas MacNeacail (then known to everyone as 'Black Angus') decided to hold the session he was chairing outside. The future of Gaelic education was discussed with hens picking away at the ground beneath our chairs. The college became the major economic driver in the south of Skye and is currently pursuing the development of a new village in partnership with the Clan Donald Lands Trust. It is designed to help reverse the centuries-old trend of emigration, something Skye has been particularly successful at in the last three decades. One of the main foundations of Sabhal Mòr Ostaig's success was the work done by its former director, Norman Gillies, who was possessed of great organisational skills, principal amongst which was the ability to persuade different bodies to invest money, not least the public agencies. Runrig's lead singer emeritus, Donnie Munro, has been Director of Development at the college for many years.

During the 1970s there were other events important to the Highlands and Islands. The new Comhairle nan Eilean Siar (Western Isles Council), established in 1975, joined all the Outer Isles from Lewis to Vatersay as one administrative unit for the first time since the Lordship of the Isles and it quickly adopted a bilingual policy. There was the publication of the retired forester John McEwan's *Who Owns Scotland* in 1977, and the founding of Fir Chlis, the first Scottish Gaelic repertory theatre company. These were all important symbols of a new Highland Scotland being shaped.

## A view of the river

When I started work in the old *Inverness Courier* building looking over the River Ness, I was determined to have nothing to do with the sometimes patronising approach adopted by some media in the south poking fun at the Highlands and Islands and what people got up to, in frequent 'Aren't they quaint?' stories. I have heard a journalist from the south argue that crofters are paid a lot of money so they can enjoy a 'quaint' existence. He didn't think to equate this to the considerably greater amounts of public money which goes to farmers, some of whom over years didn't have to take their slippers off to earn it. I recall quotes rendered in almost music hall broad Scots attributed to a crofter I knew well, whose English was at least the equal of the writer's, but obviously Scots sounded more peasant-like. When John Smith, the late Labour Party leader, was buried on Iona, one article highlighted that he was put to rest near a man who was styled as being the stammering crofter who collected the bins. The man in question I had known well over many years as one of my uncle's best friends. It was true he had a serious speech impediment and that he collected the island's bins, but this was just one of the many contracts this man of great entrepreneurial drive had won. 'A highly successful island businessman' was not a description that would have fitted the caricature of the Hebridean.

Laughing at the people of the Highlands and Islands was not part of my plan. On my first day in the job, however, I got a story on the front page doing just that. A report came in from the Inverness Harbour Trust that the Highland branch of CND had marked Hiroshima Day by floating lit candles on tiny rafts down the River Ness. The fire brigade was called as a ship was loading fuel at Inverness Harbour, and there were fears Hiroshima Day might have been marked by a more spectacular light show than planned.

## The Highland press corps

The men and women of the Highland press corps do not generally patronise the people who are their readers and sources. Most journalists based in the Highlands and Islands assume they have a dual function. They act like others elsewhere, reporting what is newsworthy and holding power local and national to account. In addition, however, they can't help but often see themselves as advocates for their area, particularly when government displays a lack of understanding of the reality of life in the Highlands and Islands. There is a sense of commitment to the communities they serve. This sense has long been strengthened by Gaelic radio, whose journalists have not only served local people but also their culture and tradition. All those covering the whole area need to be trusted in the local communities, in the certain knowledge that there could be some story in the future which requires local assistance. One telephone number can mean the difference between an article's success or failure. Knowing who to phone is the key. There can be a similar reliance on local newspapers. There are around 20 circulating in the Highlands and Islands from Shetland to Kintyre, if those in Moray – the *Forres Gazette* and the *Northern Scot* – are included. Moray was part of the old Grampian Region, which for most of my working life was covered by my friend and *Herald* colleague Graeme Smith in Aberdeen. The *Nairnshire Telegraph* of course served the needs of that county which was abolished in 1975, when it came under Highland Regional Council. Nairnshire is now only really recalled in the title of its weekly newspaper and its Highland League football team, Nairn County.

At times there has been something of a debate within Highland media circles as where the boundaries for the Highlands lie. I have always taken exception to references being made to the Highlands and Argyll, as though the former is quite distinct from the latter. The BBC sometimes says it in its road reports, and you can hear the occasional MSP repeating it along with others who should know better. In reality, they are referring to modern local authority boundaries, but in doing so they distort a couple of millennia of history – a distortion that has been worryingly gaining currency in Scotland. 'The Highlands' in Gaelic is pretty meaningless. The relevant linguistic equivalent is the Gàidhealtachd, 'the land of the Gael', which also embraces the Hebrides. It is still used. The Highland Council's official logo has Comhairle na Gàidhealtachd just below its English title. If 'the Highlands' distinguish anything today, it must surely still be the area that developed from that 'land of the Gael'. Argyll means 'the coast of the Gael', central to the story of the movement of the Gaels from Ireland. Tradition holds that Deirdre of the Sorrows, the foremost tragic heroine in Irish mythology, came to Loch Etive, which is still mostly in Argyll. Dunadd, near Kilmartin, is in Argyll and it was the power centre of the Gaelic kings of Dál Riata between the sixth and ninth centuries. Iona, where St Columba made his home on his arrival from Ireland and where later monks started work on the *Book of Kells*, is still in Argyll. So is Islay, the power base of the MacDonald Lords of the Isles. The Crofters Act of 1886, which effectively created our crofting system, specified it would apply to parishes in Argyll, as one of the eight crofting counties. This became seven when Ross and Cromarty united as one county three years later. If the national Gaelic Mòd has a traditional home, it is Oban. It hosted the first three, and more than any other venue since. Meanwhile, shinty is still played throughout the county. Renowned Highland destinations such as Glencoe and the Ardnamurchan peninsula were in Argyll until local government reorganisation in 1974–75. The Rannoch area, so important to the MacGregor clan's story, was split between Perthshire and Argyll, according to old gazetteers. The idea that Argyll isn't part of the Highlands annoys many, as do the ludicrous signs on the likes of the A9 and the A828 where motorists who have been driving through Highland scenery for hours in Perthshire north of Dunkeld and in Argyll are welcomed to the Highlands. In fact, they are entering the Highland Council area.

## Contacts

Wherever the boundaries, local contacts were/are the lifeblood of journalists covering the area, particularly those locally based. In Caithness I leant heavily on Colin Punler of the *Caithness Courier* and *John O'Groat Journal* and Iain Grant, once local freelance, now editor of those two journals. I rarely went to Stornoway without meeting the BBC's Norman Campbell and Alasdair Morrison (later Western Isles Labour MSP and minister in the Scottish Executive) and asking to be briefed on what was happening, normally in Comhairle nan Eilean Siar (Western Isles Council).

Often when I was out and about I would offer generous hospitality courtesy of *The Herald*, something my line managers in Glasgow encouraged. There was, however, a problem on one occasion when I was in Orkney for two nights and my hotel bill was sent back to *The Herald*. The news editor subsequently received a memo from the paper's director of finance asking why Mr Ross's dinner bill for the first night in Kirkwall was £6.80, but on the second night it was £112. When I explained I had taken the local freelancer David Hartley and his wife Patricia out for dinner, it was agreed that this was a perfectly legitimate exercise. Falling circulation brought an end to such hospitality on most papers.

The Highland press corps was largely locally based, however a few reporters had to work on a pan-Highlands and Islands basis while relying on freelance support in the different communities. Representatives of *The Herald* and *The Scotsman* had to take this wider view. The *Press and Journal* had, and still has, reporters in Oban, Fort William and Elgin, and used to have one in Dingwall. There was a significant BBC presence in Inverness between the English and Gaelic services for TV and radio, and I counted Jackie O'Brien, Iain MacDonald and Craig Anderson as close colleagues. Grampian, now STV, also always had a news team in the Highland capital. When I arrived first it was my old friend Izzie Fraser and today it is the irrepressible Nicola McAlley. Meanwhile, there has always been a MacPhail (Neil) in the engine room of the Highland press at the *Press and Journal* and *Highland News*, and before that as a freelancer.

Almost inevitably the *Herald* and *Scotsman* correspondents saw most of each other, as we were pursuing similar sorts of stories. In 1988, when I started, my *Scotsman* counterpart was Alex Main, who had been the *Daily Mail*'s man in the north over many years. He was also something of a local celebrity round Inverness, having been a star winger with Caledonian Football Club decades before the merger with Inverness Thistle, and then a highly successful manager of the club. He left *The Scotsman* to become editor of Stuart Lindsay's revitalised *Inverness Courier*. Alex was succeeded by Tom Morton, who had come from the *Shetland Times*. Tom and I worked closely, literally as well as professionally, as Tom had decided that Cromarty would be a nice place to take his family to live on taking up the post. He eventually went back to Shetland, then on to a successful radio career. Douglas Fraser, now BBC Scotland's business and economy editor, followed Tom and again we worked closely, he also having chosen the Black Isle as his home. We remain friends. The last *Scotsman* correspondent I worked with was Alistair Munro, who has since gone on to work for the *Press and Journal*.

While covering such a vast beat meant there had to be co-operation between the papers, and indeed with the broadcast journalists, we all got our fair share of exclusives, although obviously this book focuses on *The Herald*'s. My longest-serving partner in editorial crime, some 17 years, was Douglas Fraser's successor John Ross, who had started life on the *Press and Journal*, having trained at Thomson Regional Newspapers' college in Newcastle. Because we shared a surname and were often seen together at press conferences and the like, we were soon being referred to by others in the Fourth Estate as 'Ross and Cromarty', or more frequently, 'the Ross Bros'. The latter gained such currency that some people genuinely came to believe we were siblings. After my son Calum started working on the *Inverness Courier*, this myth seemed to become entrenched. On one occasion a photographer told John he had just missed his nephew, who had been at whatever media event they were attending. John was confused. He did indeed have a nephew living in Inverness, but he was a plumber.

I met John for the first time in May 1988, when we were both covering the General Assembly of the Church of Scotland for our respective papers. John was then working in the *Press and Journal*'s Aberdeen office while I was coming towards the end of a year or so in the Edinburgh office of *The Herald*. This was the General Assembly addressed by the then prime minister, Margaret Thatcher, in her famous Sermon on the Mound, in which she presented theological justification for the workings of the market economy and her government's policies. These were frequently condemned by the Kirk and by other denominations in Scotland, including the Roman Catholic and Scottish Episcopal Churches. John and I bumped into each other at the Assembly's close on the Friday in the Ensign Ewart pub, at the top of the Royal Mile. We were not the only ones who were in this handy hostelry discussing the week's events. John would later return to the *Press and Journal*'s Inverness office, which fairly quickly thereafter went on strike along with the paper's other journalists. He worked for some years with David Love's news agency in the Highland capital, before joining *The Scotsman*.

John and I covered many of the big stories together and seemed to be on the road most weeks, whether it was to Dounreay or Gigha. We used to have to write our stories wherever we could, whether it was on a CalMac ferry crossing the Minch, in our cars in a layby, on a small cruise boat coming back from Isle Martin, in a public bar in Stornoway, a butcher's back-shop in Lochinver or in a range of cupboards and store rooms, including one particularly salubrious one on Eigg.

On one occasion on Arran we took pity on three old gentlemen in a bar who seemed to have a rather threadbare appearance, obviously having seen better times. We insisted on buying them drinks all evening only to discover subsequently they had been directors of ICI and were millionaires to a man. We had travelled to the island to attend a meeting of the Convention of the Highlands and Islands, set up by Michael Forsyth when Secretary of State (more on him later). On this occasion no real news story was emerging from the gathering, only seemingly endless position papers from civil servants and quangos. The meeting was chaired by Donald Dewar, who was then Secretary of State for Scotland. We kept pestering Mr Dewar's press advisers for an interview with him to see if he would give us a news line which would justify having driven over 200 miles to Ardrossan to get the ferry to Brodick. Mr Dewar, a civilised man who was a reader of both *The Herald* and *The Scotsman*, finally agreed. Seconds after he arrived, however, John had to answer a rather urgent call of nature and left me with two tape recorders and a rather bemused Secretary of State.

John of course had many stories about my antics on the road, not least that after earlier celebrations with the redoubtable islander Colin Carr and others, I prematurely set light to the bonfire that was to act as a beacon for communities on the mainland, marking Eigg being taken into community ownership. This may or may not be true, but I take issue with another version of the tale which had me actually falling into the bonfire. There was however a yachtsman who had been viewing the event from his boat anchored a wee bit away. He said later that he assumed it was some form of tribal dance that was being enacted.

On another memorable occasion we visited RAF Saxa Vord on the Shetland island of Unst, the most northerly community in the UK. As one of NATO's most important Cold War listening posts, its radar tracked Warsaw Pact aircraft on a daily basis for a half century. But in July 2005 John Reid, the Labour government's Defence Secretary, announced that the island's radar, sited above the Muckle Flugga Lighthouse, would be put on a care-and-maintenance basis from the following April. This effectively was closing the base with the loss of over 100 jobs, including 69 military personnel. *The Herald* and

*The Scotsman* were invited to visit the base as it was run down, and things certainly were running down, not least its security. As we approached the base, where once we would have been challenged by armed sentries, the barrier was up and unattended. We found the guardhouse and went in to announce our arrival and to ask where we could meet the Commanding Officer. We were waved towards a building at the other side of the camp where there seemed to be a lot of desks and filing cabinets, presumably once full of top secret information. There was little sign of human life until we found the CO making a pot of tea, which he invited us to share. Later that day another senior officer asked if we would like to go up to see the radar, which of course we did. We were taken right inside the metallic hemisphere which had covered the rotating radar blades. We asked what range the radar had, and were told that clearly was an official secret 'But if you were to say xxx miles [I can't remember the figure quoted] you wouldn't be far out.' Then it was down into the bunker below, where the command post was located, to see records of all the contacts with Soviet planes, with dates and times over many years. The rundown of Saxa Vord was part of the so-called peace dividend which delivered reductions in military spending at the end of the Cold War. But for some reason our visit reminded me of the Boulting Brothers' 1959 comedy *Carlton-Browne of the FO*, about a former British colony that had been granted independence 50 years earlier, but the Foreign Office had forgotten to recall its governor.

## Runaways

Not every mission was so enjoyable. I myself became the centre of media attention one Monday in March 2003 when I spotted two runaways that police had been hunting for in the Highlands. Schoolgirl Naomi Mills, 15, had left her home in the St John's area of Worcester the previous Friday to walk to school but had never arrived. Her family did not know where she had gone. In fact she and Matthew Brooks, 22, a probationary constable with West Mercia Police, had travelled almost 600 miles to Tongue in Sutherland in a borrowed Vauxhall Astra. The car was recovered from the Kyle of Tongue after it was spotted partially submerged at low tide. They had apparently parked it on one of the slipways beside the causeway, perhaps not realising the tide would take it out on to the sand. There was speculation that the couple might have entered a suicide pact or have feigned suicide so they could start a new life together. Police refused to comment other than to say the inquiry related to missing persons.

It was one of those dry but sunny days at the end of the winter which become bitterly cold as the sun goes down. The media had arrived from all over the UK and awaited development at the causeway across the Kyle of Tongue. A search and rescue helicopter from Stornoway Coastguard had been called in to use its heat-seeking equipment to scan outhouses, bothies and roadsides in the surrounding area in the search for the pair, but nothing was found. At about 6 p.m., with the day darkening and the helicopter back at its base, I talked to Glasgow and it was agreed I should set off on my 90-mile drive home and possibly return the next day, depending on developments.

I wasn't far down the minor road to Altnaharra when I spotted them. They were dressed in dark outdoor clothing, both with black woolly hats pulled down over their heads. I passed them and looked in the mirror. They appeared completely unperturbed, engrossed in each other as they walked intertwined. I stopped and pretended to be talking on my mobile phone and they strolled past without a glance. I decided to phone the news desk in Glasgow and the police. Others said later I should have tried to interview them, but I had no idea as to their psychological state and was frightened that any approach would spook them into taking to the hills. Having spent so many years writing stories about people who had got lost and died in the wild lands of the Highlands, that was not a risk I wanted to take. There was also the fear of a suicide attempt. I was condemned subsequently by some in the media, who should have known better. My crime apparently was passing up the chance of a scoop. One commentator even said I should have been sacked on the spot and the episode be used in the training of journalists as an example of what not to do. Another accused me of working for the police rather than for my newspaper. Meanwhile, a London-based tabloid diarist styled me as a poor country bumpkin who watched the greatest story of his life walk over the horizon.

I had always understood a journalist has a responsibility towards the subject of his/her story, but if my critics didn't share that view, none bothered to explain why it would have been appropriate to breach, in such a blatant manner, the Press Complaints Commission's Code in force at the time and which clearly stated: 'Journalists must not interview or photograph a child under the age of 16 on subjects involving the welfare of the child or any other child in the absence of or without the consent of a parent or other adult who is responsible for the children.' Even the police couldn't interview without such a person being present. Clearly the welfare of Naomi Mills was an issue. It was THE issue and under the circumstances Matthew Brooks could have been reasonably described as the antithesis of a responsible adult. I doubt any of my critics would have defended me if, once approached, the runaways had disappeared into the darkness to suffer an unfortunate fate. As it was it took the police with sniffer dogs nearly two hours to find the couple who were hiding, if memory serves, in a culvert beneath the road, which in itself didn't suggest that they would have granted me an on-the-spot interview. This was confirmed when Naomi and Matthew were taken by ITV to meet me several months later at home in Cromarty. They said I had been right to act in the way I had, as they would have run away. It was a bruising experience, but members of the Highland press corps were entirely supportive.

I ended up that night going to the house of an old friend, the late Mary Beith, to write my story. Mary lived in the nearby village of Melness, where she wrote a fortnightly column in the *West Highland Free Press* on the Gaelic medical tradition. In 1995 she published her seminal work, *Healing Threads: Traditional Medicines of the Highlands and Islands*, reprinted several times, on the Beatons, the legendary medical dynasty of Gaeldom. But Mary also knew a lot about journalism. Her work for *The People* in Manchester was renowned, as Roy Greenslade, Professor of Journalism at London's City University, once recalled: 'In 1975 . . . one of *The People*'s most famous investigations – into cruelty at a vivisection laboratory – was published to widespread acclaim. Reporter Mary Beith, working undercover at the lab, smuggled in a camera to snap an iconic photograph of a row of dogs hooked up to machines that forced them to inhale supposedly "safe" non-nicotine cigarettes. The smoking beagles image is one of the most memorable ever published by a newspaper.'

Mary had won the Campaigning Journalist of the Year title in the national press awards in 1975 for that story. But she had been prouder of her work exposing the treatment of the elderly in psychiatric hospitals, dressing up in a nurse's uniform to work under cover. She also worked in Northern Ireland and was asleep in the Europa Hotel in Belfast on one of the 33 occasions it was bombed by the Provisional IRA. Her hearing suffered ever after as a result of the explosion. She later said that she could not believe the manner in which I had been attacked over the runaways. Mary wrote to papers supporting me and pointing out that, regardless of the view from London, this had been a fairly small story compared to some the Highland press corps had worked on, and that I had always been prepared to stand up to authority when necessary, including the police.

I had met Mary Beith 14 years earlier on a far more gruesome story. A widow from Milngavie, Mrs Margaret McOnie, 55, had gone missing during a holiday in Tongue. Her body was eventually found on moorland near the village. Police were anxious to interview a man using the name David Kerr who was known to have been with her. But as murder squad detectives were heading north, Kerr, in reality unemployed motor mechanic Brian Newcombe, 51, from Huthwaite in Nottinghamshire, was heading south. He was also being hunted by police in North Yorkshire for the murder of pensioner Jack Shuttleworth, 88, at Ingleton.

Newcombe subsequently returned to Tongue and struck up an acquaintance with another woman. He gave her rings, later identified as belonging to Mrs McOnie, and also spoke of buying a hotel together in nearby Durness. He was later arrested and charged. He hanged himself from the bars of his cell window at Armley Prison in Leeds that November. Newcombe left three suicide notes admitting his crimes. It was thought he had attacked Mrs McOnie from behind with a rock. It was as horrible a story as I ever covered.

### 'The Prof'

We can't leave the subject of the Highland media without a word or two about Norman 'the Prof' Macdonald, BBC Scotland's man on Skye for 20 years. His previous work as a university lecturer in Nova Scotia entitled him to be called professor. Even as a journalist his real interest was in Gaelic and historical scholarship, although he did become an authority on the Skye Bridge anti-tolls campaign, attending many of the court cases in Dingwall (preferring sometimes to drive all the way back to Skye to record his reports rather than use the studio in nearby Inverness) and Edinburgh. He could surprise those he interviewed, not least Dame Ellen MacArthur.

In June 2006 the record-breaking round-the-world solo yachtswoman was awarded the Freedom of Skye and Lochalsh. She became only the fourth person to be given the honour. Her great-great-grandfather came from Luib on the southern shore of Loch Ainort on the east side of Skye. He and two of his brothers left the island at the end of the 19th century for Belper in Derbyshire to work in the mills. But they opened a grocery shop in the town instead, where Dame Ellen's family still lived. She had the reputation of not enjoying the attentions of the press in the south and the intrusion into her private life. She was rather disarmed, however, by the Prof when she attended a press conference before being awarded the freedom of the island. Rather than pose questions to her, he shed some light on her ancestry and presented her with a copy of an extract from the proceedings of the 1892 Royal Commission into Deer Forests in the Highlands and Islands when it had met in Broadford. One of those who gave evidence to the commission was a 'Donald MacArthur' from Luib. On the subject of how he supported himself, he was asked if he had ever been a 'yachtsman'. He hadn't, though he had been at sea for two years 'before the mast'. This Donald MacArthur also told the commission that two of his brothers had gone to England. He himself was to follow them and Norman was able to present Dame Ellen with material demonstrating her descent from the same family. She was delighted and said she found the information fascinating and it helped answer another mystery: 'For years when I have been asked whether my family had any connection with the sea, I had to say no; that I belonged to a place as far away from the sea as you can get; and that I had started sailing in a pond. But now I know this is where I get my sea-faring gene.' For Norman's part, he left the Portree press conference proudly clutching a signed and inscribed copy of her book *Race Against Time* to be added to his incomparable collection of Skye-related books.

This same Donald MacArthur was to feature in another major project which the Prof was to undertake after retiring from the BBC, compiling *The Great Book of Skye – From the Island to the World: People and Place on a Scottish Island*. Donald MacArthur was the subject of one of the entries in the first volume of this extraordinary work. It contains portraits of 563 people connected to the island; profiles totalling a quarter of a million words from original sources, more than 600 pages long with more than 1,000 footnotes: the equivalent of two doctoral theses. It was the work of the Prof and Cailean Maclean, from South Uist, my wife's first cousin. Cailean had lived on his mother's native Skye for more than 30 years. A renowned photographer, he also worked as a lecturer, researcher, publisher and broadcaster. Their original idea was to produce an updated gazetteer of Skye but they were side-tracked into producing this monumental work.

To qualify for entry into the *Great Book*, the subjects had to have some connection to Skye, to be dead and the authors had to know when they died. So Agatha Christie is in it because she spent time in Broadford. But Cu-chulainn, the great warrior of Celtic myth-ology, only makes it into the appendix because nobody knows when he died, or indeed whether he even really existed. Mao Zedong has an honourable mention because of a Canadian, Dr Norman Bethune, who in 1938 joined Mao's Eighth Route Army as a surgeon in the war with Japan. Bethune's paternal grandmother was a Skye woman, Janet Anne Nicolson from Husabost in Glendale, a sister of a famous 19th-century Skye figure, Sheriff Alexander Nicolson who, besides writing in Gaelic and English, was an early climber of the Cuillin. When Dr Bethune died in China in 1939, Mao wrote an obituary 'In Memory of Norman Bethune', describing him as 'a man of importance, integrity, of virtue, who forsook self-interest for the interest of the people'. It became one of three prescribed articles during the Cultural Revolution, which intriguingly was to be translated into Gaelic in 1969.

*The Great Book of Skye* points out that Janet Bethune died in Edinburgh on a visit home from Canada in 1872 and is buried with her brother the sheriff in Warriston cemetery in the Scottish capital. If the Prof has his way this site will yet become a shrine for Edinburgh's tens of thousands of tourists who come every year from China, where the doctor retains iconic status.

Mahatma Gandhi was included because of his connection to a Skye minister's son who was an indigo planter in India. Gandhi witnessed the exploitative management of his plantation and the experience sparked the great man's embrace of radical politics. Mairi Mhor nan Oran ('Big Mary of the Songs'), Mary MacPherson, the Skye poetess of the Clearances, was profiled, as one would expect. My own granny's cousin, Angus MacNiven, has a page and a bit. He was a pioneering psychiatrist who helped develop the concept of diminished responsibility in criminals. He became superintendent of Glasgow Royal Mental Hospital Gartnavel aged 33. Something of a brilliant eccentric, he was found riding a horse in the hospital grounds, reading underneath an umbrella. When asked by the hospital authorities to explain, he said that his horse needed to be exercised, he had papers (the story in our family was it was a book) to read and it was raining. His entry into the *Great Book* was due to his mother having been from Sleat on Skye.

The *Great Book* also gave space to many of the less heralded men and women of Skye whose contribution to the life of the island down the centuries has been valued. This first volume was published in 2014. A second volume followed in 2016, and at the time of writing Norman told me that the third had also been completed.

# 3

# Sorley

ARGUABLY THE SINGLE most important qualification I had for being the Highland correspondent of *The Herald* was my choice of wife, or to be more precise my choice of father-in-law, the celebrated poet Sorley MacLean. He was to help me immensely. I consulted him so frequently on so many subjects – from Gaelic culture to philosophy, human geography and history to politics and literature – that it became a family joke he was my Google and Google Maps before Google was invented. I first met him and Mary's mother Renee in 1974 in the top flat of a fine tenement building on Morningside Road, where they were staying following his appointment as writer in residence at Edinburgh University. I was rather drunk. My only real memory is a discussion on how schools in different parts of the country favoured different universities for their pupils. We also got on to the subject of smoking, which I did at the time, and how he had never managed to master the art of inhaling. He presented me with a packet of 10 Senior Service with nine left, which he had bought having run out of pipe tobacco. My future mother-in-law's only memory of that night was that I had a hole in both my shoes.

Sorley's job at the university had come at the right time. He had been retired a year from his post as rector of Plockton High School when he was approached about the new position. His family encouraged him to take it, as he had appeared rather lost after he retired, going from being responsible for several hundred pupils to having no obvious day-to-day role. He didn't have time-consuming hobbies such as golf and his days of climbing on the Cuillin Ridge were long behind him. Any DIY was Renee's area of expertise, or for anything significant her brother Duncan's when he came on holiday.

Sorley enjoyed the work as writer in residence, meeting students who came to him for advice on their own writing. He enjoyed being part of a university community. He might well have been drawn to the life of an academic had events taken a different course. But one of the most important things about the Edinburgh appointment was that it gave him access to the Edinburgh University Staff Club in Chambers Street. In its bar he would meet friends and make new ones. Long after he had left the job, he and Renee maintained membership of the club. Any time they were in Edinburgh thereafter, which was quite often, he would head there ostensibly to reply to the many letters he used to receive, but he would get distracted and end up in the bar. It meant that Renee always knew where to find him.

One man he was particularly interested to meet in the staff club was the late John Erickson, Professor of Politics and for many years NATO's top adviser on its Soviet adversary. Erickson's two-volume history of the Second World War, *The Road to Stalingrad* (1975) and *The Road to Berlin* (1982), had greatly impressed Sorley. He had become very interested in the Battle of Kursk, fought in the summer of 1943 between German and Soviet forces less than 300 miles south-west of Moscow. It involved 6,000 tanks and is remembered as the greatest tank battle in history. The career of the Soviet commander Marshal Zhukov also engaged him. The scale of the sacrifice made by the Russian people in the Second World War always stayed with him and he would often ponder where the West would have been without it. He loved to tell the story of the female clippie on a Glasgow corporation bus who was being chatted up by American GIs. One asked did she not think she should be friendlier to the soldiers who were saving Britain from the Nazis. To this she had retorted, 'Sorry, sir, I didn't recognise your Russian accent.'

Sorley and Renee's life on Skye was different. They had bought an old cottage in Peinachorrain, one of the crofting townships in the Braes area of the island, then renovated and extended it. The mountain Glamaig was just across the mouth of Loch Sligachan, and the outline of the Cuillin could be seen up above the head of the loch. There were views to the southern end of Raasay from another window. The house sat at the foot of Ben Lee, a hill prominent in Highland history. A dispute between the community and Lord Macdonald's estate over its grazing had led to the Battle of the Braes in 1882 between local people and the forces of law and order. The residents resisted an attempt by their landlord to evict 12 crofters as part of the dispute over Ben Lee, which was due to be taken over by a farmer. They refused to pay their rents and a crowd of 150 assaulted the sheriff's officer and burned the eviction notices he brought. However, he returned almost two weeks later with 50 policemen sent from Glasgow to arrest five of the crofters. As they left Braes the party was attacked by a large crowd of men, women and children carrying sticks and throwing stones. The Battle of the Braes was the start of the 'Land War' of 1882–88, a wave of agitation across the Highlands demanding land reform. A monument was erected to the men and woman of Braes, and Sorley wrote the inscription in Gaelic and English explaining its significance: 'Near this cairn on the 19th of April 1882 ended the battle fought by the people of Braes on behalf of the crofters of Gaeldom.'

In May 1883 Gladstone's Liberal government announced the establishment of the Napier Commission, 'to inquire into the condition of the crofters and cottars in the Highlands and Islands of Scotland'. The Napier Commission's report led to legislation which granted crofters security of tenure and fair rents amongst other rights. It was the foundation of the crofting system that survives to this day.

Sorley and Renee's house in Braes had also been home to one of Sorley's forebears, Angus Stewart, who was the first person to give evidence before the Napier Commission. Stewart spoke out against landlords and their agents. But before he dared do so, he said: 'I want the assurance that I will not be evicted, for I cannot bear evidence to the distress of my people without bearing evidence to the oppression and high handedness of the landlord and his factor.' Lord Napier persuaded Lord MacDonald's factor, who was present, to give that assurance. The Napier Commission's five-volume report gave future historians a truly invaluable insight into the lives of ordinary Highland people in the 19th century. The first meeting of the Napier Commission was held in what was the parish church just a couple of miles up the road from Peinachorrain at Ollach. The building was bought by Sorley's second daughter Catriona and her husband, Donald MacDonald (always known as DR) from North Uist. They were both Gaelic teachers in Portree High School and brought up their three sons in the adjoining former manse speaking Gaelic as their first language. One of their sons is now doing the same in the same house.

It was all symbolic of just how close Sorley was to his people and their story. Every time we visited Mary's parents in Skye there were certain things we always did. One of my duties was to drive to the neighbouring township of Balmeanach to visit a former weaver Uilleam Choinnich MacDonald (Willie to me), who was very lame and didn't get out much. Armed with a half bottle of whisky at least, we would sit in his cottage for several hours. Sorley and he would range over many subjects, but one of the most frequently addressed was the Battle of the Braes, on which Willie was something of an authority (this would be largely in Gaelic with Sorley translating the 95 per cent I hadn't understood). He would want to check details of what had happened where, when and who had been involved. A highly intelligent man, Willie was immersed in local tradition and was always able to answer the queries.

I think Sorley had to see things with his own mind's eye. He was talking once to Willie's neighbour Flora Nicolson, who was recalling how her late husband had come to live in Braes after he had sailed over from his native Applecross. Sorley was interested and wanted to know more, asking: 'Do you remember by any chance if he said which way the wind was blowing that day?' Flora was apologetic that she didn't and Sorley quickly conceded that perhaps it had been an unfair question. Going out for a walk with him in Braes would take some considerable time as he would keep stopping to examine the nooks and crannies that nature had created and for each of which the Gaelic language seemed to have a name. He would have been delighted that his grandson Gilleasbuig, whom he christened 'the Philosopher Prince', had written his final honours thesis in Glasgow University on the Gaelic placenames of Braes.

New Year was always enthusiastically celebrated in Braes, but the first-footing schedule sometimes had to be amended if the Sabbath fell on Hogmanay or 1 January. If not, the MacLean house could be a busy thoroughfare from not long after the bells. The family would be mostly home, which in the early years included Catriona, as DR would be off home to Tigharry on the west side of North Uist. Catriona's wonderful singing of traditional Gaelic songs would frequently fill the room. There were often additional house guests, but the numbers would be dramatically increased in the early hours as neighbours began to appear. Some came from further afield, including friends from Earlish near Uig, the Lockharts, who would be joined by Donnie Munro of Runrig fame, whose home was and indeed is again in Portree. Flora's house was always the focus of activity on New Year's Day, when there would be another ceilidh. The New Year could go on for four or five days. One of the celebration's stalwarts was Alasdair Beaton, Sorley and Renee's next-door neighbour, who was always called Alasdair Susie after his grandmother. He had been a merchant seaman who had sailed round the world several times and had retired to his croft. He kept cattle, an important symbol of crofting activity. He often used to go out fishing in his small boat before finally crossing to the bar in the Sconser Lodge Hotel on the other side. Sorley would anxiously keep watch for his boat returning to make sure he got home safely, cursing the longer it lay beside the Sconser jetty. Another prominent Skye figure would often appear at New Year and follow Catriona's singing with his own contribution, which tended to be 'I Recall a Gypsy Woman' or 'Blueberry Hill', accompanying himself by playing the coal shovel.

Driving was not one of Sorley's greatest skills. He was at the wheel one Christmas Eve when the family was young. They were heading for Inverness when they hit ice and almost ended up in Loch Cluanie. It was probably not his fault, but the episode did nothing to instil confidence in his driving amongst his daughters. As he got older Renee did more and more, progressively limiting where he was allowed to drive. The mainland became a no-go area, but he would still drive up and down to Sabhal Mòr Ostaig when he was writer in residence. Eventually he only drove around Braes, although he remained confident in his own ability. On one occasion he was telling me that in snow and ice one should always drive in as low a gear as possible. I said I understood that while you should use low gears rather than brakes in wintery conditions, in general you should drive in as high gear as possible and try to take off in second gear. He was not at all convinced and told Renee of our debate when she came into the room. She told me to ignore her husband's views on driving, and cited how twice they were about to leave Plockton to go on holiday and he had taken the car to Kyle of Lochalsh to fill up with petrol for the journey only to crash it. Sorley had a defence: 'On the last occasion, technically speaking, Tommy [the other driver] was in the wrong. He was going too fast but, admittedly, I was on the wrong side of the road.' He blamed every road accident on excessive speed and when he was a passenger he was given to leaning over from the front passenger seat and asking, 'As a matter of interest,

Dave, how fast are you going?' He also had particular disdain for drivers who didn't dip their lights, cursing them loudly in a mixture of Gaelic and English.

Sorley accompanied me when I went to sell my car while still in Edinburgh. We found our way to a yard off the Pleasance where such business was conducted. Several men were lying on the grass smoking cigars, with fearsome-looking Alsatian dogs on chains. Sorley later described them as resembling 'minor characters from Dickens'. He was highly amused when the police appeared at our door some weeks later asking about the car. Apparently our Dickensian dog lovers had passed it to persons unknown who had taken the number plate off the Ford Escort and put it on a Ford Granada, which was then used in a bank robbery in England.

Sorley's main responsibility at home was to clean and lay the fire. He took great pride in having roaring fires to greet any visitor. His control centre for these operations was his shed, where he kept the wood, peat and kindling, with the coal nearby. He made a lot of improvements to the shed, with many reinforcements he christened 'flying buttresses' as homage to the Gothic cathedrals he loved so much. There were so many that Renee was terrified it would collapse on top of him and persuaded DR and myself to demolish it, which was actually a lot harder than we thought it would be. Sorley was later made an Honorary Fellow of the Royal Incorporation of Architects in Scotland, which he loved to attribute to his work on the shed.

The house in Peinachorrain had many visitors, and all were made welcome. Those of Highland extraction would be cross-examined on their family trees, their *sloinneadh*. This his daughters could find annoying when it was their young friends who were being interviewed. When I took my new brother-in-law Angus Macdonald to Braes with my sister one New Year, Sorley immediately went into action. Angus's grandfather Coll A. Macdonald had also been from Iona and had sat beside our own in the island's primary school. He had gone on to become a prominent minister and a Gaelic scholar. Sorley had known him and had been good friends with his son Colin, Angus's uncle, at Edinburgh University. A major in the Sudan Defence Force, Colin had been killed in the Second World War at Debra Marcos in Ethiopia, aged 29. As he questioned Angus, Sorley must have filled three pipes without lighting them, most of the tobacco falling on the floor.

There were several intriguing guests. One was a Professor Wang from Beijing, who had been sent to the rice fields in Mao's Cultural Revolution. A professor of English, the British Council had asked if he could visit. He stayed a few days during which time Sorley closely questioned him on the history of Sino-Soviet relations, which were then pretty strained. He wanted to know if there had been historical enmity over territory or whether there was an ideological dispute between the two communist giants. As far as I can recall Professor Wang said it was largely the former. He was engaging company for Sorley, who would recall his humour on the subject of the Chinese leadership. Zhou Enlai had been the father of his people but Mao had been the epoch-maker, he said. However, the latter had made some mistakes, 'for example, the Cultural Revolution, which supported the old adage about not letting your wife interfere in your business'.

Seamus Heaney and his wife Marie arrived one evening while we were there with two friends and a bottle of Talisker. He was to come back to visit in 2004 to walk with the family and others along the grassy track to the birch trees around the deserted township of Hallaig on Raasay. It was the setting and title of Sorley's celebrated poem, which had been published 50 years earlier to mark the 100th anniversary of the last people being cleared from Hallaig. What was Heaney's first visit to Raasay was over seven years after Sorley's death and 150 years since 129 people left the island in one day mostly 'encouraged' by the then landlord, George Rainy, a West Indian merchant. More than 40 of those leaving had come from Hallaig. They made their way by boat to Liverpool, from where they left for Portland in Victoria, Australia.

There was nothing Sorley himself liked better than to make his family laugh. Eyes twinkling, he would happily bear the brunt of familial ridicule, the younger his tormentor the better. That never changed to the end, even when he became very ill. His cancer seemed to be more of a nuisance to him than anything else. When he was asked by his consultant at Raigmore hospital whether he was managing to sleep at night, he admitted there was something keeping him awake – not his own impending mortality but the fact Skye Camanachd had promoted a grandson of his to the first team at not much more than 16. As honorary vice president of the club, he thought this far too early for senior shinty.

To this day numerous conversations among his six grandchildren (Somhairle, Aonghas and Gilleasbuig MacDonald; Calum and Catherine

Ross; and Donald Mackay) still begin with, 'Do you remember when *Seanair* [grandfather] . . .' and a narrative is recited of Sorley having done or said something plain daft, underlining his normal eccentric behaviour. That was true to the end. He had come to our home, to recuperate from treatment. He had been complaining about feeling the bed damp (either because he had spilled a drink or because he had been sweating) and to underline the point declared, 'Renee, it is so wet in here it's like the Pontine Marshes before Mussolini drained them.' This was a frequent element of his humour, to associate the epic and exotic with the ordinary and commonplace. The immersion heater in the house in Braes was always known as 'the Renaissance'; a friend from North Uist had the face of 'the Christ on the south portal of Chartres Cathedral'; and Don Quixote was recalled when referring to one particularly lugubrious islander known always as 'the Knight of the Rueful Countenance'. On hearing that I had given a complete wreck of a car to my uncle for use on his croft on Iona, he declared: 'How fitting that the *càr mòr buidhe* ['big yellow car' as it was always known to his first grandson] goes to lie with the kings of Scotland on Iona.'

Despite all this, Sorley of course was a serious man who wanted to talk about serious matters. When we were by ourselves no subject seemed off limits, from the personal to the political: the Land League, Gaelic, the Spanish Civil War, his war service in North Africa. But it was when he talked of his despair in the 1930s and how he came to believe the Red Army was all that stood in the way of the whole of Europe succumbing to fascism that I really began to understand the forces that had forged him. He had utter disdain for the treatment meted out to Anthony Blunt when uncovered as a spy in 1979 by certain newspapers which had once presented a rather more positive image of Hitler and Nazi Germany than they would now care to recall. He would have been proud to die fighting fascism. Very real ties prevented that being in Spain; at the time he was sending most of his teacher's salary home to Raasay, where his father's tailor's business was failing. He tried to volunteer in September 1939. His employers, Edinburgh Corporation, however, proved difficult; he was conscripted later. Wounded three times in the North African campaign, it was amazing that he ever walked again, and he carried bits of metal in his legs ever after. He saw great courage there, such as the Englishman in Egypt – 'A poor little chap with chubby cheeks and knees grinding each other, pimply unattractive face – garment of the bravest spirit.' But unlike others he managed to see courage, far away from the battlefield, in ordinary people making the best of their everyday lives.

His suspicions over the evils of fascism had begun early. He told me how he suspected the political journey on which Oswald Mosley had embarked when he left the Independent Labour Party to found his New Party in 1931, a year before he established the British Union of Fascists (BUF). Sorley had gone to demonstrate when Mosley spoke in Edinburgh about the New Party, and went there again when he came back as BUF leader. He loved to recall how he had stood up and shouted at Mosley and, when the BUF brownshirts started running towards him, he was saved by a huge man called Boag Thompson – if memory serves, an Irish-American who had fought in the Spanish Civil War. 'Boag got to his feet and he roared!' Sorley would recall with delight, this having been sufficient to repel Mosley's finest.

As Sorley wrote himself: 'Munich and the unparalleled heroism and self-sacrifice of Communists in the Spanish Civil War almost made me a Communist in 1938.' He never joined the Communist Party of Great Britain and he certainly was not prepared to support the Soviet–Nazi Pact Stalin and Hitler signed in August 1939. Half a century later he could still be scathing about the party's theoretician and general secretary, Rajani Palme Dutt, who had demanded acceptance of Stalin's new line which ran completely counter to the British left's anti-fascism stance. He had shared the view of the likes of Harry Pollitt and Willie Gallacher, who believed Dutt had put the British party into an impossible position as Hitler invaded Poland.

A man utterly untainted by any snobbery, Sorley's interest in people was genuine, whether it was a philosopher discussing the work of Immanuel Kant or a neighbour on the subject of his potatoes. He was as impressed by practical skills as intellectual ability. His old friend George Davie could almost have had Sorley in mind rather than the Scottish system of higher education when he coined the term 'the democratic intellect'. His socialism was natural, emotional. Sorley said once to me – only once – that if things had been different he might have tried to go into politics, but didn't say which party. He believed in Scottish independence, but was very alive to the charges of being Tartan Tories levelled against the SNP in the 1970s. He always paid tribute to the post-war Labour government of Clement Attlee. He memorably did so at a debate I was taking part in alongside Brian Wilson, organised by Edinburgh University's Highland Society. The motion was that Scottish nationalism was irrelevant to the future of the Highlands. Sorley was in the audience and was furious when another there invited him to opine, by describing him as arguably the greatest living Gael. Sorley said that while many would assume he would back the SNP, he had to say the huge improvement he had seen in the social conditions of so many ordinary people in his lifetime had been 'due to one thing and one thing only, the British Labour movement'. He became a member of the short-lived breakaway Scottish Labour Party (SLP) led by the then Labour MP Jim Sillars. Sorley had volunteered to join when, as a student, I was helping set up an Edinburgh branch of the party, members of which were to include poet and folklorist Hamish Henderson, journalist and writer Neal Ascherson, political philosopher Tom Nairn and a future Lord Advocate, Colin Boyd. I came across a letter recently from the SLP's organising secretary, Alex Neil, now an SNP MSP and former Scottish government minister, acknowledging the membership of one S. MacLean.

Sorley retained his suspicion of what he saw as the establishment and its trappings. He turned down an OBE, refusing to be associated with anything which celebrated the British empire and colonialism. It was a decision Renee never really understood, and we believe he accepted the Queen's Medal for Poetry in 1990 for her. He told us that he got on well with the monarch when he received his medal at the Palace of Holyroodhouse and that they had discussed their respective grand-children. I am pretty sure Sorley would have voted Yes in the 2014 independence referendum, but one can never be absolutely certain. He died before New Labour came to power, and the only observation I can remember him making about it was that he found it impossible to know what Tony Blair really believed in, which was important to him. He would, however, have been highly critical of the comparisons made between the threat posed by Saddam Hussein's Iraq and the military might of Hitler's Germany as a pretext for war.

He took great pride in saying that when headmaster he had made Plockton High a comprehensive school long before any others in Scotland; that he would present any child for 'O' Grades or Highers unless they had learning difficulties. But if he was ahead of his time in this respect, he had no time for newfangled educational thinking which understated the need for sheer hard work. Befitting a man who had read the three volumes of Thomas Carlyle's history of the French Revolution before he was 12 (he said he had run out of books to read on Raasay), he couldn't really understand students who didn't embrace what had been to him the joy of scholarship – this writer included. He was proud to receive seven honorary degrees from universities in Scotland, England, Ireland and France.

Sorley and Renee's closest friends often pondered what might have befallen him had he not met and married her. It was a question normally met with a pursing of lips and a shaking of heads, the consensus being that everyday life would have been immeasurably more difficult for him. Although she always kept herself firmly in the background as her husband was winning international recognition, Renee was his anchor. Her natural charm, humour and well-developed diplomatic instincts were disarming, her organisational skills often much needed. With her, his earlier personal torments gave way to a loving and fulfilling family life in Edinburgh, Plockton and Skye.

Renee was not the woman/women of whom he wrote in some of his most famous works. But the one poem he did write for her, 'Soluis' (Lights), suggested a new optimism. It begins:

> Nuair laigheas an ceann ruadh seo
> Air mo ghualainn 's air mo bhroilleach
> Fosglaidh camhanaich na buaidhe
> Air cho gruamach 's a tha 'n doilleir.

> When this auburn head lies
> on my shoulder and my breast
> the dawn of triumph opens
> however gloomy the darkness.

Renee had grown up in a family of four in Inverness. Her father, Kenneth Cameron, who had a joinery business, came from the Kilmuir area of the Black Isle when Gaelic was still spoken there. Her mother, Isabella Buchanan, was from Callander. They lived in the Crown area and she attended the then nearby Inverness Royal Academy. It was an Inverness unrecognisable today, with farmland almost on their doorstep where great swathes of housing now stand. On leaving school she went to Edinburgh College of Domestic Science in Atholl Crescent. She told us of how she was looking out of the college windows one day and saw some of the first German war planes to fly over Scotland in 1939. She studied needlework and qualified as a teacher. She would often talk about the war years and paint a vivid picture of the home front – from restaurants that would advertise a choice of six main dishes, when they only ever had powdered egg omelettes, to the trains packed full of servicemen. She said that despite the awful loss of friends and relations which so many suffered, the Second World War had not been a bad time to be alive; that there was a genuine feeling of everybody being in it together and the few who sought to profit by it were despised.

By the time she met Sorley in 1944 the tide of war had turned. He had been injured in the North African campaign and had returned to Scotland. He had first met her on a train with his brother Norman, but had laboured under the misunderstanding that she was going out with somebody else, thereby delaying his initial approach by some months. He was teaching English at Boroughmuir High School in Edinburgh when they married. She gave up her own teaching career on becoming a married woman, as was the norm at that time. They became close friends with the poet Sydney Goodsir Smith, both families sharing a house in Craigmillar Park for about 18 months. In the folklore of family this became known as the 'Schloss Schmidt' and was the focus of much humour. They both held Smith to be the most naturally funny man they ever met.

Although their friends of the Scottish literati, from Hugh MacDiarmid to Hamish Henderson, were around Edinburgh, family life dominated as three daughters, Ishbel, Catriona and Mary, followed. It was during this time in the Scottish capital that Sorley's masterpiece 'Hallaig' was written. In 1956 he was appointed rector of Plockton High School, so they left Edinburgh and headed to Ross-shire, where they brought up their children. There, by all accounts, they managed to sustain a policy of effortless hospitality as a broad section of humanity beat its way to the schoolhouse door.

It was the same open-door policy when they retired to Braes in Skye. The MacLean house was always a place of warmth and great *craic*, where Renee would often hold centre stage as she recounted some ludicrous episode, often involving her husband's eccentricities. There was the occasion in their room in a St Andrews hotel when the phone rang and he picked up the hairdryer that was attached to the wall and said into it 'Sligachan 253'. Then there was the speech he was asked to give to some students which ended with him counselling, 'Whatever you do, don't get trapped inside a roll of linoleum,' which apparently had been a fate that had befallen Sydney Goodsir Smith.

Sadly, during their later years in Skye, Sorley and Renee suffered the cruellest of blows when their daughter Catriona died in 1993. Thereafter their lives were dedicated to helping Catriona's husband DR bring up their three sons. Sorley died in 1996. Renee later came to live with us in Cromarty for the last six years of her life.

# 4

# Gaelic

WHEN I TOLD Sorley I was leaving the Edinburgh office of *The Herald* in 1988 to take up the job in the Highlands, he asked whether I could fill that post without speaking Gaelic. I pointed out that many of the journalists on the Highland beat did not speak the language either. But he was right: I would have been able to do the job much better had I been bilingual. My mother had a 'bit of Gaelic', as people would say. She could understand a lot, but would never speak in front of native speakers. Both her parents were native speakers, as was her oldest brother Dugald, who went to Iona Primary School speaking only Gaelic. More and more English, however, was being spoken around their home, which was being run as a guest house, as Iona was attracting tourists earlier than other Hebridean destinations. As a consequence, the younger children were no longer immersed in the language. On the Ross of Mull, just across the Sound of Iona, there was not the same early exposure to tourism and Gaelic survived much longer. There had also been a succession of teachers after 1900 coming to Iona Primary who didn't have Gaelic, unlike their predecessors.

When it came to choosing which subjects to study at Oban High School, my grandfather had advised my mother to take French rather than Gaelic, saying she would get all the Gaelic she needed at home. It was a common tale in many a home in the Highlands and Islands. English was seen as the language of success. But my mother did feel that she had lost something important and would sometimes go to Gaelic evening classes to 'brush up' when we were in Blairgowrie.

I knew only a few phrases from my granny, who was a MacNiven from the Ross of Mull. She would always listen to the church service in Gaelic as well as English. My uncle Neil, however, had married Ena MacCormick, who was from a croft at the south end of Iona. She had trained as a teacher at Jordanhill College and had been teaching on Mull. Her family had continued to speak Gaelic and she would often speak to Uncle Neil in the language, and he would reply hesitantly in Gaelic or in English. It seemed she would do this when she was trying to keep something from our generation.

Her elder daughter Marjorie, to whom I was always close, had learnt enough from listening to her parents' exchanges to catch the drift of what was being said and would promptly relay it to her cousins. Aunty Ena was the last native speaker to live permanently on the island. She could count amongst her MacCormick relations the celebrated jurist Professor Sir Neil MacCormick of Edinburgh University and his brother Ian, who served as SNP MP for Argyll from 1974 to 1979. They were sons of 'King' John MacCormick, a lawyer who in 1934 became the first national secretary of the SNP and was involved in the removal of the Stone of Destiny from Westminster Abbey on Christmas Day 1950. My mother and her siblings were also related to him as third cousins. Mairi MacArthur, my cousin who wrote the histories of Iona and restarted the Iona Press publishing imprint (now the New Iona Press) told me recently how Neil MacCormick always talked of us as being fourth cousins of his.

One of his anecdotes was about a slightly pompous academic who had expressed amazement that people in New Guinea, or somewhere, knew who their second cousins were. Neil's response was along the lines of 'Never mind New Guinea, have you never been to Mull and Iona?' On the subject of cousins, my mother and her siblings had 49 first cousins on their father's side and none on their mother's, although she had been one of seven children. Her sister Flora was the only other one to marry, but she had no children.

## Gaelic's future in the hands of learners

Sorley himself had been pessimistic about Gaelic's survival. He had long recognised that the native speakers would die off, taking their language with them as English advanced. Its only chance was that it would be learnt by others. But in the early years of the 20th century the Lower and Higher courses in Gaelic were designed for pupils from Gaelic-speaking homes who were themselves already fluent. In his important article 'Questions of Prestige: Sorley MacLean and the Campaign for

Gaelic', which appeared in the collection of critical essays published by Scottish Academic Press in 1986 in tribute to him, Aonghas MacNeacail examined how significant an issue this was to Sorley. He had been aware of successful attempts to teach Gaelic to non-native pupils in Glasgow and Argyll, most notably by the great Lewisman Donald Thomson at Oban High School, where Sorley's brother John was rector. In 1997 the celebrated scholar Professor Donald Meek, a native of Tiree, wrote about teaching of Gaelic in Argyll for the Association of Scottish Literary Studies.

> The county became home to writers who originated in other parts of the Highlands and Islands. Often these were ministers or schoolmasters. If we were to compile a list of such people, it would include modern Gaelic writers such as the Rev. Dr Kenneth MacLeod, of *Road to the Isles* fame (or notoriety), who was a native of Eigg, but was latterly parish minister of Gigha. It would also include Dr Iain Crichton Smith, a native of Lewis who has lived in Oban and later in Taynuilt for a large part of his active literary life, and who taught English in Oban High School for many years. When I was a fifth-year pupil in Oban High School in 1965–66, Dr Smith was my English teacher and the Rector of the school was the distinguished Classical scholar, John MacLean. At the same time as Iain Crichton Smith was enriching Gaelic literature with his innovative short stories and poems (and explaining the significance of Sorley MacLean's poetry!), John MacLean was translating the Odyssey into Gaelic. Both men had a great interest in Gaelic literature, and encouraged their pupils to take an interest in it too; but they also practised what they taught – and that was very impressive. With the infectiously pro-Gaelic activist Donald Thomson (a Lewisman) in charge of the Gaelic department, and Donald Morrison (another Lewisman!) also teaching Gaelic and writing short stories and Gaelic articles, Oban High School was a veritable Gaelic academy in those days!

Sorley began campaigning for a Gaelic learners' Higher paper against opposition within the Scottish Education Department, but he felt guilty he hadn't done so earlier. In his essay Aonghas quotes a letter Sorley sent to the Gaelic Society of Inverness in 1965 with a suggestion of who the society should elect as its 'chief' for that year:

> I think it ought to be Donald Thomson, both for his own sake and for the sake of the tiny group of whom he is the pioneer and the most noted: those teachers who are teaching Gaelic to pupils who do not already know it. One of my bitterest regrets is that I have been so late in raising my voice on their behalf and on the behalf of the patriotic parents who are encouraging their children to take Gaelic in secondary schools when their environment makes it next to impossible that they should be Gaelic speakers.

Sorley was highly critical of those Gaels who supported the status quo against a learners' paper. He also challenged the educational thinking behind the Scottish Education Department's position. He wrote to the civil servants highlighting the contrasting fortunes of two pupils in Plockton. One who was 'a very able and hard-working pupil who passes in Higher Latin, Higher English, Higher Mathematics and Higher Science, and fails in Higher Gaelic due to not being a Native Speaker'. The other was a native Gael 'who came to Plockton school as a Junior Secondary pupil who was not fit to sit any other Higher except English, in which a bare pass was obtained, and gets a Credit pass in Higher Gaelic because this pupil is a Native Speaker'.

The campaign for a Gaelic learners' Higher, with Sorley increasingly outspoken in support, gained momentum. He used to talk about it a lot in later life, and told me once that he had been so concerned that he might have gone too far by defaming certain prominent figures in the Scottish Education Department, and that he had transferred assets into Renee's name just in case he was ever sued. He worried a lot about many things, but he was safe enough from any legal action, and at any rate the campaign was to win through and a new course was launched for learners. His second daughter Catriona took the new Higher in 1968 and went on to study Gaelic at Glasgow University and to teach the subject in Portree High School with her soon-to-be husband D.R. Macdonald, who was principal teacher. As a result, Sorley lived to see three of his grandchildren being brought up in a house in which

Gaelic was the everyday language. I have no doubt how important that was to him, and indeed why, after interviewing Sorley at length, Aonghas concluded in his essay:

> In assessing the contribution he has made to our cultural treasury, it is entirely proper that we lay most emphasis on the literary achievements of Sorley MacLean. No doubt it pleases him, or at least does not offend him, that he should be so honoured, although the ceremonial honours so far conferred on him – doctorates from the University of Dundee and Edinburgh and the National University of Ireland – in no way reflect the extent of the recognition which he now receives.
>
> Yet when he himself recollects past achievements, it is not to the poetry he refers but to the part which he played in the campaign for the provision of a Higher Leaving Certificate examination paper specifically designed for learners of Gaelic. Not at the first glance the most likely object of pride to our greatest living poet, but the 'Learners paper' had deep symbolic significance for MacLean.

### Mary Robinson learns a Gaelic lesson in Scotland

I did myself try to learn the language properly by going to night classes, but my attendance was too often interrupted by being sent away on stories. As it was, Finlay Macleod, formerly director of the Gaelic Playgroups' Association (Comhairle Sgoiltean Araich), whose work was absolutely crucial in giving Gaelic a chance of survival, once told me it could take decades to become fluent going to just one night class a week. I did, however, meet some interesting people in the process. There was an elderly gentleman in one of my classes who stood out for asking the Gaelic teacher the most unexpected of questions. My favourite was whether she thought it was safe for him to sleep with his electric blanket on. It later transpired that he could speak Gaelic perfectly well and only came along for the company.

Whether it was an accident of history or not, one of the great achievements of the Gaelic movement in Scotland was that the cause of the language never became the preserve of one religion, or one political movement. As a result, when Gaelic came to fight for its survival in recent years it could attract support from across a wide political spectrum. Things were very different in Ireland, and remain so today. At the time of writing an Irish Language Act is still a central issue dividing Sinn Fein and the Democratic Unionists, preventing the restoration of Northern Ireland's devolved government.

This situation was something the Irish President Mary Robinson commented on when she visited Iona, Lewis and Skye in 1997. She had come to mark the 1,400th anniversary of the death of St Columba. She flew by helicopter first to Iona. It was moving to watch this most notable Irish woman pick her way through the thistles in a field to get to the abbey which had first been built by her saintly countryman and where monks began work on the *Book of Kells*, now so proudly displayed in Trinity College, Dublin. In a press conference after the church service the president told us she was conscious that Ireland could learn so much from Scotland when it came to Gaelic: 'Too often in the Irish context, Celtic or Gaelic culture has been identified with Catholicism and nationalism, which has had the effect of inhibiting those of the Protestant and Unionist tradition from claiming part of their inheritance. It is surely time to insist that our past and our culture is rich, varied and complex: that it cannot be resolved into narrow, sectarian compartments and that it is open to each of us to claim what is rightly ours.'

Mrs Robinson went on to open an exhibition on St Columba in Stornoway and then to Skye's Gaelic college to deliver the annual Sabhal Mòr Ostaig Lecture. In this she underlined how close the two countries remained, recalling a man she had as her guest in official residence in Dublin, Áras an Uachtaráin, formerly the British Viceregal Lodge. She said, 'I am reminded of the words of Sorley MacLean, whose passing last year we mourn deeply, that great poet who loved this island so well. He described the bond between us in words that say it all: "The humanity that the ocean could not break, that a thousand years has not severed."'

She recalled the founder of the Irish Land League Michael Davitt's visit to Skye in May 1887 and the welcome he enjoyed for having supported the crofters' cause against the landlords, being carried shoulder high through Portree: 'These are common experiences which mark forever the history and development of our nations even though we may have different perspectives on the turbulent events which shaped us. We cannot deny the way in which they have bound our destinies. This past still determines today the links between our countries and the comings and goings of our people.'

Mrs Robinson hoped that in considering our past, we could recognise what we had in common and cherish that: 'So often the past has been seen as a source of division and dissension and has served to under-score religious and political differences. When I became president of Ireland I spoke of a province of our imagination, a common ground on which we could come together and celebrate what we share. Perhaps we can create an island space for ourselves to celebrate what Scotland and Ireland share . . . I am particularly conscious that this may enable people of both traditions in Northern Ireland to reclaim parts of their inheritance which have been denied them.'

While Mrs Robinson was in Lewis, the Scottish minister with respon-sibility for Gaelic, Brian Wilson, launched the 'Columba Initiative' to foster closer cultural and linguistic ties between the Gaelic-speaking communities of Scotland and Ireland. It still operates today as the Columba Project. One event which is staged under its auspices is a hurling/shinty match which is played alternatively in Scotland and Ireland. In 2012 I wrote a story about it which intrigued my editors who published it under a headline of 'Shinty shock: Speak English and you will be sent off'. The players, who for the first time that year were drawn from Northern Ireland as well as the republic had to speak the Scottish or Irish forms of Gaelic when on the field. The referee had been given special powers to expel anyone reverting to English.

## Gaelic in Caithness

I don't believe there has been any real upsurge of outright hostility to Gaelic in Scotland. Even today after years of cutbacks in public spending, it would be hard to find an MP, MSP or MEP of any party to speak publicly against the Gaelic cause, although the odd one may quibble about money. If a newspaper is seeking to criticise Gaelic it is normally a columnist or commentator they have to approach for a quote, and there are some more than happy to oblige. There are also plenty of murmurings about the Gaelic tail wagging the Scottish dog and suchlike. Some civic leaders in Caithness, for example, have made quite a name for themselves over the years, trying to prevent the spread of the Gaelic language through the medium of bilingual road signs. They argued that it was on the grounds of cost, although the money involved was always pretty minimal given that the language of the Garden of Eden would only ever appear when the English-only sign had to be replaced. A cultural argument was also deployed that Gaelic had never been the language of Caithness, the county's heritage being Norse rather than Celtic. Some of these debates were revived with the confirmation that the first Gaelic medium primary school unit in Caithness would open at the start of the new school session in 2013. It was to be based at Mount Pleasant Primary School in Thurso, which was already home to an active Gaelic medium nursery.

The staging of the National Mòd in the north coast town in 2010 definitely helped dilute anti-Gaelic sentiment, and the Gaelic medium unit was one legacy of that. The history of it all is still worth revisiting, particularly the work by a respected authority on Gaelic Scotland, Dr Domhnall Uilleam Stiùbhart, who lectures on the subject at Sabhal Mòr Ostaig. A few years back he decided to delve into the apparent Caithnessian antipathy to Gaelic. Other areas like Argyll and Perthshire had largely lost Gaelic but remained proud of their linguistic tradition. The legacy in Caithness was more negative. Stiùbhart found, however, that Gaelic had indeed been the language of much of the county:

> The earliest description we have of the relative extent of Gaelic and English-speaking areas of Caithness dates from 1706, an era when a whole series of local descriptive accounts were being compiled across Scotland. Many of these were written by local ministers, with the focus firmly upon their own parish. One particular account lists where Gaelic was preached within the bounds of the presbytery of Caithness. It reported seven in all: Thurso, Halkirk, Reay, Latheron, Farr, Durness and Wick, but underlines the people of Wick understood English also. We should note the implication that, unlike bilingual Wick, the county town, Thurso parish was populated mainly by monoglot Gaels.

He added that another rather interesting source from the same time suggested just where the linguistic boundary lay. It had said: 'If ye suppose a Parallel to the hypotenuse drawn from Week [Wick] to Thurso, these on the Eastside of it speak most part English, and those on the

Westside Irish [Gaelic]; and the last have Ministers to preach to them in both languages.' Stiùbhart said: 'In other words the frontier may well have roughly followed the present-day railway line between the two towns.'

By the beginning of the 19th century Caithness was still a mainly Gaelic-speaking county; some 50.1 per cent of its 22,609 inhabitants spoke the language. 'But by the end of the century Gaelic was in terminal decline. By 1891 the population of Caithness had grown to 37,177, but the number of Gaelic speakers there had decreased to just 4,068.' The decline continued: 'In 1931 only 633 speakers were recorded, while census results between 1951 and 2001 reported almost negligible numbers. No locality had any number of speakers worth mentioning,' Stiùbhart said. He also underlined that throughout this tale many, if not most, of those who were deemed to be speaking English had in fact been speaking Caithness Scots. 'But that's another debate. Having ascertained that there was indeed such a people as native Caithness Gaels, and indeed that Gaelic was rather more widespread in the county than many believe, we must ask why there is still so much hostility towards Gaelic felt by some individuals in Caithness, and what might be done to overcome it?'

Stiùbhart thought the answer to the first was surely to do with the fact that Caithness was a rather unusual part of the country in that much of its history was shaped by a centuries-long bitter feud between families on either side of the linguistic border, namely the Sinclair Earls of Caithness and the Gaelic Mackays of Strathnaver: 'It was about land and power and was particularly bitter. Nothing unusual about that particularly in 16th and 17th century Scotland. But perhaps to a greater extent than almost any other locality in Scotland, language and culture were caught up in political affairs.'

Stiùbhart concluded in a characteristically enlightened flourish: 'Perhaps it might be time to lay this ancient enmity to rest. Caithness is one of those privileged areas of Scotland where the inhabitants can boast of a share in both of Scotland's languages and cultures: the marvellous riches both of English or Scots on the one hand, and of Scottish Gaelic on the other.'

In light of this I suggested in a 2013 blog the road signs should be trilingual in Caithness.

## Just making Gaelic up for tourists

In 2015 I wrote a *Weekend Magazine* feature headed 'Has Scotland betrayed its Gaelic heritage?' It concerned yet another of my wife's cousins, Coinneach Maclean, who was the son of Sorley's brother Alasdair, a GP on South Uist for many years. Three years earlier I had to write the obituary of Coinneach's twin brother Uisdean, who had been the first of the Raasay Maclean family I had met.

Coinneach Maclean trained as an archaeologist. But his subsequent career choices ranged from deer farming, community business development and housing investment. They gave him a deep understanding of the economic and cultural challenges facing many communities north of the Highland line. His subsequent time as deputy chief executive of the National Trust for Scotland also afforded him an appreciation of the complexities involved in the stewardship of natural and heritage assets. In his late 50s he embarked on a doctoral thesis at Glasgow University which he successfully completed. It was an important piece of work.

It exposed how Scotland's much vaunted tourism industry, which generates more than £4 billion of foreign exchange annually, either obscures the true story of Gaelic Scotland or airbrushes it out of its narrative altogether. This despite the landscape of the Highlands and Islands – the Gàidhealtachd – being the very image so often promoted by the industry. It is as though the Gaels had been all but removed from the land they had cherished for an epoch. It was no wilderness to them. Every hillock, burn and lochan had been dignified by a Gaelic name at one time; the wildlife and environment central, all remembered in poetry and song. As Highland historian Professor Jim Hunter put it in his book *The Other Side of Sorrow: Nature and People in the Scottish Highlands* (first published by Mainstream in 1995): 'For close on 1,500 years now, ever since the reciters of the Ulster sagas – drawing, perhaps, in Ireland on their knowledge of the Dalriada settlements – caused Deirdre to lament so eloquently her departure from her Scottish glen of steep-ridged peaks and pools and dappled deer and rowans and hawks and round-faced otters, our literature has consisted very largely of our efforts to explore the meaning of our place.'

But the Gaels' imprint has been remorselessly eroded. Maclean even found the process being unintentionally aided by some of those who indubitably love this land today, the mountaineering fraternity for example, who bundle peaks such as the Five Sisters of Kintail or the Three Sisters of Glencoe together for anglicised convenience. Maclean wrote in his thesis: 'Scotland represents one of the oldest sites of mass tourism, remains a significant part of the Scottish economy, and there is a substantial corpus of literature on the nature of the Highlands of Scotland. But, paradoxically, the Gael (the Gaelic Scot) is reduced to a silenced subaltern "other" under an unmediated "tourist gaze".'

As part of his research Maclean, a Gaelic speaker, went on a series of bus trips along Scotland's favoured tourist routes: Perth to Inverness via the likes of Killiecrankie; Loch Ness to Fort William and Ben Nevis; Glencoe to Rannoch Moor and Loch Lomond. He logged the historical and linguistic nonsense that often punctuated the commentary for visitors. They were told that Loch Ba on Rannoch Moor got its name from 'the noise sheep make' when it actually means 'loch of the cattle'. Meanwhile, Loch Lochy in the Great Glen was so called, visitors were told, because the ancient Gaels couldn't think of another word (Loch Lochaidh probably means 'loch of the dark water'). The air quality in the Highlands apparently 'leads to whiter sheep' and 'most of Inverness was destroyed by the last Jacobite rising'. It wasn't. The hydroelectric generating hall at Inveruglas on Loch Lomondside was explained thus: 'At this point the road used to flood with water from the hill. But this problem was cured by channelling it down in pipes, and then they decided that they could generate electricity from the power of the water flow' – an interesting perspective on the development of hydro power. Strontian had 'at least four possible meanings', when it has one – 'the snout of the fairy hill'.

In addition, 'Rob Roy was so physically challenged that he looked like a gorilla and his knuckles practically scraped the ground', and rather wonderfully 'there was a bit of controversy when Ossian published his poems a couple of centuries ago'. Ossian was a legendary Celtic warrior and bard. James Macpherson, a native Gael from Badenoch, had gained fame then notoriety in the 1760s for the literary sensation of apparently finding and translating the ancient works of Ossian. But in fact most of it was his own creation.

Maclean's own favourite was 'the relatively harmless gem that heather thatch was used instead of slate because the house walls were too weak to withstand the weight'. In reality the poor people had to use whatever material was at hand . . . Again there was the totally invented citing of the loss of the Ninth Roman Legion at Lix Toll (between Killin and Crianlarich), which was jazzed-up even more by claiming that 'the unfortunate Roman soldiers were eaten by supposedly cannibalistic Picts.' Also, Lix was supposed to represent the Roman numbers for 59. Why? Because it was 59 miles from Glasgow, of course. 'In fact it derives from the Gaelic word for a flagstone or hard slope,' Maclean explained.

His decision to write the thesis had followed another career change. He had embarked on a course, validated by Edinburgh University, designed to produce advanced 'blue badge' tourist guides. But he was shocked at some of the course content, or rather the lack of it:

> I was surprised and increasingly irritated by the almost total blanking of a Scottish Gaelic presence from both history and landscape. However, what concerned me more was that when reference was made to Gaelic culture it was treated as though it belonged to the Iron Age. The message was clear: it was a primitive language which was quite impenetrable and only capable of being mastered by gifted linguists. This in a Scotland which attracts people from around the globe, from across Africa and Asia, who manage to understand what they are hearing in English . . . It was one thing for the university to allow such nonsense to be peddled but what mattered more was that the students, who had paid good hard cash for the privilege, were being denied any knowledge that might have enabled them to effectively guide their clients through the Highlands.

He even heard one tutor reveal that when asked to speak a few words of Gaelic, 'any old gibberish will do'.

The only reference to Gaelic in the literature of the course was in a poem in Scots by William Dunbar called 'The Flyting of Dunbar and Kennedy', which hardly promoted the language:

> Mismaid monstour, ilk mone owt of they mynd,
> Renunce, ribald, thy rymyng, thow bot royis,
> Thy trechour tung hes tane ane heland strynd;
> And lawland ers wald mak a bettir noyis.

Maclean himself stepped forward and offered to give a couple of lectures by way of a general introduction to Gaeldom: 'Happily the new programme of guide training which the Scottish Tourist Guide Association initiated now has a small component on Gaelic history and culture.' Maclean had an important message for the tourist industry: 'All important tourist destinations across the world give high priority to delivering an authentic experience. Scotland is a mature destination and desperately needs to market itself on the strength of an authentic offering. At this time of raised awareness of our national identity, surely Scotland should tell its real story. For a start it would help if VisitScotland might consider paying a little more than lip service to Gaelic, given its absolutely central role in that story.'

He said the Gaelic plan produced by the agency as a public body in response to the demands of the Gaelic Language (Scotland) Act 2005 dealt entirely with 'transactional matters' such as putting up signs and gave no strategic thought to how Gaelic might be used in offering visitors an authentic experience. He suggested VisitScotland should support guide training initiatives: 'Support for quality training should be accompanied by an accreditation scheme which might prevent any Tom, Dick and Harry setting themselves up to take money from unsuspecting tourists by spouting arrant nonsense about Gaelic Scotland.'

But they are hardly alone on that front. The late Hugh Trevor-Roper, Lord Dacre, Regius Professor of Modern History at Oxford (who famously and wrongly authenticated Hitler's diaries), gleefully claimed that much of Scottish history and Gaelic culture was based on self-serving myths. Many of his arguments have been effectively challenged, not least by William Ferguson, the distinguished Edinburgh University historian, who wrote on the identity of the Scottish nation. He opined in the *Scottish Historical Review* in 2007: 'Nowhere is the absurdity of Trevor-Roper's "Scotch history" more apparent than in his essay on Highland tradition in the well-known volume entitled *The Invention of Tradition*. Nearly everything he has to say in that prolonged sneer is either mistaken or wide of the mark. How people have been taken in by that feeble stuff has puzzled me for years.'

Coinneach Maclean said: 'The problem is that too many, possibly in deference to his Oxford chair, have swallowed his ideas hook, line and sinker. It has become commonplace, for example, that his claims of an Englishman inventing the kilt are repeated as established historical fact by the likes of Jeremy Paxman. A millennium and a half of Gaelic tradition, apparently, is as naught in the face of an Oxford authority.'

Maclean for one has been doing his bit to set our record straight.

### A pink jumpsuit on the shores of Loch Nevis

Many of the stories I wrote about Gaelic concerned the politics surrounding the language and its funding, but there were others more enjoyable in which Gaelic was an element. I had an early lesson as to the usefulness of the language when I embarked with Cailean Maclean on a journey to visit Donald and Jessie MacDonald, a brother and sister who had lived their lives in a particularly lonely outpost.

This was in 1989 when Mr MacDonald estimated he was 'getting on 80' while his sister was about 10 years his senior. They had never moved away from Tarbet, Loch Nevis, apart from two years at Mallaig school when they stayed with an aunt. They took over the house, which was an inn and the croft they had been born on, and over the years had watched the remorseless erosion of a community that had been home to generation on generation of their people.

To get there we walked the seven-mile track along the northern shore of the freshwater Loch Morar before crossing over to the inlet of Loch Nevis where sits Tarbet (Gaelic scholars prefer Tarbert), named from the Gaelic for 'the isthmus between the two lochs'. On our way down we were greeted by something we weren't expecting to see, a youngish woman in a pink jumpsuit. It transpired she had answered an advert placed in *Lady* magazine: 'Help needed on hill farm. Good home and £10 a week.' It had been placed by Mr MacDonald. She had been tiring of the pressures of her career in marketing in the city of York and had decided to give it a try with the view to writing a book about Donald and Jessie's life. As a consequence, when she approached us on the path she initially didn't seem very keen that we interview her charges. However, Donald had come up behind her and Cailean spoke to him in Gaelic and there was no stopping him. Our bottle of whisky sealed the deal and we retired to their house to meet Jessie.

They told us of another time in Tarbet, when sailors and fishermen would seek the shelter of its bay, conduct business there and gather at the inn where, tradition had it, barrels would be filled with sovereigns, the fruits of their commerce. Across the bay stood the Roman Catholic chapel, the Star of the Seas. Once a month a priest would cross Loch Nevis from Inverie in Knoydart to tend to the spiritual needs of a flock which would fill the pews. From the scattered crofts children would wind their way along the mile-long rocky path up the loch to Kylesmorar, where the school provided the bulk of their formal education.

At the end of the 19th century things had started to change, with the coming of the railway to Mallaig ensuring the growth of that port at the expense of Tarbet. It could not compete. There was, and is, no road to it. Tarbet lost her people. The MacDonald croft and the empty church were all that was round the bay when we visited in 1989 save the ruins of another time. Holiday houses (one owned by Cameron Mackintosh, the London-based multi-millionaire producer of the show *Cats*) and an adventure centre (owned by the Atlantic oarsman Tom McClean) were the MacDonalds' only near neighbours by then.

There used to be a post office attached to the MacDonalds' house and fishermen told of the 'Wednesday half-day' sign which was displayed by Donald, and a brother before him, who used to run it. But it went with the people, leaving the two visits from the mail-boat from Mallaig (three in the summer) as not only the MacDonalds' lifeline but also their only reliable social contact in a week. Thirty years on I still remember that visit and often wonder what would have gone through Jessie or Donald's mind when they opened their door in the morning and looked across the landscape that had been their life, but had emptied.

### Gaelic scholars as suspects

On Gaelic-related matters I am reminded of a story I wrote more than 20 years ago which appeared in *The Herald* on Boxing Day 1997. I remember it because I thought it an interesting tale but also because of how my colleague on the subeditors' bench in Glasgow decided to improve it. He added druids to the introduction, thereby making the first sentences utterly inaccurate by at least 1,000 years. If we take the druids out, the story concerned the theft of a priceless and unique manuscript, thought to be one of the earliest transcriptions of the work of the celebrated 18th-century unlettered Gaelic poet Rob Donn. It was stolen some time in the 1960s from the National Library of Scotland in Edinburgh.

Rob Donn lived in Sutherland between 1714 and 1778, and his grave can still be seen in Baile na Cille churchyard near Durness. He was a Mackay and this was Mackay country where the chiefs managed to retain or recreate the ancestral pattern of cultural life encouraged by the old Lords of the Isles far later than any of the other clans elsewhere in the Gàidhealtachd. As a poet and observer of this, Rob Donn's work has been seen as crucial to understanding our past. In his book *The World of Rob Donn* (first published in 1979 by The Edina Press, Edinburgh), historian Ian Grimble wrote: 'Rob Donn remains the last and greatest of those who were in a position to interpret and illuminate the traditional, tribal way of life of Gaelic Scotland before it was destroyed . . . But the corpus of poetry that he did bequeath to posterity entitles him to the highest place amongst the illiterate peasant poets of Europe.' Grimble speculated that had Rob Donn been literate 'he might have been another Euripides among the Greeks'.

His work was handed down by oral tradition, being published first only in 1829, half a century after his death. But the missing manuscript appeared significantly to pre-date that first publication. Its original catalogue entry at the National Library, the fullest description there is of it, reads: 'Paper. Note-book. 7 1/2 x 4 and 5/8th ins. Bound mottled boards and paginated by the scribe, pages 1–137. Contains collection of poems chiefly by Robb Donn.' It then goes on to list an 'Account of the life of Rob Donn (Mackay)'; 25 separate entries for poems of varying length; and a final intriguing 'Note by scribe:- These Poems were taken from Janet McKay, dr. to the Rob McKay before Duncan McIntyre, poet, this 22nd of December 1800'.

The idea that they had been taken down directly by or from Donn's own daughter and in the presence of the great Argyllshire bard Duncan Ban MacIntyre (1724–1812) only increased the significance of the National Library of Scotland's loss.

Librarian Ian McGowan told *The Herald* that the manuscript had been an important document and that he deeply regretted its theft, adding:

It appears that it was in the early 1960s that it was removed from the library. That was long before my time here, but as far as I can gather there has never been any publicity about its loss. The obvious assumption is that it was somebody interested or involved in Gaelic scholarship. It is not the sort of manuscript that would interest a wide range of people.

That said, there is a market for Gaelic material; for all things Scottish in fact, and not just within Scotland's borders. It would be impossible to put any price on the manuscript at present. The market would have to be tested before you could get an idea of price.

The chances are that some unscrupulous Celtic scholar somewhere knows the whole story. In 2012 a refurbished memorial was unveiled to Rob Donn in Baile na Cille.

# 5

# History Matters

THE HISTORY OF the Highlands and Islands has been the subject of much debate and remains so to this day. It has become common for people of a certain age in Scotland to insist that the history they were taught in school was Scottish up till the Act of Union in 1707 or perhaps the Jacobite Risings 40 years later. But after the Battle of Culloden in 1746, it became English history or that of the British Empire. 'We were never taught about the Highland Clearances' is the most common exemplar. Sorley, however, had grown up immersing himself in the substantial corpus of Gaelic tradition which told of that time. In 1938 he wrote in an article entitled 'The Poetry of the Clearances':

> I have little doubt that four-fifths of the emigration from 1780 to 1880 was caused directly or indirectly by the Clearances, or by such close relations of the Clearances as rack-renting and appropriation, by landlords, of the best agricultural and pastoral land . . . All poetry reflects social phenomena, and in the Highlands of the 19th century emigration of one kind or another was the phenomenon of phenomena . . . The Highland Clearances constitute one of the saddest tragedies that has ever come on a people, and one of the most astounding of all the successes of landlord capitalism in Western Europe, such a triumph over the workers and peasants of a country as has rarely been achieved with such ease, cruelty and cynicism . . . The Leckmelm (near Ullapool) eviction in 1880 and the Battle of the Braes in 1882 mark respectively the end of the Clearance period proper and the beginning of crofter resistance.

Three and a half decades later his views were unchanged, as witnessed in the film *Sorley Maclean's Island* which Douglas Eadie directed in 1974:

Ever since I was a boy in Raasay and became aware of the differences between the history I read in books and the oral accounts I heard around me, I have been very sceptical of what might be called received history; the million people for instance who died in Ireland in the nineteenth century; the million more who had to emigrate; the thousands of families forced from their homes in the Highlands and Islands. Why was all that? Famine? Overpopulation? Improvement? The Industrial Revolution? Expansion overseas? You see, not many of these people understood such words, they knew only Gaelic. But we know now another set of words: clearance, empire, profit, exploitation, and today we live with the bitter legacy of that kind of history. Our Gaelic language is threatened with extinction, our way of life besieged by the forces of international big business, our country's beggared by bad communication, the iniquities of land ownership, the failures and unconcern of central government. Our culture is vitiated by the sentimentality of those who have gone away. We have, I think, a deep sense of generation and community but that has in so many ways been broken. We have a history of resistance but now mainly in the songs we sing. Our children are bred for emigration.

Sorley speaking these lines also appears on a track released in 2015 by Niteworks, the band founded on Skye which blends Gaelic, traditional and electronic music. That his thoughts entered popular culture in this manner will be assumed by certain figures to somehow invalidate them. He never indicated to me he had changed his mind at all. Many historians, some of whom Sorley would have been talking about, have criticised the emotion that has been attached to the subject of the Highland Clearances; they argue that their significance is grossly overstated in historical terms, or that there was an economic inevitability which somehow excused landlord excesses in evicting their tenants.

Some find it strange that I count Michael Fry as one of my friends, given that we have been on opposite sides of the debate for so long.

Forty years of us arguing, and neither has moved the other one whit. As it happened, we were both amongst the speakers at a conference at Strathclyde University in 1996 on Highland history, organised by Sir Tom Devine, who is regularly billed today as Scotland's leading historian. Sir Tom was interviewed a year ago by a Sunday newspaper. He was in the Highlands, researching illustrations for his next book, *Dispossession: The Scottish Clearances*. He said, 'I'm going to argue that the scale of dispossession in the rural Lowlands was even greater than it was in the Highlands. And this is going to create considerable controversy. That's what history is all about – argument, counter-argument.'

Just before I finished editing this book in the summer of 2018, Sir Tom wrote an article in *The Scotsman* about the late John Prebble's *The Highland Clearances*, published for the first time in 1963, which he notes remains the best-selling Scottish history book ever written, having achieved worldwide sales of more than a quarter of a million. In this article Sir Tom writes of the Clearances: 'There is indeed still much to be said about this controversial and emotive subject. In my new book, *The Scottish Clearances*, which will be published later this year, I return to the saga of the dispossession of peasant communities, not just in the Highlands but throughout Scotland between 1600 to 1900. Based on four decades of research, writing, teaching and reflection I see it as my most ambitious and challenging project to date.'

I have no doubt it will cause a stir, and so should *Scotland's Populations from the 1850s to Today* by the former Vice Principal of Edinburgh University, Michael Anderson, (Oxford University Press, 2018). Professor Anderson, who had the good sense to marry my cousin Elspeth MacArthur, is a distinguished economic historian. His book's detailed analysis of Scotland's demographic trends, which took him to 95 per cent of Scottish parishes, argues that while the Highlands may look empty today, they were always almost empty. While there was depopulation, he finds that much of it took place not only after 1850 and the period associated with many of the most notorious Highland evictions, but after 1890 and the years of crofter resistance, right through into the postwar period. He doubts that even the most apparently fertile Highland glens of today could ever have been farmed as really productive arable land before modern field drainage, land clearance and modern fertiliser techniques came into use. He believes that, as a consequence, human settlements were always fairly dispersed up many Highland glens.

This puts him at odds with the likes of Jim Hunter, whose work on the Sutherland Clearances (more of which later) found that in one glen alone, Strathbrora, there had been 62 different townships cleared in the second and third decades of the 19th century. He also worked on old military maps which indicated intensive cultivation in the Sutherland glens in the 18th and early 19th centuries. Whether or not the Highlands and Islands suffered worse depopulation numerically compared with other parts of Scotland I have never felt to be the most important issue. Rather it was the impact on the people, which Sorley described as 'the phenomenon of phenomena'. This has been recognised by others. At the time of writing, *Dispossession* had not been published but I have no doubt it will cause a stir.

T.C. Smout, who could be suspicious of the emotion surrounding the Clearances, wrote on this in the second volume of his *A Century of the Scottish People* (first published by William Collins in 1986), saying that rural depopulation was not peculiar to Scotland, never mind the Highlands and Islands. It happened across England and Wales and through Europe: 'In Scotland there was, however, a very remarkable contrast in people's reactions to the process of rural depopulation. In the Highlands, it was associated with enormous resentment: stamped with the word "clearance", with overtones of violence, oppression and hopeless suffering. In the Lowlands, there were no such associations; it just occurred and was accepted.'

But Professor Smout, who was to become Historiographer Royal in Scotland seven years after this book was published, did concede there were reasons for the difference in the Highlands:

> There were, however, two significant peculiarities in the Highland situation, especially in the first half of our period. One was that, at the very start, the element of force used to divorce men from the land was much greater than elsewhere.
> . . .
> The second distinctive thing about the mid-Victorian Highlander – it was connected, indeed, with the first, the degree of violence deemed necessary to effect the Clearances – was that many in the north-west perceived that occupation of a traditional area of land, and not acquisition of new wealth, was the greatest good that life had to offer.

In 2000 there was another engagement in the war of words between historians over the Highland Clearances. A new edition of Jim Hunter's celebrated book, *The Making of the Crofting Community*, was published. In an updated preface, Hunter, by this time Chairman of Highlands and Islands Enterprise, attacked some leading historians for siding with the landlords of the time. He did not include Tom Devine in his list.

> Their interpretation of Highland history was one which gave no credence to – in fact, virtually never cited – any Gaelic and other sources from which one can form some impression of how the Highland Clearances and associated developments were perceived by the folk on the receiving end. Instead [this] school relied on the record of estate managements, on travelogues produced by visitors from the south, on the correspondence and reports of public officials. In its setting aside of the Highland perspective on the Highland past, this school's output, I duly felt, was the precise counterpart of Trevor-Roper's 'history of the Europeans in Africa'. [The controversial Regius Professor of Modern History at Oxford said in 1963 in a series of lectures at Sussex University later broadcast by the BBC: 'Perhaps in the future, there will be some African history to teach. But at present there is none: there is only the history of Europeans in Africa. The rest is darkness.'] And it seemed to me imperative, when I commenced work on *The Making of the Crofting Community*, that this anti-Highland travesty of Highland history be overthrown in the same spirit – and with the late 20th century version of the many defences it had mounted – 100 or more years earlier – of the Highland Clearances.

Professor Devine had earlier written:

> Perhaps only James Hunter among recent writers has tried to provide some scholarly support for the more popular interpretation of Highland history. In Hunter's book, the landlords are once again cast in their traditional role as villains, dominating and exploiting their people and systematically pursuing policies of clearance and forced emigration. Hunter's analysis has

not been generally accepted within the mainstream of historical research despite its wide-ranging archival research. This
is partly because of the author's unwillingness to set landlord
activity in its social and cultural context and his failure to com-
bine demographic and economic analysis with an evaluation of
elite behaviour.

Sorley, however, held Jim Hunter and his work in the highest esteem
and would have supported his view of traditional approaches to writing
history when Hunter wrote: 'I have never grasped why some historians
– though not, in my experience, the greatest historians – see virtue in
declining to empathise with the people whose lives they survey.' He
said Sutherland was an important example:

> Why do Scotland's historians, living and working in a country
> where nowhere is more than a few hours from anywhere else,
> so neglect what Simon Schama – an outstandingly successful
> explorer of the world's past – calls 'The Archive of the Feet'?
> Nowhere is that archive more easily accessed than in Sutherland.
> Go to Strathnaver and spend an hour or two among the wide,
> sheltered fields, whose cultivators Patrick Sellar evicted in
> 1815. Travel next to the desperately exposed coastal locations
> – Strathy Point and Bettyhill, for example – where Sellar's
> men installed Strathnaver former residents on five-acre plots
> of windswept rock and bog. Nothing is more implausible, in
> the light of such a journey, than the notion that Strathnaver's
> occupants were evicted solely to enhance their wellbeing.

Fighting between academics, and historians in particular, is common.
This exchange seems modest compared to some, as anyone who has
read Adam Sisman's well received *Hugh Trevor-Roper: The Biography*
(Weidenfeld & Nicolson, 2010) will recognise. The public I believe
largely stays aloof from such exchanges, regardless of how heated they
can become. The row between Jim Hunter and other historians was
reported in the Scottish media, but it is unlikely it made much of an
impact on the majority of the Scottish people. Few who believed that
they had been denied knowledge of the Highland Clearances while at
school would accept now that the evictions were not a highly important

episode, not least, as Hunter argued, when they have the evidence of their own eyes as they look out over much of Highland Scotland.

Hunter's latest book, *Set Adrift Upon the World: The Sutherland Clearances* (Birlinn, 2015), won the Saltire Society's History Book of the Year award in 2016. In this he tells how the people of Kildonan suffered as the House of Sutherland embarked on a programme of improvement for its estate. He follows them across the Atlantic in 1813 and on their epic journey from Hudson Bay to Red River, now Winnipeg (where my sister Janet has lived for half a century), the following year. The Saltire Society stated: 'Rarely have the Clearances been written about so evocatively. Hunter's method and his empathy with those involved speaks to us with elegant restraint in an account that sweeps from the Sutherland straths to the struggles of those forced to seek new lives in North America.'

It is clear that Hunter has a different sort of authority on Highland matters from those who promote what Sorley described as 'received history'. He has spent much of his life writing 13 books, and is working on a 14th, helping us understand the lives of the ordinary people of Gaelic Scotland better, both in their homelands and when they left for the likes of North America. Crucially, he has also worked tirelessly to try to shape a meaningful future for the Highlands and Islands. He has been willing to roll up his sleeves and get his hands dirty – sometimes literally. He produced a report on the feasibility of establishing a representative body for Scotland's 11,000 crofters in the 1980s. Once the Scottish Crofters Union, now the Scottish Crofting Federation, was established he became its first director – few of his historian critics who write about Highland land can know as much about what grazes on it. He chaired Skye and Lochalsh Enterprise and served on a Scottish Natural Heritage area board. He served for six years as chair of Highlands and Islands Enterprise then became the first Director (indeed first staff member) of the University of the Highlands and Islands' Centre for History in Dornoch between 2005 and 2010, albeit part-time. The original idea was that it would be a research centre. But he was convinced within weeks that, to have any chance of viability, it had to be a teaching centre as well. He told me this year: 'With the key help of Dr Karen Cullen, my first colleague and a young and brilliant historian, we made that happen. There are eight full-time history staff now in Dornoch, a biggish industry by Sutherland standards. They teach 200-plus students across the Highlands and Islands. They teach Masters students around the world and they supervise a growing number of folk turning out first-rate PhD theses. This team is headed by Dr David Worthington. I'm quite hopelessly proud of them and their achievements.'

He also served on the board of Community Land Scotland, the umbrella organisation for the community buyouts such as Eigg, Knoydart and Gigha. Having started his working life as a journalist with the *Press & Journal* and then the late lamented *Sunday Standard*, he understands the media.

Jim Hunter is a trusted figure in the Highlands. He is a long-time supporter of Scottish independence and a member of the SNP, but is very public in his criticisms of the Scottish government. He led opposition to plans to replace individual agency boards with a Scotland-wide strategic board to co-ordinate the activities of Scottish Enterprise, Highlands and Islands Enterprise, Scottish Development International, Skills Development Scotland and the Scottish Funding Council. He denounced this as SNP control-freakery, breaching a 50-year consensus stretching back to the establishment of the Highlands and Islands Development Board. It was debated in the Scottish parliament with MSPs inflicting a rare defeat on the Scottish government, who eventually compromised, allowing a form of Highlands and Islands Enterprise board to continue but reporting to a national body. He has also been critical of the pace of land reform.

I first interviewed him for *The Herald* in January 1989 when he was living on Skye. The paper billed him as 'Architect of the crofting resurgence'. He had not been born on a croft, however, but rather into the house of a Forestry Commission trapper at Duror, near Appin. But he had crofting connections on both sides which were to bring him into contact with its traditions, and what he told me then was similar to Sorley's views on Highland history:

> The first I heard about the Highland Clearances was from my mother's father, whose parents had been crofters, but he himself was a farm manager for an estate at Kingairloch. In fact the reason I got interested in all of that was that when I did some Scottish History as an undergraduate at Aberdeen University it was borne in upon me that the received academic view of what happened in the Highlands in the nineteenth century was not

at all the same as I had been hearing from my grandfather. If I was motivated by anything I was motivated by the desire to show in an academically reputable way that the Highland view of Highland history was the right one.

He also cited the work of the highly controversial figure John Prebble as helping to persuade him that the history of the Highlands was interesting. He told me recently: 'Donald Meek gave me his copy of Prebble's *Glencoe* to read just after it came out when we were both in Oban High. For the first time I became properly aware that there was a Highland "history" in the full sense of that word. Previously, I think, I thought of "history" in terms of the foreign policy of Queen Elizabeth I or Pitt the Younger, while the Highland past was just a sort of "story", nothing really to do with the serious subject of history.'

## Historian without honour

'A thousand small streams from the north and south create the River Coe. At the Meeting of the Waters, below the Little Herdsman of Etive, it leaps westward over a rock and now the Pass of Glencoe truly begins . . .' So wrote John Prebble in his book *Glencoe*, published in 1966. It was at this same point, the Meeting of the Waters, that his ashes were scattered one Sunday in June 2002, 66 years after he first visited a place which would stay with him for the rest of his life.

The man who brought the history of Highland Scotland to more people than any other historian in the 20th century had died in January the previous year, but his wish to be left in Glencoe was frustrated by the foot-and-mouth crisis, which had limited travel and movement in rural areas. His widow, Jan, her stepdaughter, Sarah, and her two sons, and Alan Bolter, a family friend, finally travelled north to honour their commitment to him. I had also been invited to attend and had been accompanied by the award-winning *Herald* photographer Angela Catlin. We were the only other people present.

The one and only meeting I had with John Prebble had been in June 1995, although I had talked to him a number of times on the phone. I had wanted to interview him because of the controversy surrounding Scottish universities' apparent determination not to award him an honorary degree. In the January of that year journalist Brian Wilson, by then a Labour MP and spokesman, used his column in the *West Highland Free Press* to pay tribute to the historian, writer and broadcaster Ian Grimble, who had just died. He argued that Grimble, author of such works as *The Trial of Patrick Sellar* and *The World of Rob Donn*, had not received sufficient recognition in Scotland, a place, Brian said, 'where there is little academic honour awarded those who have preferred truth to the cover-up, particularly over the history of the Highlands'. He concluded: 'I was reminded by Grimble's death of a conversation I had a while back with Jim Hunter, about the similar lack of recognition accorded to John Prebble – and in particular the fact that no Scottish university has had the vision to award him an honorary degree for his immense services to historical knowledge. As a matter of principle, it is long past time for that omission to be remedied and all of us who care about these matters should say so with one voice.'

Jim Hunter and Brian Wilson have themselves been outstanding Highland champions in modern times, but they have not always agreed, not least on the issue of Scottish independence. But on the issue of the hugely popular Prebble, they did speak with one voice, as Jim Hunter confirmed to me for the article: 'There is no writer living who has done more to introduce people, in Scotland and all over the world, to Scottish history and Highland history in particular. John Prebble is a quite marvellous writer, a great stylist whose work is so accessible. He is a superb historian. I have raised the question of an honorary degree at fairly high levels within our Scottish universities, and I have never received a satisfactory answer. I simply do not know why John Prebble has not been honoured.'

Hunter had also been confused by the fact that there was hardly an academic historian in Scotland who would admit Prebble's name to their bibliography. He had always done so and as did others further afield. 'What has been interesting recently is that Linda Colley, Professor of History at Yale and widely regarded as an outstandingly original historian, has produced her marvellous work, *Britons Forging the Nation 1707–1837*. In this she draws on John Prebble's work, particularly *The King's Jaunt* about George IV's visit to Scotland in 1822. She isn't embarrassed to admit to having read Prebble,' Hunter said. It had been John Prebble's preference for dramatic reconstruction to the systematic analysis demanded by established traditions of historical scholarship which had offended academia.

He was on his annual holiday to a hotel overlooking Loch Melfort, south of Oban, when I interviewed him in Argyll in 1995. There, with the islands of Luing and Scarba pointing south to the Sound of Jura, his obsession with the past was as infectious as it was in print. But talk about honorary degrees he found both embarrassing and touching. He thought it would be presumptuous of him to assume that the Scottish universities should recognise him. But he was unrepentant:

> I don't think of myself as an historian, I am a writer. I write about what interests me. I admire academic scholarship. But I think they [academics] can be a bit arrogant about it and can be their own worst enemies. In order to write history they scrupulously avoid all the opportunities that literature gives them. They will not use what I call deductive assumption, they will not use words that arouse emotions in the reader. What they want is an intellectual reaction. But history has a longer record than that. Julius Caesar was not beyond writing phrases that aroused the spirit. What terrifies me is how historians will treat people like Stalin and Hitler 200 years from now, dispassionately and bloodlessly, trying not to raise anger.

It was Scotland's history which had embraced him, and he it. His first book was *The High Girders* (1956), the story of the Tay Bridge disaster of 1879, but his mission lay further north. *Culloden*, first published 1961, originally by Atheneum, followed by *The Highland Clearances* (Secker & Warburg, 1963) and *Glencoe: The Story of the Massacre* (Secker & Warburg, 1966), were all bought by many millions of people when they appeared as Penguin paperbacks. They continue to sell in craftshops, bookshops, chain stores and every imaginable tourist outlet. But there have been other important books in which he took some pride: *The Darien Disaster; Mutiny: Highland Regiments in Revolt* and *The Lion in the North*. There was nothing in his own background which would have pointed to such subject matters. Indeed, the first he heard of the Scottish Highlands was as a small boy in a classroom in Sutherland, Saskatchewan. His parents moved there in 1921 when he was just six. But the better life proved elusive. The Prairie provinces were already sliding into the Great Depression by the time they arrived. The young Prebble's schooling there was at the hands of a Scots Canadian, Miss

Campbell, whose hero was James Wolfe, 'The Conqueror of Canada', and who never tired telling of the role played by the Fraser Highlanders: 'Although Miss Campbell had never been to Scotland she spoke of it with an intense pride. Undoubtedly it was in these childhood years that my interest in the country formed its first imaginative roots, if only because all that she told us about that far land of mist and mountain was in so great contrast to the familiar world about us,' Prebble told me.

His family were to return to London, and thereafter, as he recalled in his autobiography, *Landscapes and Memories* (McVitie book prize-winner in 1993), he was to extend his reading. In 1933, his last year in school, he came across *The Lyon in Mourning* in which Episcopalian priest, later bishop, Robert Forbes painstakingly, and some would say extravagantly, recorded in 10 volumes the suffering at Culloden and its aftermath.

Forbes was a dedicated Jacobite and his work was partisan, exactly the sort of source material viewed so suspiciously by academic historians. Prebble defended it and said it had a profound effect on him: 'I read it in the British Museum beneath the awesome dome of the library. I had early abandoned the bold reason I gave when applying for a reader's ticket, a proposed biography of Titus Oates, and I do not think I took out another book during that first year . . . by the end of that year I was already in love with a country I had yet to see, and inspired by a history I had yet to understand.'

There was no reason why he should. His mother had been a London factory girl and his father a sailor. Neither knew much about their own past and accepted a High Anglican/Tory tradition. But Prebble came to look further back. He saw his roots deep in many generations of rural labourers, his father's people in Kent and his mother's in Hertfordshire and Essex. He looked even further back across five and a half centuries and came to identify with the agrarian radical tradition, the Peasants' Revolt, even then one of the few left in England to do so. His empathy for those on the land was a constant feature in his work whether in Kent in the 15th century or Strathnaver in the 19th. It was still part of the man I interviewed. He told me: 'I would hate to be a farmworker, but I believe that people who have a union with the soil and the country, no matter how painful or onerous, have a spiritual strength which a nation loses at its own risk.' It was hardly surprising that he said he felt 'a very warm glow' when he heard that the Assynt crofters had bought the

North Lochinver Estate two and a bit years earlier, 'But I would advise the people of Assynt to look behind every rock because what they are up against is so big, so implacable.'

From Assynt in the 1990s to Kent of the 1380s and back again, it was just one of the historical threads that Prebble could spin with warmth and humanity. He was always on the side of the common, ordinary people as they wrestled with the murderous forces of history. The Glencoe MacDonalds in 1692, the native North Americans in the 19th century, or the children of Europe 70 years ago – he saw no difference. They were all just people who didn't matter. Despite this he displayed an extraordinary empathy for the common soldier, be he in the Duke of Cumberland's army on its way to Culloden; in a black regiment in the Union Army driving the Comanches from their homelands; or with him in a truck at the gates of Belsen in 1945. He said: 'Soldiering is a filthy trade, you give it your youth. I gave it six years.' His youth had been overshadowed by the prospect of war and the memory of the Great War. 'What I knew of that obscene struggle was so terrible that I believed that it could have been endured by exceptional men only. The omnipresent survivors of its horror and betrayal – a gassed and yellow-skinned uncle gently coughing over his watch-repairing, blue-coated and maimed figures seen across the green parks of military hospitals in the Home Counties, kerbside buskers with greasy ribbons and tarnished medals – all these must be superior men from a now broken mould.'

It was hardly surprising that he, like so many of that generation who refused to accept the established order of things, joined the Communist Party, or indeed later that he was to leave it. He didn't greatly suffer from his period as a party member, although the matter was raised by Lord Beaverbrook while Prebble was in his employ as a journalist. Many of a radical bent found themselves in that state. But while A.J.P. Taylor was moved to write: 'Beaverbrook's friendship enriched me. The joys of his company are beyond description', Prebble could only manage: 'I cannot say I ever liked this man. His generosity was calculated, and his use of power was accompanied at times by a childish spite which cured any warmth.'

But a decade before he took the Canadian's shilling, he had finally made it to Scotland and to the Highlands. At 21 he had taken a ship from Wapping to Leith, a tram to Edinburgh and a train to Fort

William and then Mallaig. For two weeks he walked around Sunart, Ardnamurchan and Moidart. These lands stayed with him. In 1959 he came north to Inverness 'to write an article for the *Reader's Digest* about tartan or something. It wasn't accepted.' But he took the opportunity to visit Culloden battlefield and on impulse resolved to write about those who had died there.

In the interview he wasn't sure he would publish anything more: 'I don't know whether I have written myself out or whether I am getting old. But the last three years have been stressful. My first wife had Alzheimer's disease and it was very difficult. I am married again now. I have got two books in mind. One is an editing job. My sainted mother died at the age of 96; when she was 92 she wrote an autobiography, which I want to put together. She was a little Cockney girl who left school at eleven and a half and never made a spelling or a grammatical mistake. I am not altering a word of it, although she didn't know what a paragraph was.' The other project he had in mind was a novel about the last day or 12 hours in the life of Mary, Queen of Scots. 'What happened? Probably not much,' he said.

In 1997 he was finally awarded an honorary degree from Glasgow University, the only university to do so. This was entirely due to the efforts of Professor Edward J. Cowan, Professor of Scottish History there. Any such honour presumably would have been opposed by the late Professor Gordon Donaldson of Edinburgh University, Historiographer Royal, who had once described Prebble's work as 'utter rubbish'.

Prebble's widow, Jan, said that he tried not to let it bother him, 'But I think he got a bit fed up with the academics. Because he didn't do footnotes it gave them grounds to say he had been using his imagination. But after he died I got quite a few letters from people saying that they had started by seeing him as a novelist but ended valuing his history.'

In 2015 the National Library of Scotland announced that it was buying John Prebble's papers. Dr Catriona MacDonald, Reader in Late Modern Scottish History at Glasgow University, has been studying them. Her mother was from Harris, her father from North Uist, but she describes herself as a proud child of Partick. She told me:

John Prebble transformed Scottish history in ways that few have appreciated and even fewer have celebrated. This is, in my opinion, a gross injustice. While academics in Scotland celebrated new approaches to social history that emerged in the 1960s, heralded by E.P. Thompson's *Making of the English Working Classes*, many failed to see that under their noses a Canadian had been doing the same in Scotland – rescuing the Highlander from the 'condescension of posterity'. One exception to this rule was the Historiographer Royal, Professor T.C. Smout. What's more, unlike Oxbridge academics, Prebble was doing it in ways that genuinely reached a public audience – reached them in ways that re-set their perceptions of what Scottish history ought to be about, and what therefore its future might be. Having worked in Prebble's archive, I was struck by the intensity of the research that went in to his books, and the generosity of spirit from which he wrote. This was not – as some have suggested – victimology. It was a gentle re-visioning of a popular appreciation of Scottish history that was long overdue. Prebble's Scots did not end victims: they challenged, they mutinied, they strived. As a great-granddaughter of a man whose family were cleared not once but twice, Prebble began his work in the decade when I was born, making my route to history a more meaningful one. Few, after Prebble, would dismiss the Clearances as previous generations had done. For that I am grateful.

## MacDonalds on a fence

In January 1995 it was reported that the High Chief of the Clan Donald, Lord Godfrey Macdonald of Macdonald, was offering North Americans a chance to 'honor' their ancestors who fell at the Battle of Culloden in 1746 by buying into a Culloden Memorial Garden at his Kinloch Lodge on Skye's Sleat peninsula. It is 100 miles from the battlefield which saw the Jacobite cause extinguished. An advert appeared in the December issue that year of the *Highlander* magazine which circulates in the US and Canada, advising of an 'opportunity so special it comes only once every 250 years'. It explained: 'The centrepiece of the Garden is a Memorial Stone for all those who fell at Culloden. Placed around this stone will be individual memorials dedicated to those families whose forebears are forever linked to the tragic circumstances of that battle.

For generations to come, your personal plaque or stone will honor your ancestors or your present family members. Memorial Stones and Plaques are available to individuals, families or corporations in three options of style and size starting at $250.' Readers were advised to act quickly and that, for those who took pride in their Highland heritage, 'nothing you do today could be more important'.

Lord Godfrey also explained the site was 'as dramatic as the battle itself' and 'particularly appropriate for those whose forebears are of Clan Donald descent'. What the advert didn't explain was that Lord Godfrey's own forebear, Sir Alexander Macdonald of Sleat, was not actually at Culloden, nor were his clansmen. Despite having Jacobite sympathies, he was officially on the Hanoverian side. The decision not to take the Sleat Macdonalds out for the Jacobites may even have been taken by Sir Alexander at a house on the site of the present hotel. It is thought that Sir Alexander's role in Soitheach-nan-Daoine, 'the ship of the people', had forced him into the decision. In 1739 ordinary people were taken from the Skye lands of both Sir Alexander and MacLeod of MacLeod to be sold into slavery as bonded servants in the Americas. This rather shady business had allowed Forbes of Culloden, the Lord President of the Court of Session, to blackmail these two gentlemen into declaring themselves as Hanoverian, to avoid prosecution.

The *West Highland Free Press*'s brilliant cartoonist Chris Tyler had the last word on Lord Godfrey's memorial garden project, attracting the attention of newspapers throughout Scotland and beyond. He drew a series of gravestones with the names of sponsors on them including HYDRO ELECTRIC PLC, MARK THATCHER'S ARMS CORP, and messages such as READ THE SUN, THIS STONE IS SPONSORED BY THE PEPSI CORPORATION. McDonald's were on one shaped like the chain's capital M logo. In pride of place, however, was one with the inscription: THIS MEMORIAL GARDEN MARKS THE EXACT SITE OF THE FENCE ON WHICH THE MACDONALDS OF SLEAT WERE SITTING WHILE THE BATTLE OF CULLODEN WAS BEING FOUGHT IN 1746.

It would have been news to many Americans and indeed Scots that the Macdonalds of Sleat were Hanoverian in the 1745 Rising, unlike their clansmen of Clanranald, Glengarry, Keppoch and Glencoe. The more so that they were involved in the subsequent search for

Bonnie Prince Charlie when he went on the run across the Highlands and Islands. Even fewer would know that it was one of these same MacDonalds who was the architect of the prince's escape in what was to become one of the best-known boat trips of all time. According to Alasdair Maclean and John S. Gibson in their book *A Summer Hunting a Prince: The Escape of Charles Edward Stuart* (Acair, Stornoway, 1991): 'It was to the Prince in the cave behind Beinn Ruigh Choinnich (in South Uist) that a messenger now brought a surprising proposal from none other than Hugh MacDonald of Armadale, who commanded the MacDonald Militia company, ostensibly hunting for him in South Uist. This was to the effect that the Prince should be disguised as a woman and ferried over to Skye as maid servant to Flora MacDonald, a young gentlewoman of the Milton family of South Uist who was also Armadale's step-daughter.'

Dr Alasdair Maclean had been a renowned GP on South Uist for decades after the Second World War and was Sorley's brother. He would talk at length to his older patients in Gaelic of the oral tradition of the islands. One man, Duncan MacDonald of Peninerine, gave him the story of another of the occupants of the boat that left Loch Uisgebhagh – one Neil MacEachan, a MacDonald. He was an important Jacobite agent who was to go into exile with the prince. His son was to became Napoleon's Marshal MacDonald, later created the First Duke of Taranto. (There was a story that Napoleon never deployed MacDonald against the British Army as he didn't want him hearing the sound of bagpipes.)

Maclean wrote that this was all new to him, and when he asked his source about the more famous Flora MacDonald, 'something of the magic had gone and the flame of Duncan's enthusiasm diminished'. It became clear to Maclean that his 'schoolboy history' of Flora MacDonald had hidden a more important story which had not been in his textbooks or other historical works but had been passed down through generations of islanders.

So it was that the cross-dressing prince and his party on a June evening left from the south side of Loch Uisgebhagh on Benbecula's east coast to sail over the sea to Skye's west coast and into the immortality created by the 'Skye Boat Song' written by Sir Harold Boulton in 1884. Yet many visitors to Skye believe the famous journey had been from the mainland, probably from where the Skye Bridge now stands.

Nothing has marked where they left Benbecula, but that should be addressed soon by Stòras Uibhist, the community owners of South Uist and much of Benbecula. A heritage trail is planned celebrating the island's history, including the escape of Bonnie Prince Charlie and the sinking of the *Whisky Galore!* ship SS *Politician* in the Sound of Eriskay in 1941. The chairman of Stòras Uibhist, Angus MacMillan, told me just before I retired: 'There is still nothing to mark the spot, but the true story is important to these islands.' More too could be done on the Skye side. According to Neil MacEachan's *Narrative of the Wanderings of Prince Charles in the Hebrides*, they first landed in Waternish on the north of Skye, where they rested for an hour before taking off in their boat again heading north-east, landing in Kilbride on the Trotternish peninsula. There is no sign to mark either spot.

Myths endure about much of Highland history, repeated by some unlikely people. Channel 4 News came up to the Highlands before the 2015 general election to examine the SNP surge in the north. As part of his package, the estimable broadcaster Jon Snow went to Culloden, which he described as 'the scene, 270 years ago, of the last great battle between the English and the Scots'. Had his researchers gone in to the National Trust for Scotland's impressive £10-million visitor centre, they would have learned that the battle in April 1746 was most definitely not a battle between the English and the Scots. The interactive exhibition debunks the notion it was such an engagement, underlining that it was part of a civil war which threatened to engulf the whole of Britain. There were Scottish soldiers and Gaelic-speaking clansmen on both sides, as there were Englishmen. But the myth about Culloden being a Scots/English conflict endures despite the efforts of the National Trust and others. It is certainly not the only chapter of Scotland's story to be distorted, or indeed that of the Jacobites.

# 6

# Religion

I HAD MANY discussions with Sorley about religion. He had been brought up in the Free Presbyterian Church, known as the Seceders (apart from on North Uist where it was called An Eaglais Bheag, 'the Wee Church') and not the 'Wee Frees', which is a term too often used to describe all Highland Presbyterians. The Wee Frees are those who stayed in the Free Church created by the Disruption of 1843 and did not follow the majority in 1900 who joined with the United Presbyterian Church to become the United Free Church. The Free Presbyterian Church had been effectively founded by the minister from his native Raasay in 1893, just 18 years before Sorley's birth. The Free Church of Scotland had broken from the Church of Scotland in 1843 over the issue of patronage or the role of landowners in appointing local ministers. The Free Church itself was disrupted exactly 50 years later over the issue of an internal measure called the Declaratory Act, which the conservatives saw as weakening the Church's commitment to the Westminster Confession of Faith. They seceded from the Church, led in the first place by two Free Church ministers, Donald Macfarlane, the minister on the island of Raasay, and Donald Macdonald in Shieldaig. They were the embryonic Free Presbyterian Church of Scotland. Both ministers lost their manses and their churches.

Sorley was not a believer himself, but would never disparage anyone who was. On an odd occasion he would go with Renee to the Church of Scotland in Portree to keep her company, but he was always interested in hearing ideas. To the end he would defend the Seceders or FPs and the Free Church of Scotland (Wee Frees) against uninformed comment and misrepresentation. Included in that was James Hogg's *Confessions of a Justified Sinner*, which he saw as a hellish calumny in its exaggeration of the hypocrisy of Scottish Calvinists. He would recall the wonderful preachers who would come to Raasay for the Communions, hugely important social as well as religious events. He would marvel at their intellectual powers and ability to preach for hours, often without notes. One in particular stood out for him: Argyll man Neil Cameron (born in Kilninver near Oban; went to school in Kilchoan, Ardnamurchan and Onich, south of Fort William), who was to be the long-standing minister in St Jude's in Glasgow. Sorley also loved to tell of 'The Blind Munro', the Skye catechist (1777–1830) who had reputedly memorised the Bible, or a good part of it. Donald Munro was born near Portree. Blinded by smallpox at the age of 14, he was one of the island's foremost fiddlers, particularly in the Trotternish district. But he forsook playing for the Bible. Munro was to become known as the father of evangelical religion in Skye. His preaching was so powerful that he once persuaded his listeners to show their renunciation of all forms of worldly pleasures by bringing their musical instruments to the head of Loch Snizort for a public conflagration. A veritable mountain of fiddles and bagpipes was said to have been consigned to the flames.

Sorley never mocked religious belief. But he would also say that anyone who truly believed in the prospect of an eternity of physical and mental torture, as some had preached in his youth, would go insane. Given the stakes were so unimaginably high, he was always amused by the story of the Skye character who had applied for membership of the Free Church. (In much of the 20th century, only perhaps 10 per cent of church attenders – the section which had a strong hope that they were born-again – took communion as members. The majority were adherents and didn't take communion. Nowadays, the majority of those who attend the Free Church, and between a quarter and half of those who attend the Free Presbyterian Church, are communion-taking members and not simply adherents. Members are those who hold most ardently the Churches' teaching on salvation.) This particular man was an unlikely candidate for full membership and he had heard that he had been refused while standing in a bar in Portree. 'I wasn't hellish particular anyway,' was his response, suggesting that he may not have fully accepted the teaching on his eternal fate.

The role religion had played in the sadder periods of Highland history, however, weighed heavily on my father-in-law. This was apparent in a powerful paper he wrote for the Gaelic Society of Inverness in 1938 entitled 'The Poetry of the Clearances'. It ran to more than 30 pages in Volume XXXVIII (1937–1941) of the green-bound works that are the *Transactions of the Gaelic Society of Inverness*. It was republished in 1985 by Acair in Stornoway in its *Ris a' Bhruthaich: The Criticism and Prose Writings of Sorley MacLean*. He had been talking of the 'absurd tendency to blame the factor more than the landlord' for their role in the Highland Clearances, then wrote:

> But the religious factor was of far more consequence in the weakening of popular resistance, and it increased in importance as the Clearances progressed. Thus the fact that there were so many more examples of resistance to the Clearances in the period between 1780 and 1820 than in the period between 1820 and 1870 is partly accounted for by the spreading and deepening of the religious revival after 1820. It may be that the clergy's silent acquiescence and even occasional open support for the landlord has been exaggerated, but it is probably true that not one in ten of the Highland clergymen supported the crofters in any tangible way. The ministers of the Established Church were economically attached to the landlord, and few of them attacked their patrons, while some of them actively supported the Clearances, preaching to the people that their sufferings were God's judgement on them for their sins, and that resistance to constituted authority was sacrilege. The connection of the landlords with the Established Church undoubtedly helped to drive great numbers into the Free Church, but a church that considered the world a vale of tears, earthly affairs of little account and original sin one of the two central things in human life could advise only submission and resignation and an escape to religion.

Nothing Sorley said to me 40 years later suggested he had changed his mind on these points, although he would praise those ministers who had been noble exceptions and had spoken out.

A journalist covering the Highlands and Islands didn't necessarily need such a deep understanding of Church affairs, but did require some knowledge of religious history. Not least where the traditionally Presbyterian communities were and those which were still the preserve of the Roman Catholic faith. In the Outer Isles these were respectively either side of a north/south divide in the archipelago, with Benbecula the meeting point. There just over half the people share the RC faith of the islands to the south (South Uist, Eriskay, Barra, Vatersay), while about 45 per cent are Protestant, mostly Presybyterian like their northern neighbours (Grimsay, North Uist, Berneray, Harris, Scalpay, Lewis). But as the Visit the Outer Isles website is at pains to stress: 'The difference in Christian denominations in the Outer Hebrides has, however, caused little division amongst inhabitants, and they have lived peacefully side-by-side for centuries.'

Of course, for long enough the different island communities south of Harris had limited contact with each other, apart from fishing, until a series of bridges, causeways and new ferry services brought them closer together. The first link to be completed was the 82-span South Ford Bridge from Benbecula to South Uist, completed in 1942. The five-mile North Ford Causeway from Benbecula to North Uist opened in 1960. My late brother-in-law, D.R. MacDonald, told me how, after the North Ford had just opened, he and friends from the west of North Uist travelled down to South Uist for the first time to attend a dance at Iochdar. They were slightly nervous, but they received the warmest of welcomes. In 1983 a new two-lane causeway was built to replace the South Ford Bridge. In 1990 a causeway was opened, linking Barra to Vatersay.

## Floating on a Sabbath sea

Religion has long been important in the Highlands and Islands and has thrown up many a tale. One favourite episode which I liked to remind *Herald* readers about every so often was the Floating Church on Loch Sunart. It was a corrugated iron shed on a barge paid for by hundreds of local people who used it for worship for 30 years from 1846 because the landlord refused to give them land to erect a building for the newly created Free Church of Scotland. After the Disruption in 1843, many of the people of Ardnamurchan joined the new church. The peninsula was owned by Sir James Riddell who by and large was a considerate man, but was extremely worried by the new Church which he held had 'bid defiance to the powers that be and broken up society from its very foundations'. He refused land for a Free church so the people used to worship in the hills above Loch Sunart. These were determined people who resolved to find an answer and the answer was a church of the sea. About £1,400 was raised and an order placed in a shipyard in Port Glasgow. In the summer of 1846 the church was towed north and anchored in Loch Sunart. For the next three decades every Sabbath was marked by hundreds of people making their way to worship in small boats.

Many in Scotland automatically associate Highland Presbyterianism with strict Sabbath observance and its impact on public transport. It was the Westminster Confession of Faith in 1647 (born out of the Long Parliament when the forces of puritanism were in the ascendancy) which laid down the rigour of Sabbath observance which Scotland clung to until the end of the 19th century, and in much of rural Scotland well into the 20th. The Confession went largely unchallenged as 'the principal subordinate standard of faith', subordinate only to the Bible. In Chapter 21 of the Confession the purpose of the Sabbath was made clear: for 'holy rest from worldly employments and recreation'. It stipulated that the whole time should be taken up with the worship of God which could only be interrupted by the duties of necessity and mercy. The Old Testament Sabbath observance of the Jews was being carried over into Christianity. The Confession was seen as a development of Calvin's work in the 16th century. As T.C. Smout described in *A Century of the Scottish People 1830–1950*, the Confession's insistence on rigorous Sabbath observance carried weight throughout most of Scotland for most of the 19th century: 'To natives and foreigners alike, the Scottish Victorian Sabbath was the outward and visible sign of the Church's inward and spiritual sway. A universal stillness fell over Glasgow and Edinburgh (except in the unredeemed slums) at the time of divine service and pervaded small towns and villages from dawn to dusk.'

Sabbath observance started to retreat in Scotland as the 20th century progressed. My own parents were slow to change. When I was young we went to church, stayed in our Sunday 'best' clothes and visited relations. We were not allowed to play with friends or listen to the radio. My two older sisters would often secretly defy the broadcasting ordinance, the draw of Radio Luxembourg being too great for them. Despite it all, I have no memory of Sundays or any other day being unhappy or joyless because of our parents' religious beliefs, which were shared by many. The draw of our first TV (a Murphy with a lid on top you opened to turn it on) helped liberalise our Sundays. I was to stop going to church myself when a student, which I know broke my father's heart. To this day, however, I have good friends, and indeed a sister, who are committed Christians and still hold the Sabbath dearly, although not necessarily in the same way as our parents' generation.

In 1965 the Caledonian Steam Packet Company (CSPC which was part of British Railways, having been established as the maritime arm of the Caledonian Railway in the 19th century) introduced the first Sunday ferries to Skye across the Kyle of Lochalsh, with the Rev. Angus Smith, then of the Free Church, famously lying down on the slipways in protest, earning him the title of 'Ferry Reverend'. By 1988 Caledonian MacBrayne (which incorporated CSPC and David MacBrayne) had decided to introduce the first scheduled Sunday ferry service between the Presbyterian islands of Harris, North Uist and Skye the following summer. On the day of the announcement in September I interviewed Colin Paterson, CalMac's managing director, on the phone. He was a man I came to admire greatly, but I didn't really help him that day. The fishermen on the island of Scalpay had threatened to blockade nearby Tarbert, the main settlement and ferry port for Harris, to prevent CalMac's £7-million ferry *Hebridean Isles* from docking on the Sabbath. I asked Colin what he would do in that event. He replied: 'I suppose that the Royal Navy is ultimately responsible for ensuring that the shipping routes are kept open, and if absolutely necessary we would be willing to call them in.'

The next day the *Glasgow Herald*, as it still was, had a front-page story with the heading 'CalMac may ask Navy to protect ferry'. Whether the Scalpay men were truly prepared to resort to such tactics in defence of their traditional Sabbath was not clear at the time. More recently, some in Harris have said that it was only ever threatened for propaganda purposes. But the Scalpay spin seemed to have the desired effect, as we learnt that the Scottish Office officials had taken it seriously enough to counsel the publicly owned CalMac to proceed with great caution over a Sunday sailing to Harris. Colin was himself a Church of Scotland elder in Helensburgh and had no desire to offend anyone's religious convictions, but insisted he was responding to local as well as tourist demand. However, Professor Donald Macleod of the Free Church College in Edinburgh stated that the importance of Sabbath observance had long roots: 'Well, it is the Fourth Commandment and has the same standing as any of the others. It was first given legal backing following the Emperor Constantine's conversion to Christianity in the early part of the fourth century and has had such backing ever since.' In the end CalMac dropped Harris but went ahead with Sunday ferries to North Uist, and on 21 May 1989 the *Hebridean Isles* left Lochmaddy bound for Uig on Skye.

There was huge contingent of journalists, almost 40, from all over the country. A photograph of us all was later published in the *Press Gazette*. We had sailed out to North Uist on the Saturday and convened in the ferry's bar. On arrival I recall a reporter from one of the London tabloids saying he needed to go and interview 'the vicar' and was somewhat confused to learn that if he meant the Presbyterian minister, there were three to choose from on the island. These men of the cloth had already attracted some comment by organising a public meeting 'to consider and oppose' the Sunday sailing to North Uist. When the ferry left Lochmaddy on the Sunday at 11.32 there was no protest demonstration as church worship had commenced half an hour earlier. Some local residents did turn up to wish the service well. One of them was Angus Maclellan from Balranald on the west side of the island. He told us: 'I am a member of the Church of Scotland, but I think that if we are to keep our young people here we must be willing to live in the 20th century. If that means a Sunday service, so be it.' That was how many islanders viewed the issue. The community needed future generations to build a life there, but it was a highly sensitive issue. The Western Isles Council, which had a built-in majority of councillors from Lewis and Harris, had padlocked the linkspan, which it owned, so the ferry had to use its side ramps. On arrival at Uig there was a group of about 50 protesting on the pier under a banner which was being held by two ladies recently arrived from Oxfordshire. One said she was there out of respect for her crofting neighbours' Sabbatarian sensitivities while the other objected to the noise. A few journalists (including this writer and my good friend Torcuil Crichton then of the *West Highland Free Press* and now Westminster editor of the *Daily Record*), decided to make the return journey to Uist. On arrival another crowd had gathered to welcome the ferry and, some said, their island's entry into the 20th century. But it was difficult not to spare a thought that night for the many households on the island who had been saddened by the day's events.

## Lord Chancellor on trial and Free Church glasnost

Highland Presbyterianism stayed in the national headlines for the rest of that week. The Free Presbyterian Church was holding its national synod in Inverness and voted by 33 votes to 27 to suspend the UK's Lord Chancellor, Lord Mackay of Clashfern, for attending the Roman Catholic funerals of two fellow judges. The suspension was to remain in force until Lord Mackay repented. The subsequent row led to a split in the Church with some of those who supported Lord Mackay leaving and forming the Associated Presbyterian Churches, whose nickname was the 'Split Ps' to distinguish it from the FPs and the Wee Frees

The synod was covered by media around the world. The *Jerusalem Post* reported: 'In 1986 he [Lord Mackay] went to the Westminster Cathedral Roman Catholic Requiem Mass for Lord Russell, having previously attended a requiem mass for Lord Wheatley – actions which, given the Free Presbyterian view of the Pope as "Antichrist, that man of sin, that man of perdition" did not much please the Church's ruling body. Having condemned the Roman Catholic mass as "the most blasphemous form of religious worship that Satan ever invented," the Church's synod voted, albeit narrowly, to suspend Mackay for six months from his position as an elder, the suspension to be lifted "upon Lord Mackay's expression of repentance." But the good lord, who once memorably praised his church as manifesting "the most tender love that has ever been described," immediately responded that he could not possibly repent and was therefore leaving the Free Presbyterians for good.'

Sitting in that church in Inverness watching the national synod at work was an experience I won't forget. It was so different to anything I had witnessed in the Church of Scotland in the mid to late 20th century, and almost certainly spoke to the Kirk a century earlier.

Because of such stories there has long been an apparent media licence to ridicule Highland Presbyterianism, while remaining largely silent on other denominations and faiths which, to a rationalist mind, advance equally preposterous ideas. The fun some feel free to poke at the Presbyterian Churches would arguably never be directed to the Roman Catholic faith, never mind Islam. On one occasion during the BCCI crisis on Lewis, of which more later, some journalists attended a prayer meeting in Stornoway which had been billed as a 'day of humiliation', which did not mean self-flagellation or anything of the like, simply an evening prayer meeting. I told my news editor I thought it inappropriate to go into one church simply to laugh at or at best patronise its worshippers, however gently, which seemed inevitable.

However, changes were afoot. I wrote in August 2013 that it was difficult not to be intrigued by the new-found determination of the Free Church of Scotland, one of the bodies popularly held to epitomise religious intolerance and a censorious view of life, to publicly engage more fully with the wider world. It no longer addressed only the narrow concerns so frequently and enthusiastically lampooned in the media. I wrote:

> Last week Free Church ministers in the Highlands wrote to Transport Secretary Keith Brown urging him to dual the A9 as a matter of urgency – because they didn't want to conduct any more funerals from accidents on the road. The week before a Free Church minister in Dundee was billed as the first Scottish church leader to publicly condemn the homophobic Vladimir Putin regime over its treatment of minority groups in Russia. Rev. David Robertson denounced Putin as 'a fascist communist whose autocratic reign is the very antithesis of everything Jesus Christ is about'. While still opposed to gay marriage and accepting the 'biblical teaching' about homosexuality, he was clear: 'It is our responsibility to care for and protect any homosexual who is faced with that kind of bullying. We unequivocally condemn it as of the devil, rather than of Christ.' It is just not the sort of statement that would have been expected from the Free Church a few years back. But some sort of glasnost within has been increasingly obvious.

In April that year the Free Church displayed genuine ecumenical credentials in appointing a Church of England minister to its congregation in St Andrews. The month before Free Church ministers on Skye wrote an open letter to their MSPs urging them to reverse the Scottish government's decision to lease the shooting and fishing rights of the Raasay Crofters' Association to a stalking firm in South Ayrshire, something they would have held themselves aloof from in the past. In 2012 the Church resisted calls of a boycott of the visit of Richard Dawkins, the world-famous atheist, to the Hebridean Book Festival on

Lewis. Stornoway Free Church minister Rev. Iver Martin welcomed the visit as an opportunity for debate.

So what was happening in the Church born in the Disruption of 1843, which has 12,500 worshipping in 104 congregations across Scotland? According to a Church spokesman, the Free Kirk had always spoken out: 'However, there have been some significant changes which mean that we are being heard a little more. Professor Donald Macleod [former Free Church College Principal] once said that the press would only be interested in our opinion of the nuclear bomb if we announced that it should not be dropped on the Sabbath. The Wee Free stereotype of at best a quaint backward Highland Church and at worst a bunch of dour hypocritical joyless mean-spirited Tartan Taliban is now being challenged and seen for what it is – sheer prejudice.'

## Another misunderstood denomination

The much publicised early retirement of the Rt Rev. George Sessford, Scottish Episcopal Bishop of Moray, Ross and Caithness in 1993 over the issue of the ordination of women was seen as a matter of little consequence to the vast majority in Scotland. Many viewed it as the Caledonian end of an internal dispute in the Church of England. Growing up in Blairgowrie I would unthinkingly refer to St Catharine's Scottish Episcopal Church down the road as 'the English church'. I was to realise my error, and that of many others, when researching an article on the Scottish Episcopal Church following Bishop Sessford's departure, some of which I paraphrase below. Arnold Kemp told me he thought it one of the most important pieces I had written. In this I was tutored by the Very Rev. Allan Maclean, then Provost of Oban's Episcopal cathedral. He is now the 16th Chieftain of the Macleans of Dochgarroch, a cadet branch of the clan based at the north-eastern end of Loch Ness, but has long been a significant Highland historian well known to Sorley.

What I learnt was that 'the English Church' was/is a historical myth, but one which has been fuelled in recent years by the influx of Anglicans, particularly to the Highlands. Between 1982 and 1992, for example, the membership in the episcopal diocese of Moray, Ross and Caithness actually rose from 4,318 to 4,569, a 5.8 per cent increase, in stark contrast to most other Churches and to the Episcopal Church nationally, which recorded a 19.8 per cent drop.

Most of Scotland held the Episcopal Church to be the English Church long before the phrase 'white settler' had any meaning here and before it created profoundly unhealthy attitudes among many Scots. It is a view that has hurt and still hurts. Whatever it was to become, the fact is that the Scottish Episcopal Church was a very Scottish Church whose roots can be traced back through Highland Jacobite blood for at least 300 years. It can lay a claim to descent from Columba's Iona equal to that of any other Church. Even today, travelling from Oban to Fort William by way of Appin, Ballachulish and Glencoe, you can see just how much the Church is still part of these communities.

Episcopacy, or church government by bishops, came to assume a place in our Presbyterian demonology. But it wasn't always so. In the early years of the Reformation, superintendents were appointed above hard-pressed ministers, and Professor Gordon Donaldson, the Historiographer Royal who died 25 years ago, effectively proved that these were bishops in all but name. T.C. Smout, who succeeded him in his royal appointment, wrote: 'Indeed, in 1572, the Concordat of Leith [an agreement on how the Church was to be organised] made the Scottish Church quite explicitly Episcopalian by arranging to fill the old sees with Protestant bishops as they fell vacant, the Crown nominating the candidates but the General Assembly holding them under its discipline. John Knox in his old age gave the Concordat his blessing – qualified, for he feared that by this arrangement the bishops would become tools of an unsympathetic Crown, but nevertheless a blessing.'

The bishops certainly were not universally trusted in 16th-century Scotland. But their troubles really began in 1574 when Andrew Melville returned to Scotland after six years in reformed Geneva. Melville held that episcopacy, with the minister elevated above others, was unscriptural as there was no biblical evidence that the early Church had been hierarchical, although Episcopalians have always held that the status of the apostles made it so.

In the next 100 years, Episcopal/Presbyterian fortunes ebbed and flowed within Scotland's national church, but there was a constant quest for unity. In 1610 an apparently workable compromise was introduced by the Crown whereby bishops would become the recognised presidents of presbyteries and synods while the Crown would provide increased financial help to the Church on the ground. Although opposed by the Melvillian minority, it won a fairly wide acceptance that might have lasted had not Charles I displayed his complete ignorance of Scottish opinion, Episcopalian and Presbyterian. He announced in 1636 and 1637 details of a new Church policy that took no account of the religious facts of Scottish life, General Assembly, presbytery or kirk session, but tried to introduce a new prayer book recalling the mass and the more Roman Catholic practices of the Anglican Church under Archbishop Laud.

In protest, the National Covenant was signed in Greyfriars church-yard in Edinburgh in 1638 by representatives of the Scottish people, appearing to unite all. The Covenant took care not to attack the bishops, although many Presbyterians who signed were still determined to achieve their end. The initial royal reaction, to treat all signatories as rebels, then to prepare to move an army towards Scotland only to back down and recall the first General Assembly for 20 years, helped them. The General Assembly abolished bishops. A civil war ensued that was to end in Charles losing his head and Oliver Cromwell ruling the land. In 1660 Charles II was restored to his father's throne, and again there was an attempt to integrate bishops into the Presbyterian structure. This did not have the popular support it had had in 1610, and around 300 ministers were ejected for refusing to accept the new episcopacy. Thirty years later, however, with the House of Orange on the throne, the tide was to begin its final ebb for Episcopalianism within Scotland's Church. In 1690 a new constitution for the Church of Scotland was prepared by the Convention of Estates and affirmed by King William III. It again abolished bishops and restored the authority of the General Assembly over the now familiar Presbyterian structure. The Church of Scotland was established, and membership of it alone was lawful.

It was too much for some of the old Episcopalians to swallow, and an estimated 500 clergy gave up rather than submit. It was these Scotsmen, who would never have doubted their own Protestantism, who effectively began the Scottish Episcopal Church. Of course, it wasn't quite as neat as that, particularly in the Highlands, according to the Very Rev. Allan Maclean, who shared with me his encyclopaedic knowledge of Highland history and objective view of his own Church's role in it: 'In the Highlands, as elsewhere, while the Episcopalian/Presbyterian divide was about systems of Church government, it was also clearly about adherence to the Stuarts. The two went hand in hand. Those who tended to support the Stuarts were Episcopalian, unless they were among the small number of RCs. There is a great misunderstanding about this. The vast majority of Jacobite clansmen were Episcopalian, not Catholic.'

It is a misunderstanding that weaves its way through Scottish history. It has been helped on its way by the man responsible for the Massacre of Glencoe, Sir John Dalrymple, Master of Stair, whose 17th-century reference to the MacDonalds of Glencoe as a 'Popish' clan has meant that they are popularly held to have been massacred as Roman Catholics. There is no historical evidence that the Glencoe MacDonalds were Episcopalians at the time of the massacre in 1692 but, as the late Rev. Kenneth Wigston who served in St Mary's, Glencoe, from 1985 to 1993 pointed out: 'In 1713, we learn that the whole catechisable population of Glencoe is given as 229, all Episcopalians. It is inconceivable that just 21 years after the massacre the population, had they been Roman Catholic then, should have been converted to the old, disestablished Episcopal Church of Scotland just at a time when her own priests were sufficiently occupied with their own congregations. There would have been none to spare converting Roman Catholics to Episcopalianism.'

Episcopalian attachment to the Stuart family was to prove disastrous, not just in Glencoe. In 1707 the Act of Union carried an associated document which stated that the Church had to be Presbyterian. But five years later Queen Anne passed an Act that restored patronage to the Church of Scotland (lairds appointing parish ministers), which was to lead to the Disruption of the Church of Scotland 135 years later and the establishment of the Free Church of Scotland. Associated with that was the Act of Toleration which allowed the Episcopal Church to exist in Scotland. As a legal entity, therefore, the Scottish Episcopal Church dates to 1712.

The 1715 Jacobite Rising, however, clearly demonstrated the close link between Scottish Episcopalianism and Jacobitism, underscored by the politically suicidal practice of having the exiled King James confirming appointments of bishops. This was all too much for the House of Hanover which, in 1719, passed the first penal law that held 'no person should be permitted to officiate in an Episcopal meeting-house where nine or more persons are present in addition to the minister's household, unless they prayed by name for King George'. This offence carried a six-month prison sentence. Some Episcopalians were prepared to pray for King George in what became known as qualified meeting houses. Those who were not were the 'non-jurors', and the fiercest of these were fervent Jacobites.

After the '45, things became even worse for the Scottish Episcopalians, with the second penal Act reducing the maximum number at a service to five. Henceforth, Scottish clergy would be ordained by a bishop of the Church of England or Ireland. Meanwhile, the Duke of Cumberland, victor of Culloden, was merrily burning Episcopal meeting houses throughout the Highlands, regardless of whether or not they prayed for his father. After Bonnie Prince Charlie's death in 1788, however, the Stuart line was in terminal trouble, headship of the family having passed to Henry of York, a cardinal. Many Jacobites saw little point in carrying on, and in 1792 the government felt that the penal laws could be repealed.

According to Allan Maclean, 'There were some pockets that remained Jacobite throughout the eighteenth century: Aberdeenshire, the fishing villages of Angus; certain parts of Perthshire; on the Black Isle, Arpafeelie, which is basically North Kessock; Highfield, which is Muir of Ord, and Fortrose. Inverness itself was quite a strong centre of episcopacy and, of course, North Argyll.'

While the fortunes of the Episcopal Church waxed and waned in the rest of Scotland, it clung on tenaciously in north Argyll and, indeed, still does. It is something Maclean has studied. 'There were 14 churches built between the island of Luing, just south of Oban, and Fort William: Cullipool on Luing, built for quarriers from Ballachulish; Oban; Connel; Bonawe, again because of the quarry there; Fasnacloich at the head of Loch Creran; Appin; Duror; Kentallen; Ballachulish; Laroch; Glencoe; Kinlochleven; North Ballachulish and Fort William. Episcopal schools were built in nine of these communities, and two are still open, in Oban and Glencoe. Indeed, the churches are still operating in all but Cullipool; Connel, where it is now used as an antique-shop; and Fasnacloich, which is a private house.'

So why was this area comparatively successful in holding its faith? The Stewart chiefs in Appin were very Jacobite, as were the MacDonalds around Loch Leven, and the Camerons, but there were other Jacobite areas where the Church did not flourish. Maclean believed there were several reasons:

I don't accept that the Episcopal Church survived in Scotland because the lairds started to send their children to English public schools. I think it more important that people were going to work in England or joining the armed forces or the like. They came into contact with the Anglican Church and some perhaps found it more attractive than the starkness of early nineteenth-century Presbyterianism. There were other reasons here in north Argyll. One undoubtedly had to do with the activities of Bishop Forbes, an ardent Jacobite. In the 1760s he did two tours of the Highlands, to Caithness and Inverness, then came down here. In Ballachulish he confirmed 373 people in a single day. He managed to revitalise something that was already there. Then, in the nineteenth century, there was Bishop Chinnery-Haldane, who had a romantic vision of the Episcopal Church in the Highlands and appeared determined that those in the Church should be kept in the fold. He had a very rich wife and they settled in Ballachulish. He was very generous, helping with schoolmasters' fees, building schools, supporting the clergy all around this area.

It all paid off and the Episcopal Church for a large part remained the Church of the local people in that area.

Maclean estimated that of the 300 families associated with Oban Cathedral, one third had Appin origins, the remainder being split almost evenly between other Scots and people from England or elsewhere. He didn't accept that all English incomers automatically converged on the Episcopal Church: 'Many actually go to the parish church, the Church of Scotland, I think because of the community aspect of the parish.' He did agree, however, that the influx of people from England had been a lifesaver for the Church, preventing the dramatic decline suffered by others. That was to reinforce the popular view of the Church as English.

It may be an uninformed view, but it has to be said that the Scottish Episcopal Church has not done enough over the years to emphasise its Scottishness. Within living memory it had a native Gael as a bishop, but still appeared to turn its back on the Gaelic culture in contrast to some notable Roman Catholics and Presbyterians. It was the Jacobite Church, but allowed itself to be seen in modern times as that of the

English establishment or of a few affluent Scots. It sprang from the very heart of the Scottish Reformation, but is now seen almost as a symbol for the 'Englishing' of Scotland. It should be looking not to Canterbury and Wells, but to Ballachulish and Appin.

This would seem to be reinforced by work done on the 2011 census. According to the 'Thinking Anglicans' website's analysis, 'One of the most surprising things is that many people in Scotland identify themselves as Church of England or Anglican, rather than Episcopalian, or belonging to the Scottish Episcopal Church.' The figures in the table are: Church of England 66,717; Episcopalian 21,289; Anglican 4,490; Scottish Episcopal Church 8,048; Church of Ireland 2,020; Church in Wales 453. These compared to 1,717, 871 for the Church of Scotland and 841,053 for the Roman Catholic Church out of a total Scottish population of 5,295,403.

# 7

# Politics and Politicians

I ATTENDED MY first meeting of Highland Regional Council in August of 1988. I found it very different from the local authorities I had been most acquainted with for my work on the *Times Educational Supplement*, most notably the old Lothian and Strathclyde regional councils. They were run on strict party lines, with the ruling group deciding before the councils met how their councillors would vote. In the council chamber in Inverness there were Labour, Liberals (since March that year Liberal Democrat), as well as SNP members and the odd Tory, but they had mostly stood as Independents, as had the vast majority of councillors. They tended to divide along geographical lines, with the likes of the Caithness members defending local interests, which at that time meant clear support for Dounreay. There were some wonderful characters, not least Sandy Lindsay, an ardent SNP supporter who was the Aviemore councillor but won national publicity by seeking planning permission to demolish the huge statue of the first Duke of Sutherland on Ben Bhraggie which towers over Golspie in Sutherland. Permission was refused but Sandy was delighted that the man who was foremost in the demonology of the Highland Clearances was back in the news.

Early on it appeared to me there was one councillor who seemed to be consistently pursuing a rather more radical agenda than the others. I assumed he was in the Labour Party or the SNP, but this was Dr Michael Foxley, a Lochaber GP/crofter/councillor and proud Scottish Liberal. Over the years some suggested we looked alike with our relatively longish hair and beards. We never saw it ourselves, but the late great editor of *The Herald*, Arnold Kemp, once called up the night editor after the first edition had been published and told him, 'You have really screwed up. You have put a photo of Dave Ross on the front page.' Arnold had not met Michael at that point.

Dr Foxley has been one of the great characters of the modern Highlands, although he himself was born in Dulwich and grew up in the south-east of England. His paternal grandparents lived in the heart of Kent, and he made 'almost magical visits' to stay with them. His father was an architect who rose to be vice president of the Royal Institute of British Architects. It was his mother's side, however, which was to have the biggest impact on his life. She was a MacDonald whose family had lived around the crofting townships of Treslaig and Achaphubuil, across Loch Linnhe from Fort William and Corpach, since the 18th century. As a child he would head north every year to spend the summer with his cousins who lived there. His mother was to die in a freak drowning accident on Christmas Day 1976, when she got caught by the tide off the Kent coast. She is buried in the old graveyard at Kilmallie, Corpach.

Dr Foxley's politicisation, however, owed less to the Highland Land League than to the students of the London School of Economics (LSE). He told me:

> I studied medicine at the Middlesex Hospital, but I couldn't get into its residence so I was one of three exchange students who went to the LSE. The LSE students were very radical and a few weeks after I arrived I was down there demonstrating against Vietnam and occupying college buildings, trying to change the world and fight injustice. There was an extraordinary atmosphere at that time, although not many in the medical course knew much about it. I remember going back to the medical school from one of the sit-ins while my classmates, who were largely former public schoolboys with private incomes, were on their way over to the occupation to duff up the protesters.

His trips to the Highlands were to awaken him to the challenges his cousins and friends were facing in getting a house or a job in Lochaber. He grew angry about the vast stretches of land where once communities had been, but had long since been taken over by sporting estates. He was angry enough to build his life in the area, first as a GP, but then living and working one of the family crofts with hill sheep and cattle, as well as his medical work. He organised a demonstration in

1991 which stopped traffic going through Morar. This to protest at the broken government promises over the upgrading of the A830 Fort William to Mallaig road, billed as the worst trunk road in the country, because much of it was twisting single track in poor condition. I once came down it in the cab of a huge articulated lorry carrying fish south, marvelling at the driver's skills while sympathising with all who were coming in the opposite direction. Foxley's protest was modelled on the action campaigns he had seen mounted by Native Americans in British Columbia and Quebec in defence of their tribal lands. I was there and it was clear the motorists had every sympathy with the cause.

I always wanted to compare Michael to another doctor who had come from this part of Scotland, Archibald Cameron of Lochiel, the last Jacobite to be executed for his role in the 1745 Jacobite Rising. But it always took more space explaining it than was merited. We can say at least that Dr Foxley always had a similar disdain for the government of his day as did Dr Archie. The Crown Estate was another frequent target of Foxley, which was once famously described as 'the worst kind of unelected, upper-class club'. He was critical of its very existence, but also in particular of its stewardship of the fish-farming industry, which he believed could have helped sustain crofters rather than be taken over by multinationals. He has been an impassioned advocate for the cause of land reform, as the people of Eigg and Knoydart bear witness, and for Gaelic. His wife Mairead is local from a well-known family of musicians and is a Gaelic medium teacher. Their two sons speak the language.

Michael almost single-handedly won a senior secondary school for Ardnamurchan at Strontian, saving pupils a long tortuous journey to Fort William. One of his council colleagues told me many years ago, 'Michael actually does the work of three normal councillors. I just don't know how he does it. He can't sleep very much.' With the explosion of wind-farm development, he was determined to establish a formula whereby the local community most affected would receive significant investment. In 2011 he won the Scottish Local Politician of the Year in *The Herald*'s annual political awards for his efforts on issues such as this and the threat to coastguard stations, emergency tugs and the reform of the Crown Estate. He stood for election to the Scottish Parliament as a List MSP, but lost out because the Liberal Democrats were successful in winning constituency contests. He was, however, to become vice convenor and then leader of the Highland Council. He won the President's Award at the party's national conference in 2012 in Brighton in recognition of his 'huge contribution'. He couldn't attend, however, because he was in Inverness, denouncing his party's leaders in the Tory/Lib Dem coalition to the Commons Scottish Select Affairs Committee in its inquiry into the Crown Estate.

The Liberal Democrat hierarchy gave up trying to keep him in line. He voted Yes in the independence referendum of 2014. One of the early straws in that wind was his shock that the Lib Dems were willing to go into coalition with the Tories in Westminster in 2010 when they had found it unthinkable to do the same with the SNP three years earlier in Holyrood. Since Michael stood down from the council in 2017, his appetite for public service has been maintained. At the time of writing he was the Chair of Further Education Regional Board for the Highlands and Islands and a Director of Colleges Scotland. He was a board member of the Court of the University of the Highlands and Islands, as well as the Scottish Fire and Rescue Service, the Crown Estate Scotland, NHS Highland and Mallaig Harbour Authority. He also chaired the Highlands and Islands Forestry Forum.

Dr Foxley lost his political mentor in 1995 with the death of Duncan Grant, a retired forester who was a councillor for North-west Skye, having previously represented the Lochalsh area. A Gaelic speaker, Grant was a native of the island. He led a small band of mainly west-coast councillors on Highland Regional Council, including Foxley, who fought against the imposition of tolls on the Skye Bridge. They were to be outvoted 38–7 by their colleagues, some of whom had travelled by way of two toll-free bridges to Inverness to vote for tolls for the people of Skye.

Foxley and Grant really started the resurgence of Gaelic in Lochaber, pushing for three Gaelic medium units in the early 1990s, the retention of Gaelic in secondary schools and bilingual signage, first in Ardnamurchan and then on the Mallaig road, despite significant opposition. Future convener, the Achiltibuie councillor David Green was also very supportive of their efforts in the cause of Gaelic.

Duncan and Michael were a well-kent double act, one which I might say contrived to lock me out of the hotel where we were staying in Golspie on the occasion of the Scottish Crofters Union's annual conference in the Sutherland town. Duncan was a wily political operator and told me that one of his greatest achievements was to persuade Michael to limit the number of causes he was pursuing, saying, 'I advised him to use a rifle rather than a blunderbuss.' Duncan had a great sense of humour, telling me: 'Michael can be very persuasive – for example, he persuaded the council to buy a lighthouse [Ardnamurchan], which I am sure will be very handy.' This always reminded me of one of the Para Handy tales by Neil Munro, in which Para and Dougie attend a farm sale near Lochgoilhead. A lot of drink has been taken and the story continues: 'The lamentable fact must be recorded . . . the mate of the *Vital Spark* [Dougie] had become possessor of a pair of curling-stones – one of them badly chipped – a Dutch hoe, and a baking-board. Para demanded of him "What in the world are you going to do with that trash?" Dougie scratched his neck and looked at his purchases. "They didn't cost mich," he said; "and they're aye handy to have aboot you."'

In 2014 the Liberal Democrats lost another great Highland figure when John Farquhar Munro died aged 79. Friends and acquaintances knew the former MSP hadn't been in the best of health for a while. Most shared the feeling that his passing took something of importance from Highland life. The tributes were immediate and generous: a true Highland gentleman, canny, crafty, mischievous, his own man, principled and brave. But it was the fundamental decency of the man which always shone through, with Scottish politics the richer for it. To the people of Skye and Lochalsh, the old parishes of Kintail and his native Glenshiel and beyond, JF, as he was always known, was one of their own. He held the constituency of Ross, Skye and Inverness West – which stretched from Neist Point on Skye to Cromarty on the north-eastern tip of the Black Isle. He was reputed to have clocked up more than 500,000 miles in his blue Mercedes number plate JFDID, and indeed JF did. On the old Skye and Lochalsh District Council to the Highland Council and on to the Scottish Parliament, he fought hard for Gaelic, land reform, crofting, transport – the issues which remain crucial still to the indigenous Highlander of a reforming bent. His role in helping rid the Skye Bridge of its tolls (about which more later) was absolutely critical. His threat to resign from his party over the issue was no empty gesture, and the leaders of the then Labour/Lib Dem Scottish Executive knew it. He himself had always hated the tolls, but paid them because he was a JP. His wife Celia, his constant partner in and out of crime, had not – a decision he entirely supported despite her ending up in Dingwall Sheriff Court along with other Skye and Kyle Against Tolls (SKAT) activists.

JF rocked his own party and others when he came out and backed Alex Salmond as the best candidate for First Minister before the Holyrood elections in 2011. Some took this to be a sign of advancing years. More in the Highlands saw it as him paying a political debt – the SNP leader's intervention to save the National Centre of Excellence in Traditional Music at Plockton High School from closure. Mr Salmond didn't forget, when he spoke following JF's death: 'John Farquhar Munro was always his own man, campaigning beyond party loyalties, which is one reason he will be remembered with respect and affection right across the political spectrum.'

JF's life's story had been well rehearsed at the time: the merchant seaman who tried to stow away on the *Queen Mary* to get back to Britain from the US; a civil engineering and quarrying contractor; bus operator; heavy haulage contractor; crofter – he played every role and more. Sorley knew him well from his days in Plockton and liked him very much. JF remains one of only two native Gaels to have been elected to Holyrood, the other being Labour's Alasdair Morrison in the Western Isles. He had hoped that there would have been more. In 2003 he won the Free Spirit/Maverick category in the *Herald*'s Politician of the Year Awards. It is likely that he was, at some point, sounded out about a place in the House of Lords. If so he would have smiled and said something about being content to remain a commoner. There are different forms of nobility.

## Lib Dem heartland

During much of my time the Highlands and Islands have been the closest thing the Liberal Democrats have had to a heartland in Britain. With five out of the six Westminster seats north and west of the Highland line, it was their biggest clutch of contiguous constituencies anywhere in the UK. It stretched right across the old Crofting counties, from Shetland to the Mull of Kintyre at the mouth of the Firth of Clyde. In the Western Isles, it was always a different story. There it was Labour and the SNP who would always fight robust contests to represent one of the most remote electorates in the land. It was a particularly important prize for both of them.

Things changed a little in 1997 when the great figure of Scottish Liberalism, Sir Russell Johnston, retired as MP for Inverness, Nairn and Lochaber after 33 years in Parliament. His seat had been Britain's only four-way marginal. Only 1,741 votes separated the four main parties in 1992, and with slightly redrawn boundaries the new seat of Inverness East, Nairn and Lochaber looked the most difficult for the Liberal Democrats to defend, and so it proved, with Inverness social worker David Stewart taking it for Labour. Stewart was seen by many as a worthy victor because of the amount of work he had put in during the previous election campaigns. There was also the great tide of hope sweeping across the country that Tony Blair symbolised renewal. David Stewart was to lose to Danny Alexander, later Chief Secretary to the Treasury, in the 2005 election. By then opinion was running high against Labour in much of the Highlands over the invasion of Iraq and David Stewart's support for it. This was particularly true amongst erstwhile Liberal and Liberal Democrat voters. David Stewart was to return to front-line politics in 2007 as a Highlands and Islands List MSP in the Scottish Parliament, where he remains, taking up some important causes.

It is often forgotten that the most northerly parliamentary seat on the British mainland, Caithness and Sutherland, which later embraced Easter Ross as well, was held by Labour from 1966 until 1981, with Robert Maclennan attracting many of the votes from the industrialised workforce who had come north to work at the Dounreay nuclear facility. He was a junior minister in the Labour government of 1974–79, but in 1981 defected to help found the Social Democratic Party along with the 'Gang of Four' (Roy Jenkins, David Owen, Bill Rodgers and Shirley Williams). He was one of the few SDP MPs to keep their seats in the 1983 general election. He was succeeded by John (Lord) Thurso, whose grandfather, Sir Archibald Sinclair, held the seat for the Liberal Party between 1922 and 1945, serving as Secretary of State between 1931 and 1932, becoming leader of the Liberal Party in 1935 and distinguishing himself as air minister in the Second World War.

The former party leader Jo Grimond won the Orkney and Shetland seat for the Liberals in 1950. It had been held by Whigs and Liberals of some description since 1818, apart from two Tories and an Independent. It has been Liberal or Liberal Democrat ever since Grimond, with Jim Wallace and then Alistair Carmichael retaining it. The last named was to come perilously close to losing it in 2015 as the SNP swing, which had consumed all his party colleagues in Scotland, came within 817 votes of him. In 2017 his majority returned to safer levels with 4,563 votes.

Many of these Liberal and Liberal Democrat parliamentarians could claim to be the descendants of a radical liberal tradition in the Highlands, which was born in the years of land agitation and the Clearances. It threw up many significant political figures, not least Donald Horne Macfarlane, who in 1885 became one of the first Crofters' Party MPs to be elected. He and four others (representing Inverness-shire, Ross and Cromarty, Caithness and Wick burghs) had been backed by the Highland Land League, which was campaigning for relief for those struggling to survive the unforgiving economic stranglehold of the landlords and their sponsored evictions.

Originally from Caithness, Macfarlane had been an MP for Carlow County in Ireland as a member of Charles Stewart Parnell's Home Rule Party. He was a convert to Roman Catholicism and was the first MP of the faith to be elected to Westminster from a Scottish seat. To win Argyll he had to overcome opposition from two powerful forces: the Presbyterian Churches and the landlords. He did so with an electorate dramatically expanded by the Reform and Redistribution Acts of 1884 and 1885, which saw the number of voters in Argyll rise from 3,299 in 1880 to 10,011 in 1885. He won a remarkable 48.6 per cent of the vote, soundly defeating the Liberal candidate in the process and, more narrowly, an Independent. He lost the seat in 1886, but in that year Gladstone's Liberal government passed the first Crofters Act, delivering many of the reforms the Crofting MPs had sought. He wasn't finished, being re-elected at the 1892 general election as a Liberal/Crofters candidate and being knighted in 1894.

The Crofters' Party had gradually merged with the Liberals, providing a cornerstone of this radical tradition of Liberalism in the Highlands. In my view it survived, most recently through the likes of Duncan Grant, John Farquhar Munro, Michael Foxley, former Argyll MP Ray Michie, her father John Bannerman, and of course Charles Kennedy.

Because of the changing nature of the media and his enthusiasm for it, evidenced by appearances on the likes of the satirical show *Have I Got News for You*, Charles Kennedy was arguably the most widely known and identifiable Liberal Democrat figure in Britain during his lifetime. But, despite what critics and political opponents often said about

'Champagne Charlie', there was a great deal more to him than that. He showed great courage and determination in opposing the invasion of Iraq in the face of remorseless momentum towards war engineered by Tony Blair's Labour government. He was subjected to near-hysterical attacks on him by the Tories. This should be remembered.

## The Night of the Long Sgian Dubhs

In the early hours of 8 May 2015 Charles's remarkable 32-year career as an MP ended at the general election count in the Highland Football Academy in Dingwall, where he saw his 13,000-plus majority disappear. It was a result he accepted with quiet dignity. Within a month he was dead. There had been great media interest at the Highland count, where the fate of Chief Secretary to the Treasury Danny Alexander was also sealed. A former party leader, Charles was repeatedly approached for interviews as his defeat became obvious, but declined them all, saying the night belonged to the SNP victor, Ian Blackford. He would speak only from the platform after the official result had been announced. When he did, he had a characteristically Highland allusion to underline the historic nature of the results: 'Tonight, if nothing else, we can all reflect in years to come, perhaps tell our grandchildren, we were there the Night of the Long Sgian Dubhs.'

Not for the first time Charles had given the media a good line. He had been doing so ever since 1983, when at 23 he became one of the youngest MPs since the 21-year-old Pitt the Younger in 1781. He died aged 55 at home in Lochyside near Fort William not long after the election. While the SNP surge had been widely predicted ahead of the 2015 count, nobody really knew if it would sweep Charles away with the rest of his party on the Scottish mainland. It was thought he might just be the one who could defy the odds, not only because of the size of his majority, but because many would find it very hard to vote against him. Anyone who had seen him at meetings in village halls in the small communities of his far-flung constituency, from the Small Isles to Glencoe and Ardnamurchan to the Black Isle, understood. He had a sheer genius for just appearing ordinary: one of us, a thoroughly reasonable and decent guy. It wasn't an act. But he himself talked of the number of constituents who were still greeting him warmly, only to admit they would be voting SNP. There was talk of moves within the

Liberal Democrats to see if they could get him to Holyrood. Others held he was bound for the House of Lords. Neither would have suited him. The last time this writer, a constituent, spoke to him before the election was at full time in a Ross County game in Dingwall. With almost prescient symbolism, he was walking in the opposite direction to the emerging crowd. I didn't interview him, just commiserated with him following the death of his father Ian at 88 not long before. Ian had been a famous musician and stalwart of the crofting cause. He used to take his fiddle to political meetings when his son was beginning his political career. At the age of 80 he and Charles appeared before the Scottish Land Court in a dispute over access to a proposed 56-house building development near Fort William. As local crofters they both stood to benefit financially, and both were in favour of more housing. They were, however, concerned at the prospect of croft land being lost. During the proceedings Mr Kennedy Snr went off at a complete tangent telling about an eccentric who had come to live in the area many years earlier. This man apparently had developed a theory for perpetual motion. His son very gently intervened, saying: 'I don't think the court needs to hear this just now, Dad.'

Despite his great passion for his home, Lochaber lay outside his constituency. That was until boundaries were redrawn before the 2005 general election to create the constituency Ross, Skye and Lochaber. Then he was able to vote for himself just down the road from the family croft for the first time since 1983, when he had defeated the then Tory energy minister Hamish Gray for the new Social Democratic Party. He represented huge tracts of the Highlands at one time or another. Many constituents had been grateful for his help down the years, some who had been dismissed as being unstable or wasters. Charles once confided that he tried to follow the advice of the late Sir Russell Johnston: 'Russell told me never to dismiss apparent nutters or no-hopers because every so often they will be right or will be telling the truth,' he said.

One constituent from the Black Isle who had been wrongly jailed for drugs offences more than 20 years ago told me how Charles had repeatedly visited him in Perth Prison when all others had washed their hands of him. When Charles eventually helped win his early release this man would never hear a word against his MP thereafter, despite not being a typical Liberal Democrat supporter. Charles had also been supportive of a huge range of local campaigns down the years, from fighting the Skye Bridge tolls to opposing genetically modified (GM) crops on the Black Isle and cuts in the local BBC, where he had worked briefly. That was after he had graduated from Glasgow University and before he took up a Fulbright Fellowship to carry out research at Indiana University in the USA.

Skye councillor Drew Millar, who was one of the leaders of the Skye Bridge campaign and had been a Lib Dem before falling out with the party locally, said at the time of his death: 'He was very supportive of the campaign and helped keep the issue alive in Westminster. He was also supportive when I announced I was voting Yes in the independence referendum, and even when I left the party. He just said I was entitled to my view. He was a thoroughly Highland gentleman.'

After the election there had been concern as to how Charles would react to his defeat. He had been seen regularly buying drink when shopping locally around Caol and in Fort William. When news of his death was reported, there were fears that he could have taken his own life. However, Willie Rennie, Scottish Liberal Democrat leader, did much to dispel such speculation, saying he had met him 12 days earlier in Glasgow to discuss the future of his political career. 'He had so much yet to give. He was remarkably calm [about his defeat]. I don't know whether he saw it coming. He was a very laid back, very modest man who went with the flow. He was accepting the result and just thinking what else he could contribute. I am sure he was desperate to take part in the European referendum we are going to have. He would have been a major voice in that.'

Alastair Campbell, Tony Blair's former spin doctor who had problems with alcohol himself, had also been in touch with Charles not long before his death. He wrote online: 'Going by the chats and text exchanges before and after his election defeat, he seemed to be taking it all philosophically. Before, he took to sending me the William Hill odds on his survival, and a day before the election I got a text saying "Not good. Wm Hill has me 3–1 against, SNP odds on, they're looking unstoppable." Then he added: "There is always hope . . . health remains fine." Health remains fine – this was a little private code we had, which meant we were not drinking. A week later, health still fine, we chatted about the elections, and he did sound pretty accepting of what had happened.'

Meanwhile, some close associates dismissed the widely held view that Charles had been drunk when he had appeared on BBC's *Question Time* in March that year. Chairman David Dimbleby and fellow panellists including *Private Eye* editor Ian Hislop, star of *Have I Got News For You*, appeared protective towards him. But Conn O'Neill, Charles's election campaign manager, said that he had been upset after being told earlier that his father had been taken to hospital after breaking his hip and was about to undergo emergency surgery. He had refused to allow his aides to make the information public, not wishing to appear to use his family as an excuse and wanting to protect their privacy. Ian, who had been suffering from dementia, died the following month.

John Farquhar Munro had been close to Charles. His widow Celia told *The Guardian* she had tried to help the ex-Lib Dem leader with his drinking. She said alcoholism was a 'fearful thing'. Her husband had been a member of Alcoholics Anonymous and had tried to help over the years. 'One can only assume that in the end he still couldn't reach the help he needed,' she said.

At the time of all the publicity about how his drinking was affecting his leadership of the party at the end of 2005, most constituents remained loyal. Many of the people I met in the communities in his constituency, including my own, were well acquainted with the human cost of problem drinking and just felt great sympathy for their MP, his estranged wife Sarah and their son Donald, born earlier that year. Most said it would not affect how they would vote. His struggle with drink had not been a secret. I received a phone call once from a London tabloid daily paper, many years earlier, looking for stories about Charles's behaviour at the Highlands and Islands Press Ball. I wasn't able to help the paper in its investigation, telling them truthfully that my own memory of the event was rather impaired. Most who had been there would have been similarly afflicted.

More damaging was a growing recognition that in the years before his death Charles had become less attentive to his constituency work. By the time of his death it had been years since I had talked to him about Highland stories. In the early days he would have been one of the first people I would have contacted and he was always willing to help. I was fond of Charles.

His funeral took place in the building where his mother had been organist for more than 40 years and where his father would play the fiddle at weddings. St John the Evangelist RC church in the village of Caol, near Fort William, was packed to overflowing with more than 500 people who had come to mourn their local son.

Another hundred people were outside in the sunshine, where they listened to the funeral mass over loud speakers. Parish priest Father Roddy McAuley said Charles was a 'much loved and respected parishioner' and would be 'sorely missed', and recalled when he would come to worship. 'In this church, Charles was one of the "backbenchers". He didn't always sit in the same pew but he always sat at the back of the church.'

By the time of his funeral it was known that Charles had died after suffering a major haemorrhage as a result of his battle with alcoholism. His ex-wife Sarah Gurling and their 10-year-old son Donald were among the mourners. Senior Liberal Democrats Nick Clegg, Danny Alexander, Sir Menzies Campbell, Sir Malcolm Bruce and Michael Moore were also at the service. Scotland's Deputy First Minister, John Swinney, former Prime Minister Gordon Brown and Alastair Campbell were present, joined by Charles's new partner Carole MacDonald. His friend Brian McBride delivered the eulogy. He said that he had known Charles had been special from their first meeting 40 years previously. They had met when Mr McBride, chairman of fashion online retailer ASOS, had been president of Glasgow University Union and had been judging a schools debating competition in Elgin in which Charles was taking part as a 15-year-old from Lochaber High School. He said: 'There was something very special about him. Even at that young age we could all see what a prolific debating talent he was. He had a huge public service ethos, as an MP, party leader, a university rector. He wasn't doing these things for the money – he was there to serve. Everything he did, every challenge he faced, was not about him, it always started with what it would mean for other people. A hugely sensitive man in private, no ego at all, and never putting himself first, proud of his roots, his family, his friends, there was never a second side to him. I doubt I will ever see his like again – one of the few public people who walked this earth and didn't really have a single enemy.' McBride went on to say that only Winston Churchill and John Smith had been so universally mourned. Sir Menzies Campbell, who succeeded Charles as Liberal Democrat leader, said the former MP was able to connect with people, and was 'as at ease canvassing in a street like this as he was taking George W. Bush to task' over the Iraq war, as they both had done on a visit to Washington.

Following the service, which lasted more than an hour, a lone piper accompanied the hearse and coffin from the church with Ben Nevis and Glen Nevis in full view. The local crowd broke into applause as the hearse was driven past in a final tribute to one of Lochaber's foremost sons.

Caol had done him proud. It was a village that grew in the second half of the 20th century. In 1945 there were only five crofts including the Kennedys' where there are now more than 3,000 people living. After the church the hearse headed for Loch Lochy along a single-track road past Achnacarry Castle, seat of Lochiel, Chief of Clan Cameron, and where commandos trained in the Second World War. Then it was on to the old graveyard at Clunes, where Charles's parents Ian and Mary already lay.

## Donald Stewart

Twenty-three years earlier I had attended the funeral of another political giant of the Highlands and Islands, when the people of the Western Isles, joined by many from all over Scotland, gathered in Stornoway to mourn Donald Stewart. He was a former leader of the Scottish National Party and the islands' MP for 17 years. More than a thousand people attended the funeral in Stornoway Free Church, while hundreds waited outside to honour the town's former provost. He had become the SNP's first candidate to be elected at a general election and at that time its most successful, winning five consecutive contests. The service was conducted in English apart from Psalm 130 which, at the request of his widow Chrissie, was sung in Gaelic to the tune 'Martyrdom', her husband's favourite.

The church, thought to house Britain's largest Presbyterian congregation, gave Donald Stewart a special send-off. Traditionally the Free Church of Scotland delivers little in the way of eulogy at funerals. The Rev. Murdo Alex Macleod, however, broke a century and a half of convention to pay generous tribute to a man who used to sit in his church every Sunday he could. Mr Macleod said:

> We mourn the passing of a great and honourable man, who even at the height of his illustrious political career, in the words of a past parliamentary colleague, refused always to

put political expediency before principle. During the 17 years he served as MP for these islands he endeared himself to all he came in contact with in his constituency and beyond. In this community he aligned himself wholeheartedly with those people who sought to defend and maintain what was the very best of Christian values. He was an implacable but courteous opponent of those who, by their actions, showed little sympathy for such Christian convictions. It is little wonder then that the man who gave himself to the best interests of the community is so sorely missed. Generations to come will acknowledge, as we do today, that a man of Donald Stewart's worth, who sought to resist every attempt to overthrow the set, ordered traditions in this community rendered yeoman service, worth remembering, worth treasuring and worth following.

After the service more than 500 male mourners formed a procession, taking turns to carry the Saltire-draped coffin through Stornoway past the offices of the Western Isles Council, where flags flew at half mast, on out to the graveyard at Sandwick. Cars and lorries vacated the road to allow the procession to proceed. The SNP had hired a plane to fly representatives to Stornoway, and Highlands and Islands MEP Winnie Ewing was there. She herself of course was something of an electoral phenomenon, having been elected an MP twice, an MEP for the Highlands and Islands four times and an MSP for the same constituency.

Labour's front-bench spokesman Brian Wilson was also in Stornoway for the funeral. He said afterwards: 'Normally when political dignitaries die their funerals are marked by the presence of other political dignitaries. Today was different. Politicians were there but it was the island people who turned out, the people of the community.'

The Western Isles, however, could bitterly divide Labour and SNP supporters. The determination on the part of both to hold or retake the seat has been intense for decades. There can be no more hard-fought electoral battle between the two anywhere in the land. It has a special place in Labour history, being their first non-industrial/urban seat, while, as already highlighted, it was the first the SNP took at a general election. It has long held a significance all of its own in that party's sense of itself. The 23,000 voters are spread from the Butt of

Lewis in the north to Vatersay in the south and St Kilda in the west, although no one has registered to vote in that particular outpost of British parliamentary democracy. Resident military and National Trust for Scotland personnel prefer to use proxy votes.

Created in 1918, the Western Isles seat has never been held by a Tory, although a Liberal/Conservative coalitionist was returned for a brief period during the politically unsettled years of the early 1920s. Since 1935 it has been held by either Labour or the SNP. It was a 21-year-old student at Edinburgh University, Malcolm K. Macmillan from Lewis, who began it all with his election in that year, starting a parliamentary career which was to last 35 years. Lloyd George, by then the Father of the House, introduced Macmillan to the Commons, and it was Donald Stewart, the Provost of Stornoway, who forced him from the place by winning the 1970 election for the SNP by just 726 votes.

Donald Stewart was a popular figure and increased his majorities in 1974, 1979 and 1983. He retired in 1987, but could not pass the torch to his party's successor candidate. Calum MacDonald took the seat back for Labour with a healthy majority of 2,340 votes. Angus Brendan MacNeil won the seat back for the SNP in 2005 and has held it since. It was a similar pattern at a Scottish parliamentary level. In 1999 the first MSP for the islands to be elected to the new legislature was Labour's Alasdair Morrison, who held it again in 2003. However, the SNP's Alasdair Allan won the 2007 election and the two subsequent counts. Both were to become ministers in their respective administrations.

### Flying the Labour flag

When it comes to Labour Party figures in the Highlands and Islands, one of the most significant and influential must be a man who, ironically, failed three times to be elected as an MP for one of the area's constituencies. Brian Wilson appears to be a 'Marmite' character, arousing strong opinions. I have known him for a very long time and he has been very helpful to me on many occasions. I didn't and don't agree with him on a wide range of issues from Iraq to devolution or the Skye Bridge campaign, nor do I share his preoccupation with the SNP. I find it hard to understand, however, that anyone could gainsay that he has made a huge contribution to Highland life. His role in the founding of the *West Highland Free Press*, his journalism and campaigning on issues such as land reform and Gaelic were crucial to these causes, but represented only one strand of that contribution. As a government minister he launched Iomairt aig an Oir, the Initiative at the Edge project, to pool all public sector resources and focus on particularly fragile areas which had failed to respond to three and a half decades of work by development agencies. He established the community land unit within Highlands and Islands Enterprise the day the residents of Eigg took control of their island. This was a firm statement that there was now political will behind local communities taking control of their land, something that had to be spelt out to certain important officials. He worked hard for the Gaelic cause. The Columba Project, building contacts between Gaelic speakers in Scotland and Ireland, was also one of his creations. Since leaving politics his role in first saving then resurrecting the Harris Tweed industry has been immense. He lives with his family on Lewis.

## A rebel with so many causes

Another Labour man more than worthy of mention was Angus Graham, the former vice convener of Western Isles Council who died in 2008 aged 60. He was the most combative of politicians in any debate but generous and charming when they had ended. He lived on his croft with his wife Isobel and their family in the Back area of Lewis. He was one of the organisers of the Scottish Crofters Union, helping secure financial stability by running a Stornoway branch of the insurance brokerage that the union franchised from the National Farmers' Union of Scotland. Originally from a family of Govan Gaels, Graham lost his mother early, thereafter going to Lewis to live with his aunt, his mother's sister, and her husband. He told me how on leaving school he had gone to the agricultural college at Balmacara in south-west Ross-shire but had been expelled because he had wanted to stay with a sick cow in calf rather than participate in the amateur dramatics so beloved by the then principal. He was worried about going back to Lewis with the shame of the expulsion, but he had been relieved when his uncle said, in Gaelic, to his aunt of his disgrace, 'You can take a kick from a good horse!' Angus's father organised for him to go to sea shortly after, and he left the Clyde as a teenager to sail round the world before he saw Lewis again. During the oil construction boom of the 1970s and 1980s he worked across the Highlands and Islands from Sullom Voe to Kishorn. He also worked for a while as a Harris Tweed weaver. Following a by-election in the Gress ward in Lewis, he became a councillor in 1983. He was another who was tireless in his public service and for many years chaired the Low Pay Unit, a joint initiative of the Convention of Scottish Local Authorities, the Scottish Trades Union Congress and the London-based Low Pay Unit, which closed in 2008.

He was always willing to be quoted and was the man the media would go to in many political controversies. He was a frequent critic, for example, of Highlands and Islands Enterprise, and would receive several phone calls from reporters every year when the agency published its annual report. He would always contrast the significantly improving economic fortunes in and around Inverness with the continuing fight against depopulation in the Outer Isles. He hated seeing the young leave the islands and was vociferous in the interest of local fishing boats against the more powerful vessels from the north-east of Scotland. Angus was impatient at the rate of change in the islands, and indeed across the country, so much so that he could be highly critical of the Labour Party. He sought nomination as a Holyrood candidate but was not selected.

In 1995 he was desperate to join the campaigners on the Greenpeace ship *Altair*, which had been shadowing tugs pulling *Brent Spar* to its planned dumping ground 230 miles west of Orkney. The oil giant Shell, however, gave in to international pressure and abandoned its highly controversial plans, if memory serves, before Angus could arrange his transfer to the vessel. He famously fell out with Scottish Natural Heritage (SNH) in 1997 to the extent he was removed as a member of the agency's North-west Regional Board because he publicly criticised its opposition to the super-quarry at Lingerbay on Harris. But he always believed his hostility to a scheme to grant the Countess of Sutherland's family up to £150,000 for not felling pine trees in a 350-acre woodland at Loch Fleet, near Golspie, was the real reason for his removal. SNH had been concerned that the estate's desire to harvest the 100-year-old Scots pines would destroy Britain's prime habitat for a rare species of plant, the one-flowered wintergreen, which was on a designated Site of Special Scientific Interest (SSSI). The story was complicated by the fact that Lord Strathnaver, whose land it was, sat on the SNH main board. Angus had a very public row with the Regional Board chairman, writer and scientist Sir John Lister-Kaye, which journalists loved. He and I would talk often on the phone. I miss hearing his voice.

## John Pollock

Another significant Labour figure appeared not long after I had started in the Highland correspondent's job. I had known John Pollock for many years when he was the General Secretary of the Educational Institute of Scotland (EIS), the leading teachers' union.

He had retired and had been invited to address the Skye and Lochalsh local Labour Party in Broadford. He sent shockwaves by announcing his belief that only independence within an integrated Europe could protect the interests of the Scottish people. Devolution wouldn't be enough and only Labour could deliver. His Labour credentials were peerless. He had been, quite literally, bounced on the knee of Red Clydesider and legendary Independent Labour Party MP Jimmy Maxton, and had also sat at the feet of Nye Bevan, the health minister who set up the NHS in Attlee's postwar Labour government. Pollock had chaired the Scottish Labour Party twice, the STUC once and was influential within the TUC. He had turned down one of the safest Labour seats in Scotland to become general secretary of the EIS in 1975. He oversaw its transformation, with membership at 50 per cent of the teaching profession in Scotland rising to 80 per cent under his leadership. It had become the largest purely Scottish affiliate of the STUC and one of the most successful teachers' unions in Europe. It led the fight that made Scottish teachers the first public-sector group to force the Thatcher government to turn.

Pollock was an outstanding public speaker who was described as the greatest Labour Secretary of State for Scotland the country never had. His face was known throughout the country. However, only 22 turned up that night in Broadford. Various explanations were given – The Proclaimers were playing Portree; Seamus McGee and his six-piece Irish Showband were at Kyle of Lochalsh; and apparently there was a 'big wedding' on in Edinbane. Had more turned out, they would have heard him publicly challenge many of Labour's sacred cows. He pointed to a catch-22 for the then leader Neil Kinnock in his attempt to make Labour more attractive to the voters in the south-east of England, which meant Labour supporters had to ask: 'Will a transformed Labour

Party with policies relevant and attractive to the voters in the affluent south of England have any direct relevance to the needs of Scotland?' Even if Labour came to power in Britain through economic crisis, he doubted that Scotland would be a priority. But Europe presented Scotland with the opportunity of independence without the isolationism previously preached by the SNP, so hated by so many in the Labour Party. Many thought this was the start of something, but Pollock's public profile remained low and he died while on holiday with his family in Majorca in 1995. He was 69. His speech on Skye was forgotten, his subsequent silence unexplained. He didn't live to see Labour returned to power, the Scottish parliament established, Europe in turmoil or the independence referendum. But he would have had a take on it all which probably would have surprised us.

## Michael Forsyth's Celtic Twilight

Another who could surprise was Michael Forsyth. He became Secretary of State for Scotland in July 1995 and remained in that post until the general election in May 1997, when the Conservatives lost to Tony Blair's resurgent Labour Party. Tories had not been particularly popular in the Highlands, and there was no reason to think that would change under Mr Forsyth, later created the Lord Forsyth of Drumlean, who was seen as being on the right wing of his party. He was to astonish many, however, by entering his own Celtic Twilight. He launched it with his proposal to hand over control of the publicly owned crofting estates to local crofting trusts. Significantly he also exhorted private landlords to follow his example, thereby implicitly suggesting to some that the local community either had a right to the land or could make better use of it.

His enthusiasm for the Highlands continued, leaving many utterly bemused. This was not the Michael Forsyth we knew. Nothing in his earlier career had even suggested such concern.

Yet against stiff opposition from the Forestry Commission, which had been more than happy to sell to the commercial sector, he decided to let the people of Laggan try to take control of the nearby 3,500-acre Strathmashie Forest. At a meeting of the Scottish Grand Committee in Inverness he put the prospect of a Highland university firmly back on the agenda. His predecessor and Scottish Office officials had made clear it would have to wait until some unknown point in the future. I received a phone call from a Scottish Office civil servant after this meeting asking if I had notes of what exactly Mr Forsyth had said on the subject, as he and his colleagues had no detail. We later learnt he had asked an opposition MP to ask a question about the university before he entered the council chamber where the convention was being held.

At Stirling University in the spring on 1996, in a speech which was virtually unreported, Mr Forsyth declared: 'Let us confront our past honestly, warts and all. Gaelic culture has been subjected for centuries to a repression unashamedly aimed at its obliteration. This cultural genocide cannot be laid at the door of the English; its inheritors were Lowland Scots.' This was a deal stronger than his Labour predecessor Willie Ross, who, in 1965, declared in the House of Commons, when setting up HIE's predecessor the Highlands and Islands Development Board (HIDB): 'For two hundred years, the Highlander has been the man on Scotland's conscience.'

The same day Mr Forsyth announced he would be setting up a Convention of the Highlands and Islands which would embrace MPs, local authorities, public agencies and other bodies operating in the area. He would chair the convention which still meets today. At the Scottish Grand Committee in Dundee a few weeks later he abandoned earlier proposals to change grants for crofters. This would have saved the Treasury money, something he had always been keen to do, but the Crofters Commission and Crofters Union had warned it would lead to depopulation and dereliction of crofting areas.

Mr Forsyth found money to help with a causeway between the island of Berneray and the much larger North Uist after his minister Lord James Douglas-Hamilton had been left to tell islanders earlier in the year that the best they could hope for was to compete against others in the Challenge Fund. He also dropped in by helicopter to give moral support to the islanders of Eigg, taking a fairly direct swipe at the stewardship of Messrs Schellenberg and Maruma. He went to see the Assynt Crofters.

In September Scottish secretaries used to go to North America or the Far East to look for inward investment which had always been presented as a crucially important part of the job. In that month in 1996 Mr Forsyth went to Mull, Tiree, Orkney, Lewis, Harris – or at least Harris airspace – Berneray, North Uist, Benbecula, Barra, Rum, Eigg and Islay. Despite it all, few seemed ready to accept his commitment at face value that the road to Daliburgh could lead to Damascus. His strategy was unclear. The Tories may have believed they had a chance in the Inverness East, Nairn and Lochaber seat, perhaps even Argyll, but nobody else did. Mr Forsyth was fighting for his political life in Stirling, where the crofting vote was unlikely to help. He was said to have been influenced by the arguments of Highland historian Jim Hunter whom he met on Skye. Hunter is understood to have advised the politician that the Tories might be better viewed in Scotland if they did not instinctively defend absentee landowners, however questionable. He also suggested Mr Forsyth consider resurrecting the Highland Panel. This had been created in 1946 and comprised MPs, councillors and other prominent figures to advise Secretaries of State on Highland matters such as crofting. It is likely this led to the creation of the Convention of the Highlands and Islands.

Mr Forsyth was also more than happy to engage with the Highland press. I had asked for an exclusive interview for *The Herald* with his predecessor as Secretary of State Ian Lang to discuss the Highlands and Islands, but initially got no response. When I pursued it some months later I was told I could interview Lord James Douglas-Hamilton, whose minister of state's brief included the Highlands. With Mr Forsyth in charge at St Andrew's House a few years later, I decided to try again for an interview with a Scottish Secretary. Within an hour of submitting my request, I got a message to say that Mr Forsyth would phone me at lunchtime. In the resulting telephone conversation he told me he was going to ask his Scottish Office officials to examine ways to direct more money to the local authorities in the Highlands and Islands, at the expense of the Central Belt. This again was to be news to his civil servants:

> I haven't actually told my officials yet, but one of the things that struck me over the past few weeks is that I just wonder whether the basis on which we allocate resources to local government, and the basis on which we decide capital programmes, is entirely right and whether it is perhaps not too skewed to centres of population. That may be right, but if you look at the huge impact that can be made on those communities, it is something that I would like to look at again. By its very nature a local authority like Orkney, Shetland, or the Western Isles has a very limited base on which to draw resources. Authorities like

Argyll and others have all these enormous costs and difficulties arising from maintaining small populations on islands.

He was aware that such a proposal would not go down well within the then Labour-dominated Convention of Scottish Local Authorities (COSLA) and he could understand why, but he thought is was 'time that the voice of the Highlands and Islands was given a little bit more strength'.

I talked to Michael Forsyth for the purpose of this book and asked him to reflect on his time as Secretary of State and his interest in the Highlands looking back 20 years. He confirmed that he had indeed acted unilaterally when he announced the relaunch of the university project.

On the University of the Highlands and Islands, I just couldn't get anywhere. The universities were all lobbying against it, the officials were against it. I could just see the whole thing disappearing into a three-year review. I thought we will just announce we are doing it, then they will have to get on with it. So that's what I did. It has done well, but the original vision has not really happened. Perhaps it was slightly before its time. There may be time yet. At that time education was very much at the front of my mind and I was trying to get power for headteachers, self-governing schools, all the things the SNP now say they are in favour of, but at that time it was all very controversial and frustrating. We were way ahead of England in educational performance, although we are now behind. It seemed to me that education was one of the things that people associated with Scotland and particularly the Highlands, the work ethic and the belief in education, not just to get you a good job, but as something that was worthwhile in itself. That was embedded in the culture and was recognised internationally. I felt we had a comparative advantage and I believed that if we could find the way of delivering higher education to local communities it would give people a chance that had been denied them. But at the same time, using the new technology [the internet was just beginning] the University of the Highlands could deliver courses around the globe. If you can teach particle physics or plumbing in Benbecula, you could probably do it in Brazil. But that hasn't really happened with centralisation and the taking away of local colleges. I thought Labour Secretary of State Tom Johnston did a brilliant thing after the war when he just said everywhere in Scotland is going to be connected to the National Grid. I felt we should have been doing the same in the Highlands with broadband, ADSL as it was in those days. That could transform these economies. It wasn't just about bringing in tourists. It was about distributing education and providing the workforce with the skills.

Perhaps unsurprisingly he was critical of the Scottish Parliament: 'One of the disappointments [with devolution], however, has been that contrary to what was advertised on the tin, a lot of stuff has been centralised. You see that with the emasculation of Highlands and Islands Enterprise, the concentration in the Central Belt and the unification of the police forces. The Highland police were brilliant and entirely suited to what they were doing in their communities. Things have gone backwards. I suppose we have Gaelic on police cars in the Borders, but that isn't really quite what it was about.'

An enthusiastic climber who has climbed some of the world's most famous mountains, including peaks in Antarctica and Africa, he became interested in Gaelic while getting started on Scotland's mountains (he once worked as a seasonal barman in the Clachaig Inn, the climbers' howff in Glencoe). He believes more could be done to promote the language: 'It was rock and mountain climbing that got me in touch with the Gaelic language. In that mountaineering fraternity there is a lot of Gaelic culture (re. names of mountains, etc). I think I was the first Secretary of State to go to the Mòd. I remember saying to my officials we must go to the Mòd and they said, "What?" If you think about England and the Cheltenham Music Festival, it gets coverage but the Mòd is not celebrated on a UK basis yet it is a wonderful music festival, but it doesn't have anything of the profile of say the Welsh Eisteddfod.'

Lord Forsyth has his very own perspectives on the land question, community ownership and Highland history.

I had a big disappointment on the crofting. I discovered, as Secretary of State, I was the biggest crofting landlord in Scotland by a long way, and all that history about the Highlander is the man on Scotland's conscience – I do feel that actually. Remember the early Tory party was Jacobite, and I have sympathy given the way the Hanoverians destroyed the [Gaelic] culture. There was this whole bitterness of the Clearances and a lot of, in my view, rewriting of history and this whole issue of the land. I thought, 'Here we are, we have all these crofts which are costing us a lot to run, why don't we give them to the crofters?' It was a bit like the Skye Bridge. I just misunderstood things. I thought people would jump at the chance [of getting crofts]. There were conditions. They would have to mend the fences and have 99-year leases, but nobody took up the offer until the West Harris crofters [in 2010]. It rather drove a coach and horses through arguments about people being driven from their land. I misunderstood that. Perhaps I was taken in by the propaganda.

I don't mind people owning large tracts of land if they look after them and operate in what people might describe as a paternalistic manner, look after local people, understand their responsibilities. But we have had some horrendous examples of horrible landlords, mainly from outside Scotland. There were interesting things going on, what Jim Hunter was talking about, and the people at Laggan. People were embarking on planting trees, which struck a chord. When I was young I had won a Labour [Westminster City Council] ward, much to my surprise, in Pimlico. One of the things I suggested was setting up a charity and getting people to plant trees. The Westminster Council officials said, 'Oh no, it doesn't work, what happens is the trees die if they don't get watered.' But I said if they are sponsored people will look after them, and that's exactly what happened. Thousands of trees have been planted and it has become the Westminster Tree Trust. That experience made me think if communities themselves are given the power and responsibility it is amazing what can be achieved. That was the root of that. It is the same as why I was in favour of selling council houses; it was not to raise money. I would support more communities taking control. But I am not in favour of challenging people's property rights. The rule of law which protects property rights is central to the free society.

Lord Forsyth also has his own perspective on the Skye Bridge and the long-running anti-tolls campaign:

I will tell you a funny story which to me summed up the relationships between civil servants in Edinburgh and remote communities. It had actually been Ian Lang and Lord James Douglas-Hamilton who had been responsible for the Skye Bridge. It was quite controversial because of the tolls. They don't care today but in those days we decided we couldn't ask the Queen to open the Skye Bridge because it was controversial and we didn't want her getting, in any way, associated with a project there was a row about. James Douglas-Hamilton sent me a note saying if the Queen was not going to open it, I should as Scottish Secretary. I sent him a note back saying, no, it had been his project and he should do it; however I ended up doing it. It was only when I turned up on the day to be greeted by Robbie the Pict and about a thousand demonstrators that I realised what an astute politician James Douglas-Hamilton was.

I couldn't really understand the controversy because the tolls were the same as the ferry fares. I couldn't get my head round what was going on here. The tolls were the same as the ferries and after about 20 years it would be toll free. What was the gripe? About four or five months after it opened, up comes a note in my box saying, 'Good news, Secretary of State. The Skye Bridge has been a great success. It has increased activity in the economy by 25 per cent. The traffic across it to the island has gone up enormously and there is a press release saying this.' I sent a note to my private secretary saying do not let them put out that press release, and get them all in for a meeting. They arrived and were rather sheepish. I said can't you see this has nothing to do with the economy? They disagreed, but I said I now understand why there was so much opposition. They looked blankly and I said, 'Clearly the locals weren't paying to travel on the ferry, and that's why the numbers have gone up.' Years later I went to a 60th birthday and [Lady] Claire Macdonald was there as well and she said, 'Well of course they weren't all paying.' So I ordered an immediate audit of CalMac and found there was a lot of that going on. Then of course

In Peter Jolly's back garden

Sorley MacLean (Photo by Cailean Maclean)

On top of the world at Cape Wrath (Photo by Peter Jolly)

Assynt crofters John MacKenzie, Bill Ritchie (sitting) and Allan MacRae (Photo by Paul Hackett, courtesy of *The Herald*)

On Gigha (Photo courtesy of *The Herald*)

With Uncle Neil on Iona

Coinneach Maclean on tour
(Photo by Dipesh Gosar)

Cromarty from the sea

On board the ferry to Eriskay before the causeway was built

With Renee and Sorley in Galway when Sorley was awarded an honorary degree by the National University of Ireland

Cromarty Rising campaigners outside Holyrood (Photo courtesy of Greg Fullarton)

Jim Hunter near the Ballachulish bridge (Photo by Gordon Terris, courtesy of *The Herald*)

An oil rig passes the Royal Hotel in Cromarty

With John Ross interviewing one of the residents of the island of Rum

Brian Wilson, Maggie Fyffe and Colin Carr on Eigg (Photo courtesy of *The Herald*)

'The Prof' (Norman Macdonald) interviews Drew Millar at the Skye Bridge (Photo by Cailean Maclean)

THIS MEMORIAL
GARDEN MARKS
THE EXACT SITE
OF THE FENCE ON
WHICH THE
MACDONALDS OF
SLEAT WERE SITTING
WHILE THE BATTLE
OF CULLODEN WAS
BEING FOUGHT IN
1746

HYDRO
ELECTRIC
PLC

McDonald Burger

THE
READ
THE
SUN

THIS STONE
SPONSORED
BY THE
PEPSI
CORPORATION

MARK THATCHER
ARMS CORP

*West Highland Free Press*'s cartoon (courtesy of Chris Tyler) on MacDonald clan chief's 'once in 250 years'
offer to North Americans to 'honor' their forebears at the time of Culloden

# Dounreay waste store shocks council

## Rusty storage drums overflow nuclear dump

By DAVID ROSS
Highland Correspondent

THE sight of thousands of drums of nuclear waste scattered on the surface of Dounreay's waste pits shocked Highland regional councillors yesterday.

Following the planning visit, they turned down an application to extend one of the plant's pits.

Some of the drums of low-level waste had been lying rusting since 1985. Others were stacked on top of an existing waste pit and covered only by tarpaulins held down by steel pipes and concrete blocks, with wire netting to prevent birds from interfering with the waste.

The planning committee subsequently convened in Thurso Town Hall and rejected, by 12 votes to 10, a planning application from the Caithness plant to extend one of its waste pits. However, the debate is not finished.

Vice-convener Peter Peacock said it was shocking the way the waste had been abandoned. Planning committee vice-convener Councillor Michael Foxley described it as disgraceful.

Inverness councillor Clive Gnotman successfully moved that planning permission be withheld until the plant developed a proper waste management policy. "If this was a quarry, we would tell the owner to go away and get his act together."

There was also concern that granting planning permission on this scale could open the door to the nuclear waste agency Nirex returning to Dounreay in search of a site for Britain's first nuclear waste repository.

The issue of Dounreay and its nuclear activities sharply divides the council but even the plant's most ardent supporters on the council were admitting privately last night that the visual impact had lost Dounreay the application.

They were, however, still incensed by the vote and have already tabled a counter motion for the full council in two weeks' time. Caithness Councillor Bill

Mowatt said afterwards: "This will only cost Highland council taxpayers more money and put jobs at Dounreay at risk."

The Atomic Energy Authority had requested the 12,000 cubic metre extension to Waste Pit Six to allow it to accommodate the waste that had accumulated on the surface and to allow it to deal with the waste resulting from decommissioning work.

Mr Ken Butler, AEA's head of safety, emphasised to the planning committee that all the waste which would go in the pit was low-level waste such as used gloves or overshoes.

He conceded, however, that the build-up of drums on the surface had been due to a "misjudgment" on how long it would take to introduce a compacting process for the waste.

"We are aware of the buckling of drums that you all saw this morning and we are not proud of it," he said. "Some are considerably corroded but there has been no radioactivity escaping from them, measurements are always being taken and the waste is stored within the drums in heavy duty polythene bags."

Opponents of the application were in favour of careful surface storage of the waste in the same way as Dounreay already deals with its intermediate waste and argued this was council policy, although chief solicitor Malcolm MacRae said officials were at a loss to know what precisely that policy meant.

Mr Butler said that this approach could cost £60m over 30 years, compared with the £2m to £5m involved in the pit extension.

One who was delighted by the committee's decision was Mrs Lorraine Mann, of Scotland Against Nuclear Dumping. "This was the only decision which could safeguard the people of the Highlands from having materials, which in almost every other country in the world would be high-level waste, dumped in pits."

Mr Roger James, Dounreay's site manager, said he was disappointed. "This decision today impacts on our ability to deal with the very problem that everybody wants us to address."

Highland regional councillors inspect one of the overflowing waste pits while on a planning visit to Dounreay yesterday. They subsequently rejected an application for an extension to one of the pits.

*The Herald* front page from April 1 1993, which made the public begin 'to realise how Dounreay had abused the secrecy it had enjoyed'

Protestors against oil transfers on the beach at Nairn (Photo courtesy of Greg Fullarton)

the politics drove it and we spent a fortune buying it out from the Bank of America. Because the traffic was so much better, it would all have been paid for in 11 years, but it just went to show that things are never quite what they seem.

He also took a different view from civil servants on how to deal with Scottish history in the modern day:

The other thing I got into trouble over was that I wanted to do something to mark the 250th anniversary of Culloden. You would not believe the opposition in the Scottish Office from officials. They saw it as a very sensitive issue. 'Are you sure you want to do this, Secretary of State?' I was basically trying to set in motion doing something with the battlefield site, and a lot of that has now been done.

It was part of the same theme for me, that quite shockingly most schoolkids think that Culloden was about the English killing the Scots. That's what made the civil servants in the Scottish Office get very twitchy about marking Culloden. We did do some stuff to mark it, but they were desperate to keep it as low key as possible because they thought it was sensitive. Well, I think people should know it was a civil war and that there were more Scots on the Hanoverian side than the other side. And I had to cope with the film *Braveheart* as well. It became apparent that people confused the Wars of Scottish Independence in the 14th century with Culloden in the 18th century and had no understanding as to what this was all about. They didn't understand there were Jacobites south of the border and that Bonnie Prince Charlie, had he not been badly advised at Derby, could have been in London. The king had already packed his bags. People didn't understand. I think that is still the case. After the 1745 there was a determination to destroy Highland culture, and to bury it. And there was no appetite for raking up bad history. So much better to present it as us versus the English. It is still one of the things that depresses me about Scotland – that the youngsters and so many people just don't understand their own history, and it gets turned into this horrible anti-Englishness.

## Cairdeas

We have also witnessed the establishment and fairly rapid subsequent demise of two new political parties in the Highlands and Islands. In 1998, the Highlands and Islands Alliance or Cairdeas ('friendship, goodwill') was launched on Skye. It fielded candidates on the Highlands and Islands list in 1999 who were going to job share. But few voters were persuaded and Cairdeas disappeared. But it did come up with some fairly original policy ideas.

First there was MSPs job sharing; then a Highland bank; a community owned airline; an assembly of all Highlands and Islands MPs, MSPs and MEPs to consult the local people on policy; councils using planning powers to encourage supermarkets to use local produce; a watchdog to make quangos and the public sector more accountable. Cairdeas produced a prospectus, not a manifesto. To a large extent it was fronted by two or three activists. Top of the gender-balanced list was anti-nuclear campaigner Lorraine Mann, prominent for her work on Dounreay. Her job-share partner was playwright/marine consultant Eddie Stiven, who had moved to Glenelg. The second job-sharing pair were Anne Baxter from Bunessan on Mull and Peter Hunter, who worked for the Low Pay Unit.

Meanwhile in 2013 the Alliance Party of Scotland was launched in Inverness with a plan to field candidates in 2016 to stop the spread of wind farms. But it folded in May 2014. Footnotes perhaps in the political history of the Highlands, but they did represent a level of dissatisfaction with the established parties.

# 8

# The Land: Assynt

EARLY IN 2018 an important submission was made to the Scottish Parliament suggesting amendments to the planning legislation which was on its journey through Holyrood. This may not sound the most newsworthy of developments, but it was to the effect that there should be provisions to facilitate the repopulation of at least some of the land people were cleared from in the 18th and 19th centuries. The proposal came from Community Land Scotland (CLS), the umbrella organisation for community buyouts such as Eigg, Knoydart and Gigha. *The Herald* reported:

> It remains one of the most controversial periods in Scotland's history – a dark legacy of upheaval that still provokes passions to this day. Now long-forgotten townships destroyed by the Highland Clearances are set to be reborn under ambitious plans put before the Scottish Parliament. Campaigners have called for Scotland's deserted glens to 'once again ring to the voices of children playing in their landscape' as they laid out proposals to inject life back into rural areas.
> CLS – which represents Scotland's community landowners – has proposed amendments to new planning laws currently going through Holyrood in an effort to right some of the wrongs of the past. It wants ministers to be able to compulsorily purchase land for the purpose of resettlement, and also called for communities to be handed powers to buy up land that has sat neglected for three years or more – insisting current policies don't do enough to promote repopulation.

Repopulating cleared land had long been something of a dream of land reform campaigners. A new impetus was given to the idea some years ago when Scottish Natural Heritage (SNH) completed an exercise at the behest of ministers in which almost four million acres, mostly in the Highlands and Islands, were defined as wild land. This was to inform planning policy. It was not a designation founded in law but it served to underline the importance the Scottish government was attaching to ensuring certain areas were protected from development, not least involving wind farms. When SNH put its Wild Land Map out for consultation in 2013 there was support from recreational groups, but criticism from others with a different association with the land. The Crofters' Commission said people such as crofters, who for generations had worked the land in remote and rural landscapes, were being 'rendered invisible' and challenged the very essence of the concept of wildness. It said: 'Having established that some areas of land appear to be "natural, uncultivated, desolate or inhospitable", it is then assumed such a quality is desirable, without any explanation of how it has been established that such a quality is felt to be desirable, and by whom.'

Professor Jim Hunter argued that Highland land had supported people for over 50 centuries, and it was only in the last two that the voice of man had not been heard. Rob Gibson, then the SNP MSP for Caithness, Sutherland and Ross, who had written about the Highland Clearances, said he believed pressure to protect huge tracts of the Highlands and Islands was largely being driven by people, often living in towns and cities, who were against wind farms: 'Alas, in my view, clamour for "wild land" protection is a response to a predominantly urban view of wildness focused on by a well-publicised anti-development lobby. This has led to a vocal minority railing loudly against wind turbine building.' He had matched a map of clearance sites which were identified over several editions of his book *The Highland Clearances Trail* with SNH's wild land map. There was a striking overlap. Although not a fully scientific exercise, he said it pointed to 'the need for a map of settlements across rural Scotland that used to exist to see the places where human communities lived and thrived'.

I wrote a leader for *The Herald* on the subject in which I recalled the Canadian writer the late Hugh MacLennan, whose forebears had to leave Kintail. He knew the difference between wilderness and emptiness: 'Above the 60th parallel in Canada you feel that nobody but God has ever been there before you, but in a deserted Highland glen you feel that everyone who ever mattered is dead and gone.'

In March 2018 research by the James Hutton Institute revealed the working-age population in rural Scotalnd was projected to plummet by a third by 2046. It would be important to Scotland if her parliamentarians were to find a way of putting lights back on in at least some of our empty glens. That it is even being talked about owes much to the people who led the way with community buyouts in the last two and a half decades. They drew the road map for others to follow, but it is worth remembering the huge challenges they faced. The first navigational point on that map is the tortuous but stunningly beautiful B869 road in Sutherland which takes you by way of townships such as Achmelvich, Clachtoll, Stoer and Drumbeg to a spot near the Kylesku Bridge. Not quite halfway along this road there is a turn-off to the local Stoer Primary School which sits above the small reedy freshwater Loch Neil Bhàin. History was made in the building on a December night in 1992, when the modern community land movement was effectively launched by 100 crofters in Assynt.

Members of the Highland press corps were already in Lochinver as Scottish fishing boats from the North-east, which had long operated out of the Sutherland port, had blockaded French vessels also using Lochinver. This was in protest at the workings of the European Common Fisheries Policy. But it is interesting to recall in this time of Brexit-dominated debate that many of the local people said their sympathies lay with the French. We were told that although the Scottish boats had been using Lochinver for decades, there was little interaction with their crews. They would go home to the North-east at the weekend and return the next week with all their provisions. But just as we were sending our stories on the blockade, we were told by local campaigners to get up to Stoer Primary as something important was about to be announced. The Assynt Crofters had won their campaign. BBC Radio Scotland's Iain MacDonald had already driven back the near 100 miles to Inverness (or possibly Wick; he can't remember) with his tapes on the blockade but then had to turn around and rush straight back to Assynt.

There was an air of excitement in the school hall, packed with local people that night. The leadership of the recently founded Assynt Crofters Trust (ACT) entered to great applause: Chairman the late Allan MacRae, Vice Chairman John MacKenzie, Secretary Bill Ritchie and legal adviser Simon Fraser. The last two said a few words. Bill Ritchie quoted from my old friend Iain Fraser Grigor's book *Mightier*

*Than a Lord: The Highland Crofters' Struggle for the Land* (Acair, 1979), which, understandably, he said had inspired him. John MacKenzie declined to speak. Then Allan MacRae addressed the gathering. His great-grandfather had been cleared from land at Ardvar to make way for a sheep farm which had once supported 500 ewes, all long gone. He said: 'Well, ladies and gentlemen, it seems we have won the land. It certainly is a moment to savour . . . My immediate thoughts are to wish that some of our forebears could be here to share this moment with us . . . In winning the land, Assynt crofters have struck a historic blow for people on the land throughout the Highlands.'

It certainly was clear to me and other observers amidst the celebrations that something highly significant had just happened. There had been community-owned estates in Skye and Lewis for some time, those in the former offered for sale to local people by the government in 1908. In 1923 the industrialist and philanthropist Lord Leverhulme donated the parish of Stornoway as a free gift to its inhabitants, and on his instructions the Stornoway Trust was established to administer the estate. But Assynt was the first community since the days of the last land raids – Knoydart in 1948, which was ultimately unsuccessful, and Balmartin on North Uist in 1952 (of which more later) – where crofters had sought to take control of their own destiny. Allan MacRae said at the time of the buyout, 'I can't see how we can do any worse than what has gone before.' It was a view shared by many.

## A troubled past

Assynt was a story we had been covering since the early summer of 1992, when it was announced that the 21,000-acre North Lochinver Estate would be sold in seven different lots. The prospect of multiple ownership, with crofters paying rent to three, four or even seven different landlords, shocked the local branch of the Scottish Crofters Union (SCU) which had around 100 or so members on the estate, and they resolved to try to buy it themselves. They issued a statement talking of their 'anger and determination to resist the attempted sale in small lots . . .' The ACT was formed and launched its public appeal on 28 July that year. Their cause was to strike a chord, winning support throughout the land. Bill Ritchie still remembers feeling humbled by the whole process: 'There was so much support and goodwill. What people were saying in their messages to us was so moving, supporting us, I was crying when I was opening the envelopes. One old woman said she had no money but did have some stamps she wanted us to have. There were donations from ordinary people up and down the land, from pubs and clubs. It just made us feel we had got to win this.'

In part this was a popular response to the legacy of the Highland Clearances. The Assynt Crofters' cause was seen by many as a move to reverse in some small way that sad history. Assynt had been Macleod country, but later it had belonged to the Sutherland family whose name remains prominent in clearance demonology. Many of the forebears of the men and women of the ACT had been driven from the better land towards the sea, to the rocky periphery where they were to cling to their lives in these parts for another century or so. But not all did. Norman McLeod was born in Clachtoll in 1780. A minister, he was to lead a band of people from Assynt on an extraordinary 14,000-mile odyssey to Nova Scotia, Australia and Waipu in New Zealand, where he died in 1866. There were other later manifestations of discontent. In 1887 a farm which had been cleared at Clashmore was razed by its former residents. Dykes were pulled down, farm buildings burned to the ground and troops were ordered to restore order. In 1913 the Sutherlands sold Assynt to a local 'man made good' in Canada, but it was back on the market again in 1935.

This time there were two interested parties, the Duke of Westminster and the Vestey family. The former bought Assynt for his prospective son-in-law, William Filmer-Sankey. He, in turn, demonstrated his deep attachment to the area by getting in touch with the Vesteys to offer for sale the croftlands near the coast north of Lochinver. The source of the Vestey wealth was the Liverpool brothers Edmund and William Vestey, who set up a trading company in 1897. They shrewdly took full advantage of the then-new refrigeration techniques to ship vast quantities of beef from America and Argentina. William Vestey had bought a peerage, for a reputed £25,000, in Liberal Prime Minister David Lloyd George's notorious 1922 honours list. The family ended up owning most of Assynt, but over the years started to sell off different parcels. In the late 1980s the 21,500 acres under croft (the so-called North Lochinver Estate) were sold to Scandinavian Property Services Ltd (SPS) for more than £1 million. How exactly SPS ever thought it could develop land covered by crofting regulations was unclear, but few were surprised that within three years it was bankrupt and liquidators put the estate on the market at £473,000.

A quarter of a century after the buyout Bill Ritchie recalled: 'We missed a chance when Vestey sold to the Swedes in 1989, but when they went bankrupt, we were ready in 1992. There was anger. We had been paying our rent to a bunch of speculators in a foreign country who had no interest in the land. I got the brochure from the selling agents which was full of beautiful photos and said, "Perhaps even people are alien in this landscape." We got so angry, especially the likes of Allan and John, whose people had been cleared. It strengthened our resolve.'

Things did not go the crofters' way, however. Whether it was the liquidators Stoy Hayward or SPS's main creditors, the Ostgota Enskilda Bank of Stockholm, we never knew, but somebody didn't want to sell to them. As I recall it was another journalist, I think Tom Morton, and myself who broke the news to Allan MacRae that the crofters' second offer had been refused. He was working at a small stone bridge near the entrance to Lochinver. He turned to us with a trowel in his hand and rather alarming anger in his eyes, and said, 'They just don't want us to have the land!'

Three offers were tabled before the crofters won it for £300,000, and then only after they had demonstrated that if they weren't going to get it they would make sure nobody else would want it. By using their rights to buy their crofts established in 1976, they had prepared to take over the few jewels in the estate's crown: Torbreck House and the angling-rich Manse River system. Without these assets few would be interested. I faxed articles to Sweden to ensure that the Ostgota Enskilda was aware of legal restrictions imposed on the land by the crofting legislation, and what the loss of Torbreck would mean. Stoy Hayward received the same information.

## Key players

Having observed local campaigning over 30 years, it is remarkable how, so often by sheer accident, the right people seem to appear at the right time to act as leaders, bringing different skills to the table. This was certainly true in north-west Sutherland in 1992.

The ACT chairman, Allan MacRae, was the stuff of Assynt. His croft was at Torbreck and he worked as a stonemason/builder. His father, known locally as Johnny Glen, had been a shepherd/stalker who was general manager for the Little Assynt sheep farm for much of his life. Allan worked on farms in the south of Scotland and in the construction of hydroelectric dams. According to an appreciation of him on the Lochinver page of the *Scottish Villages* website, 'While working in Lochaber he took part in the Ben Nevis Hill Race, which attracts up to 500 contestants every year, coming in first once and second on four occasions. From Lochaber he would cycle home to Assynt every fortnight to see his folk and think nothing of it.' Allan was found dead in the hills near his croft in June 2013. He had taken his own life. Perhaps fittingly, the alarm was first raised on Monday night when he didn't appear at a board meeting of the ACT. His death stunned local people and his many friends in the crofting community. He was 73. An excellent biography of Allan – *The Assynt Crofter* by Judith Ross Napier, formerly of the *Northern Times* and the *Press and Journal* – was published by Acair at the 25th anniversary celebrations of the buyout.

Vice Chairman John MacKenzie had trained as a marine engineer and was in business. He grew up in the south as part of the Highland diaspora, but his roots were in Culkein, Drumbeg, and he decided to move back. He said at the time, 'My mother's people had been cleared as well and I decided to go back to try to contribute something worthwhile to the community, which I haven't managed to do until now.' John was to take charge of the ACT's hydro scheme.

Bill Ritchie, meanwhile, had no connection with Sutherland. A native of Edinburgh and an Oxford graduate in jurisprudence, he arrived in Lochinver 20 years before the buyout and secured a croft in the hills above Achmelvich beach. He was to become a prominent figure in the Highlands as a member of the Crofters Commission, a member of the north-west area board of SNH and an active player in the SCU. The Highland press corps would head to his early eco-house for briefings, which were always worth the long drive.

On one occasion the drive was very long. I had been called to Aberdeen to join colleagues Graeme Smith and George MacDonald for a business dinner hosted by *Herald* editor Arnold Kemp. Not a great deal of business was discussed as I recall, but the next morning I drove the 196 miles to Bill's house, then 90 back home to Cromarty. Arnold had made clear over breakfast that he saw the Assynt Crofters' campaign as an important story, and I was right to pursue it. He trusted my judgement, as indeed did most of editors and news editors during my time on *The Herald*, which was important to me.

All three of the Assynt leaders and everyone else connected to the campaign paid tribute to the contribution of one other man in particular, Stornoway solicitor Simon Fraser. Perhaps ironically, it was a Tory government that led to Simon's direct involvement in Assynt. In 1989 Russell Sanderson, a Scottish Office minister in Margaret Thatcher's government, took up the suggestion from the SCU that government-owned crofting estates be given to their tenants. In 1989 Lord Sanderson announced the piloting of the idea on the Skye and Raasay estates.

In the end the crofters there were content to remain tenants of the Department of Agriculture and Fisheries for Scotland. But the SCU had commissioned rural development charity the Arkleton Trust to report on the legal and practical implications for them. Simon was one of two lawyers involved and he developed a model of a community trust as a company limited by guarantee, which would work for local people seeking to buy their land. The Assynt crofters called on his expertise, as did most of the headline buyouts in the years that followed. He became their trusted adviser and friend.

Another big man physically and intellectually, he died in January 2016. Nobody had contributed more to the cause of land reform in Scotland. He was to spot early a loophole in Holyrood's 2003 Land Reform Act, whereby landowners could circumvent the impact on their assets of a community buyout by arranging long leases with companies, established or newly created for the purpose. He contacted me about it and we raised the issue in *The Herald*. This 'interposed leases' loophole was subsequently closed by legislation, in no little part because of Simon's discreet lobbying. He told me years after the buyout that he had never really believed that Assynt would work until he went to a meeting at Highland Regional Council's HQ in Inverness with ACT secretary Bill Ritchie. He said Peter Peacock, the council's vice convener, who later became an MSP and Scottish education minister, had called in his service directors and basically asked them how the council could help make Assynt work.

Peter Peacock recalled that meeting in detail for the first time for the purposes of this book:

There were Bill and Simon representing Assynt and myself and the late Jimmy Munro, then Chair of the Economic Development Committee. There were also senior officials from economic development, finance and legal services. I was clear before we went into the meeting that I wanted to help the Assynt buyout. It seemed to me that this would be highly symbolic and could be the catalyst for other potential developments. The people of Eigg for example were still experiencing deeply troubled times under private ownership. Their time was still to come. I believed Scottish land ownership patterns, particularly in the Highlands, were quite absurd. They were holding back people's ambitions and grossly unfair as a matter of principle. They were a legacy of the time of clearance. There was an urgent need of land reform. It was something the council talked about. I said to Jimmy we would need to shut up about land reform in future if we didn't help the Assynt Crofters, as we would have no credibility.

A man of considerable political skill, Peter admits now that at the back of his mind was also the notion that if the democratically elected Highland Regional Council backed Assynt, other public bodies would be embarrassed into giving support, in particular the development quango Highlands and Islands Enterprise (HIE). The council and HIE had long shared an uneven relationship, which at times could reveal a mutual irritation.

After the meeting when Simon and Bill had left, I simply told the officials I wanted this to get a fair wind for funding and to find a way of doing it, up to about £100,000. The mechanism was quickly agreed. There would be a £90,000 low interest loan from Highland Prospect Ltd, the council's investment company, plus £10,000 from the council itself. I remember a discussion of what would happen if the loan was not repaid and I said, 'At that point it would become a grant!' In short, we would just have written it off. As I was also the Chair of the Budget Group on the council, part of the deal was that I would top up the funding of Highland Prospect in the coming Council Budget by a similar amount. This helped Jimmy Munro.

It was the first assistance the ACT had received from the public sector. Others did indeed follow: a £20,000 grant from SNH; £1,000 from the old Sutherland District Council; and a £50,000 grant from Caithness and Sutherland Enterprise (CASE), part of the HIE network. CASE chief executive at that time was Andrew Thin. One of the famous family of booksellers, he went on to be one of the most prominent players in the field of Scottish quangos – a Crofters Commissioner, Convener of the Cairngorms National Park Authority, Chairman of SNH, Chairman of Scottish Canals and of the Scottish Land Commission. I spoke to him for this book and he said:

> Caithness and Sutherland Enterprise was a government-funded organisation charged with promoting economic and social development in the far north. Easy to forget that in those days unemployment was running at upwards of 15 per cent in some parts of 'the patch', and in the more remote bits of the north-west even basic housing standards were way below what we now take for granted. Population levels were in long-term decline, and there was a general air of neglect and despair among many of those remaining. Against this background there had been rumblings for a while about the responsibility of large landowners to help stimulate economic and social development, and several claims of the opposite happening either through benign neglect or through the exercise of what amounted to monopolistic control over land and assets needed for development. The owners of North Lochinver Estate had gained a certain reputation in this respect, though it was never easy to separate fact from fiction in what was claimed.
>
> The first that I heard about the Assynt Crofters' buyout was a phone call from Bill Ritchie asking me to come over and meet with some of the local crofting tenants. There was talk of the estate coming on the market and being bought by yet another absentee owner. We met at Bill's house and there was an atmosphere of great excitement in the air, verging almost on a sense of revolution. Bill himself used that word, which illustrates how novel the whole idea was in the circumstances of the early 1990s. Bill had a legal background, and he had mapped out a route whereby the crofters acting collaboratively

through their individual rights to buy could, in effect, block the sale of the estate by threatening to exercise their rights all at once and take control of the land, pretty much all of which was in crofting tenure. He knew that it might be difficult to coordinate this in practice, but it created leverage over the sale and opened the door to a possible purchase by local crofters. The meeting wanted to know what help they could expect from Caithness and Sutherland Enterprise.

My initial contacts with my superiors in Inverness were not encouraging. Quiet moral support behind the scenes perhaps, but not a suitable use of public funds. Within the board of Caithness and Sutherland Enterprise there were also diverse opinions. Some were strongly supportive, while others seemed to see community ownership in terms of some collectivist ideal that would 'never work in practice'. All that changed, however, with the publication of a major piece in the *Daily Telegraph* [written by my old friend Jenny Shields], describing the proposed buyout group in terms of initiative and enterprise, of local people reversing decline by their own guts and endeavour. I was told at the time, though this was never evidenced, that an instruction came through to Edinburgh and then Inverness from the highest levels encouraging support for the group. This was relayed to me, and all of a sudden Caithness and Sutherland Enterprise was able to move into openly supportive mode. In the event we can claim very little credit for what ultimately happened. We contributed £50,000 and a great deal of advice and encouragement, but the success of the initiative was locally derived and driven. Many of us also contributed personally to the crowd-funding exercise that followed, and we were at the party to celebrate success. But what we all learned, and it came to matter many times over in future buyouts, is that community buyouts do drive economic and social development, and they are a valuable tool of public policy in this area. A point not lost on today's Scottish Land Commission.

The funding for the Assynt Crofters also included £1,000 from Gaelic rock band Runrig, £1,300 from local Liberal Democrat MP

Robert Maclennan and £1,000 from the Skye-based *West Highland Free Press* (the paper's chairman, Labour MP and later government minister Brian Wilson said: 'All we are doing is putting our money where our mouth has been for a very long time.') Donations came in from all over Scotland and well beyond. Virtually every journalist covering the story received phone calls asking for an address or even to forward cheques. The Fourth Estate also contributed, including a modest sum from me. In the end the crofters themselves raised around £100,000, public donations the same and the remainder of the final purchase price of £300,000 was in grants and loans.

At the height of the Assynt campaign in October 1992, I wrote:

> It is difficult to overstate the importance of the current campaign by 100 Sutherland crofters to buy the land on which they live on the North Lochinver Estate. There is a great deal more riding on it than just the future of 21,000 acres of crofting land in and around the Stoer peninsula. The private ownership of Highland land has been an emotive issue for so long that the debate has become sterile. Few outside the estate owners themselves really believe the maintenance of human deserts or the ownership of communities to be right. There have been good landlords, some very good, but even they could never be completely disassociated from the immorality of the clearances which carved out their estates, and that perhaps is a shame. But to challenge such a fundamental as property rights was always seen as something only the powers of government could undertake.

Highlanders could have been excused for thinking that was exactly what was in Secretary of State Willie Ross's mind when setting up the Highlands and Islands Development Board (HIDB) in 1965: 'If there is bitterness in my voice I can assure the house there is bitterness in Scotland too when we recollect the history of these areas . . . We have nine million acres where 225,000 people live, and we are short of land . . . Land is the basic natural resource of the Highlands and any plan for economic and social development would be meaningless if proper use of land were not part of it.'

By the time of Assynt, after more than a quarter of a century, nothing had changed. Many thought that the act which set up the HIDB would be the key to doing something about the worst abuses of landlordism. The board was given powers of compulsory purchase but these proved to be no more than those of a local authority and therefore insufficient to force a bad landlord to sell. In the late 1970s the board sought more powers but an election intervened. In 1979 the Tories were returned and the new Secretary of State, George Younger, rejected the board's approach on the extraordinary grounds that since the HIDB had never used the powers it had – which it couldn't, because they were not sufficient – there was no point in extending them. Without a change of government, the land ownership debate was going nowhere, and it went nowhere. The opposition parties produced policy documents describing how they would circumscribe the powers of the landlords, but without power they remained just interesting reading.

## Land raids

In marked contrast to the years after the First World War, in the likes of Lewis there were only two land raids after the Second. The more famous was Knoydart in 1948 when seven men, including the parish priest, occupied a number of fields on the estate, which at the time was owned by the erstwhile Nazi sympathiser Lord Brocket, and proceeded to stake out would-be crofts. The raid was not a success, not least because of a lack of will on the part of the Attlee Labour government, despite all its other achievements. Neither was Knoydart's subsequent history as it was bought and sold and carved up without benefit to its people who proceeded to leave in numbers.

In 1991 a cairn commemorating the raid was built outside the hall in Inverie on a piece of land not held by the then estate owner, a Surrey property developer, who refused to have it on his land. In Gaelic and in English the cairn bears the message: 'Justice! In 1948, near this cairn, the Seven Men of Knoydart staked claims to secure a place to live and work. For more than a century Highlanders had been forced to use land raids to gain a foothold where their forebears lived. Their struggle should inspire each new generation of Scots to gain such rights by just laws. History will judge harshly the oppressive laws that have led to the virtual extinction of a unique culture from this beautiful place.'

The raiders had also been immortalised by the celebrated folklorist Hamish Henderson years earlier in his song 'The Seven Men of

Knoydart', a play on the Seven Men of Moidart, the seven companions who landed with Bonnie Prince Charlie at Loch nan Uamh on 25 July 1745. Hamish's song's opening verse is:

> It was down by the farm of Scottas Lord Brocket
> > walked one day
> When he saw a sight that troubled him far more than
> > he could say
> For the seven men of Knoydart were doing what they
> > planned
> They'd staked their claims, they were digging
> > drains on Brocket's private land.

Four years after the Knoydart raid, the crofters of Balmartin in North Uist wanted to extend their crofts because of the extreme hardship involved in trying to survive on their existing holdings. They looked covetously to the 850-acre Balelone Farm which was then owned by one Lieutenant-Colonel Henry John Cator of Woodbastwick Hill, Norwich. He had significant estates in other parts, but was not minded to give up any of his Hebridean holding to help the islanders. The Department of Agriculture informed them there was nothing the then Tory government could do to help. In late 1952 the people of Balmartin wrote to the Labour MP for the Western Isles, Malcolm MacMillan: 'We are going to raid the farm of Balelone on the 28th day of November. By so doing we shall give the whole world an opportunity to judge the righteousness of our request and actions. We have nothing to hide. It is our intention to give ample warning to all parties concerned and to conduct ourselves in as orderly manner as possible in the circumstances. This is no idle talk on our part. We are on no account going to turn back.'

On that day four men set out for Balelone, climbed the fence as the gate was locked, and staked out the land they wanted. (I met one of these raiders, Donald Alick MacDonald, at Catriona and DR's wedding.) After further official dialogue they had their way and they kept the land. Scotland's last land raid was a success. It was to be just 10 days short of 40 years later that the crofters of Assynt won their land.

In that time the debate over land ownership had become increasingly tired. There seemed to be an acceptance that there was something fundamentally wrong that so much land, particularly in the Highlands and Islands, could be owned by so few people, many of them absentee landlords, and some foreign. But the options for reform seemed limited – the status quo or some measure of land nationalisation, for which there was little political appetite in Whitehall or elsewhere. The Assynt Crofters showed there was another way. Within a decade there was a land reform act passed by the Scottish Parliament in Edinburgh, enshrining rights of crofting townships to buy their land, and affording certain rights of land purchase to non-crofting communities.

When Vice Chairman of ACT John MacKenzie addressed the Gaelic Society of Inverness in March 2011, he said, 'I want to pay tribute . . . to David Ross of the *Herald* newspaper and Iain MacDonald of BBC (Scotland). Much of the success of our campaign to raise public financial support and political enthusiasm was due to their help.' John MacAskill, in his account of the Assynt buyout *We Have Won the Land* (Acair, 2011), wrote that the strategy was to conduct the campaign through the media: 'to make clear the determination of the crofters to discourage other potential purchasers and to secure the support of the public, both moral and financial. The media reporting of the campaign was almost wholly sympathetic to the crofters and [Bill] Ritchie is in no doubt that it was vital to the eventual success of the campaign. The steering committee worked closely with a number of journalists and made important use of "off the record" briefings. David Ross of *The Herald* and Iain MacDonald of BBC (Highlands) were of crucial importance to the Trust in helping the steering group to map out its media strategy.' I was flattered, as I am sure was Ian.

Bill Ritchie was also overheard joking some years later that the buyout campaign had meant that he no longer believed in the impartiality of the Scottish press, adding, 'And thank God for that!'

He told me 25 years later:

> The important thing about Assynt, indeed all the buyouts, was the release of energy and huge excitement. There was land to allow young local people to build houses, half a dozen or so to start. In the early years there we got something like eight new young crofters, as others were persuaded to retire. The biggest achievement is that we are financially self-sufficient, and we have maintained that for 25 years. The income is from deer

management, fishing, croft rents and then there is our hydro scheme. John MacKenzie was the key man on the hydro. He got a company to put up the money to build it, if it got the income for the first 15 years. But after that it started coming to the Trust, which can now offer support to township schemes. Before the buyout there was no inducement to be enterprising, we were allowed to graze our sheep. That was it. But after it we had control of the land, the deer, the fishing, tree planting. I think we planted 800 hectares of native woodland, which was roughly 10 per cent of all the crofter forestry. The crofters were compensated for the loss of grazing, which was significant. Our township alone had an income of £6,000 a year for 15 years. The woodland is just about at the stage to be opened up, which will give shelter to deer and cattle, firewood, walking, not to mention the environmental benefit.

But the last word on Assynt should be from John MacKenzie, who spoke to me in early 2018:

As we look back, it cannot be denied that we succeeded in achieving our principal aim at the time, which was to take control as a community of our own temporal destiny and to safeguard into the future our crofting way of life. It is almost without doubt that had the liquidators of the then absentee foreign owners of our land succeeded in their ambition of breaking up the estate into seven separate lots, while giving no consideration to the potential implications for crofting of the proposed sale arrangements, our situation today would have been very different to what it actually is. Whatever the imperfections of our current situation might be, and there are indeed some, the use and intrinsic benefit of the land of our fathers is governed by an elected board of whom most still are indigenous locals. There is also now in place an annual revenue stream capable of ensuring the long-term future of the Crofters' Trust in contrast to the prophesies of doom being uttered in 1993 by those who were totally opposed to the notion of the Highlander being in control of his own destiny. We have achieved much in 25 years yet there is still much to do.

# 9

# In the Footsteps of Assynt

THE ASSYNT CROFTERS took legal possession of their land on 1 February 1993. Four months later 21 crofters on Skye seemed to be on the verge of following in their footsteps by pursuing the purchase of the 4,500-acre crofting townships of Borve and Annishader, part of the Skeabost Estate. It is the buyout everyone forgets, apparently overshadowed by those that went before and after it. But in many ways it was one of the most workmanlike. The estate was owned by Major John Macdonald and his son Charles. Major Macdonald suggested the purchase to the crofters after a failure to achieve an agreement with them over a project under the 1991 Crofter Forestry Act. This was introduced to enable tenants to plant and retain ownership of trees planted on common grazings, on condition that agreement was reached with the landlord.

The first offer from the crofters of £14,000 was refused, so it was increased to £20,000. The crofters had raised most of the money themselves and had a top-up loan from the Highland Fund, but agreement was only struck in principle in December 1993 and was recorded on 31 January 1994. Major Macdonald's grandfather, Lachlan Macdonald, was reputed to be the richest man on Skye in 1874 when he took over lands at Bernisdale. He behaved in a manner uncharacteristic of the landowning class in the 19th-century Highlands. He cancelled all arrears of his tenants and allowed them to fix their own rents. These had remained largely unchanged.

Sorley, however, had told me of a Skye tradition that Lachlan Macdonald, for all his later good works, had broken: the *cairidh* (fish-trap; *yair* in Scots), which allowed local people to catch fish caught in the tide. It had not been forgotten. I mentioned this in a piece only to receive a phone call from Major Macdonald denouncing me in the strongest terms for traducing his forebear and insisting that it wasn't true. Others, however, were to confirm Sorley's account, but it was revealing that a landowner in the second half of the 20th century held so dearly the reputation of a forebear a century earlier.

Despite it being a low-key affair, again *The Herald* devoted space to tell the story of Borve and Annishader.

## Eigg

Eigg has been inhabited at least since the Neolithic period, but the island nearly lost her people two decades ago when a population that had stood at 500 two centuries earlier was down to the last 64. In June 1997 the historic community buyout was completed. Brian Wilson had just been appointed a Scottish Office minister when he stood on a hillock up from the jetty on Eigg and said: 'Over the past 30 years, stewardship of this island has come to symbolise much that was wrong about the free market and land. The challenge now for everyone involved in this great undertaking is to create a symbol of hope and achievement, which others will be inspired to follow.'

They did just that. In 2017 the islanders were joined by friends and guests to mark the 20th anniversary of the community buyout of Eigg for £1.5 million, which reversed the chronic depopulation which had blighted the island. Since 1997 many of the obstacles to island life under previous private owners have been removed. Tenants have been given security of tenure, homes have been modernised, new houses built, businesses started, woodland made productive. But perhaps the most impressive achievement has been the development of an award-winning green energy grid – a mix of hydro, wind turbines and a photovoltaic array which ended islanders' reliance on diesel generators. With such enterprise the population had risen from 64 to 105, a near 65 per cent increase since the buyout.

But things could have been so different for Eigg, originally a Clanranald MacDonald island which was sold nine times under private ownership. Its previous long-time controversial laird Keith Schellenberg, who had threatened some with eviction, sold the island to the German artist Marlin Eckhard Maruma for £1.6 million in 1995. Maruma promptly sold off the island's cattle, but not before he had taken out loans against the island at punitive rates of interest in Hong Kong and Liechtenstein. Eigg had become a pawn in a game of international land speculation.

Maruma's tenure was to be short-lived. The island duly came back on the market in July 1996 at £2 million, and the Isle of Eigg Heritage Trust launched the appeal the following month. There were distractions: a body claiming to be The Pavarotti Foundation wanted to buy it for 3,000 musical students which would have increased the island's population by 4,615 per cent. The next week it was reduced to 300. Then there was the Luxembourg firm Compagnie de Participations, who wanted it for a holiday project, and a man whose Surrey-based private bank had gone into administration in 1992 owing £10 million to 1,000 depositors. He wanted to farm on Eigg.

Meanwhile the lottery-financed Heritage Memorial Fund refused to assist a buyout if the local people were to control the island. Apparently, the islanders were not to be trusted to look after their own future. Yet a year earlier the same body had given the Churchill family £13.25 million for the retrieval of its papers.

Simon Fraser's services were again called on. He would later recall that the stakes were higher on Eigg than in Assynt. So many island residents had not enjoyed the Assynt crofters' security of tenure. If things went wrong they could be evicted.

To get round the problem of any possible concern over islander control, Simon came up with a solution – the Isle of Eigg Heritage Trust (IEHT), a company limited by guarantee with a membership of three organisations: the island residents' association, the Scottish Wildlife Trust and the Highland Council. The trust survives today. But in the end the islanders' public appeal attracted 10,000 donations from across the country and beyond. These ranged from children sending their pocket money to the £750,000 (circa £900,000 with gift aid tax relief) from an anonymous benefactress in the north of England. The only one who definitely knows her identity is Maggie Fyffe, long time IEHT secretary and driving force of the buyout. She has always refused to divulge the benefactress's name, but was in touch with her just before the 20th anniversary.

Maggie herself had arrived on the island in 1976. She was originally from the former mill town of Bolton, growing up amidst Coronation Street-style housing. Her first career choice was the civil service or more precisely the GPO Telephones section. The idea of her ever being a budding Sir Humphrey amuses her greatly, and a few others, to this day. Sitting in her croft at Cleadale looking out towards the island of

Rum, she recalled the long and often very winding road that took her to Eigg:

I left Bolton, went to live in the Lake District where I worked in a youth hostel but I was getting the itchy feet syndrome. I went to Israel first, then to Morocco. After that I was working in Gibraltar and that was when I met Wes [her husband] who had come from Northern Ireland to do much the same as me. We were off to Afghanistan after that which was fascinating and was quite peaceful then. We came back to the UK and went to Skye, where we could get jobs easily enough, but couldn't find anywhere to live. So we ended up back on the east coast, where my mum was from – Aberdeen. We got a job on a farm outside Banff where Wes was a dairy man and used to get up at 4 a.m. to milk the cows. We then got involved in a craft shop around there and that's when we met Keith Schellenberg, who wanted to set up something similar on Eigg. He invited us to come to Eigg. Initially it was really good fun. I was delighted to live in such a beautiful place, to have a safe environment to bring up children and to be part of a small community – the politics of landlordism had yet to make an impression upon me. In the early years there was a feeling of optimism with a large propor- tion of the community being employed by the estate either on the farm, renovating old buildings for tourist accommodation or in the newly established Craft Centre. However, that feeling soon began to disappear to be replaced by a general air of inse- curity – no one had a contract of employment and quite a few families lived in tied cottages.

By 1981 we were lucky enough to have bought a derelict cot- tage with attached croft tenancy and although it was a relief to have a secure place to live, it ironically coincided with my hus- band and several other local men being made redundant. There were constant injustices but in general people were unwilling to speak out in case it would jeopardise their house or job. Most people working for the estate felt they were being manipulated but due to a chronic lack of independent housing and alternative employment faced the option of leaving Eigg or moving into a caravan which is what a substantial number of families did.

The year 1994 was when things changed radically. We woke up one morning in January to learn that Schellenberg's vintage Rolls Royce had been destroyed in a mysterious fire. Schellenberg pointed the finger at incomers and the numerous libellous statements, and his insistence on differentiating between islanders and incomers to the press, angered the community considerably. The native islanders issued a powerful statement which started: 'We who have been born and brought up on the island would like to refute utterly the ludicrous allegations about the community here. The island has a small but united population of local families and incomers who are between them struggling to develop a community with a long-term future against the apparent wishes of an owner who seems to want us to live in primitive conditions to satisfy his nostalgia for the '20s.' It was to mark an important change in our relations with the media, which was to be so important at the time of the buyout.

Nobody will ever know if the buyout would have been possible without the massive donation from the anonymous benefactress. Maggie Fyffe will always remember it:

It was a phone call and it started off rather uncomfortably because she said she had read an article which didn't exactly paint the best picture of me. But she then said she would like to donate money. Initially she said five hundred and I thought she meant five hundred pounds, but it started to dawn on me she was talking about half a million pounds. Then, when she discovered we weren't getting money from the lottery, she increased the figure to seven hundred and fifty thousand, and with gift aid that made it almost a million and with no strings attached apart from her anonymity. I was incredulous. It was a miracle. She asked to see our business plans and said it all made good sense to her. She kept in contact. She phoned to say she couldn't come to last year's celebrations. Funnily enough, I didn't hear from her at Christmas. As far as I know she has never visited the island, but one of her friends did come for the first anniversary of the buyout.

Make no mistake, mounting a community buyout isn't a decision to be taken lightly. There's a huge amount of work involved and Eigg's success is undoubtedly due in part to the many hours put in by volunteers. Has it been worth it? Most definitely! People are returning to raise their own families on the island and businesses have been starting up, there is a feeling of security. It's like night and day.

Simon Fraser loved Eigg, and on buyout day he spoke of what it represented to him: 'It is a triumph for all that is good in humanity and certainly one in the eye for everything that is mean-spirited and self-seeking.'

But what has remained a mystery is why Eigg, of all the buyouts, has attracted such mean-spirited comment from some. At one point one columnist even suggested a posy of flowers presented by a child to Princess Anne on a visit to the island should have been checked in case it included some drugs. One of the most pernicious ideas was that the public purse had footed the £1.5 million purchase of Eigg. In fact, only £17,500 from Highlands and Islands Enterprise was public money. There was even an internal debate whether it should be accepted, with Michael Foxley opposing it. Some right-wing commentators have long appeared hopeful that a community buyout will collapse, with Eigg topping their wish-list. One argued it would have been cheaper for the taxpayer to have bought a Ferrari for everybody on the island. He had divided the £7.8 million spent on a new slipway and a new CalMac car ferry (£5.5m), by the number of residents. It was revealing that the same equation was not applied to the slipways for the far smaller populations on the privately owned Muck – £4.5 million; the National Trust for Scotland's Canna – £3.2 million; or Scottish Natural Heritage's Rum – £4.2 million. All four Small Isles benefitted from the investment by Europe, Edinburgh and the Highland Regional Council, in the ferry and jetties. But only Eigg was deemed undeserving. The subsidy myth persisted, even when Eigg began to enjoy full employment. Grants did support developments such as its green power grid, a new teashop and woodland projects. But these grants were open to all. Its continued success certainly remains one in the eye of the critics Simon Fraser had in mind. The islanders have remained close to those who helped them. It was telling that when Gordon Fyfe (no relation of Maggie – only one f) retired as the Highland Council's communications manager, he was granted the freedom of the island 'in recognition of his outstanding Public Relations service and support to the community of the Isle of Eigg during their purchase of the island'. It meant a lot to him.

## Knoydart

On the day that the inhabitants of Eigg took over their island in June 1997, the Scottish Office announced that it was setting up a community land unit in the Highlands and Islands Enterprise headquarters in Inverness to help other communities seeking to take over their land. The person put in charge of the new unit was John Watt. A quiet man, not everyone realised just how much he did for the community land movement. It was to him that a community aspiring to own its land would initially talk. Mr Watt would provide feasibility studies, valuations and often simply encouragement. The hours of work and the miles he drove in the cause were prodigious. His commitment meant he helped scores of communities acquire the land they sought. The first was just across the water from Eigg – the Knoydart peninsula.

The residents there have also lived to some extent in the shadow of the crofters of Assynt and the islanders of Eigg. But remarkable progress has been made by the most remote community on the British mainland since the locals took over from a pair of fraudsters. Crucially, within the first decade they managed to reverse a centuries-old trend by increasing Knoydart's population, and by almost 60 per cent. There are now more pupils in the tiny school than for generations, more jobs, more businesses, more houses, more locally produced renewable power, more investment and more hope than anyone can remember. And this against the background of the saddest of histories.

You can only get to Knoydart by hiking the 18 miles from Kinloch Hourn or by taking the regular ferry service from Mallaig. Most choose the latter, but few will take the time to look to the north-east as their boat enters the mouth of Loch Nevis and ponder the words of Donald Ross, describing the view that met him from that point in 1853: 'As far as the eye could see, the face of the strath had its black spots, where the houses of the crofters were either levelled or burnt, the blackened rafters lying scattered across the grass, the couple-trees cut through the middle and thrown far away, the walls broken down, the thatch and cabers mixed together, the voice of man was gone.'

Ross, a journalist and lawyer, had travelled to Loch Nevis from Glasgow to report on the clearance of Knoydart by Josephine MacDonnell, the widow of the 16th chief of Glengarry who had been left with serious debt and a young son. She resolved to clear and sell Knoydart so it could be turned over to sheep and deer. Many of the 1,500-strong community had already gone to Canada, but between 400 and 500 remained. At the end of August 1853 the evictions began. Parties of men with axes, crowbars and hammers visited each township, forcing the people out and destroying their houses. Many had to be dragged down to the boats to be ferried across to the *Sillery*, the ship sent to take them away. Sixteen families took to the hills rather than leave, and when the *Sillery* finally sailed they came back down to the shore. During the succeeding weeks they built shelters for themselves, only to have them pulled down by men from the estate.

Ross had come at the suggestion of the local priest, Coll MacDonald, who had written to him: 'Today, the 22nd of October, is the stormiest day we have seen this year, and yet the servants from Inverie are after making their rounds, destroying the shelters of the outcasts! All those poor creatures are there exposed to the raging elements. The officers and servants have broken their huts six times with the first warrant. If this is legal, you know best. Oh do not, I beseech you, lose sight of the poor who are living without shelter in this dreadful weather.'

Ross did not lose sight of them and campaigned on their behalf, but few could understand the strength of what tied these people to their land, what sense of place could make them endure what they did.

It was just one of many dark chapters in Knoydart's story. Knoydart was MacDonnell of Glengarry land whose people there had suffered hellish cruelty a century earlier in the aftermath of Culloden when they were visited by a force under the Duke of Dorset's third son, Lord George Sackville. The often wrongly abused historian John Prebble recalled this in his *Landscapes and Memories – An Intermittent Autobiography* (Harper Collins, 1993). He referred to the account by Michael Hughes, a volunteer in the 20th Foot regiment, of his time in the Hanoverian Army:

He [Hughes] had a soldier's respect for some of the vagrants who would not kneel or wear a blindfold when they were shot, but his narrative says nothing of the worst atrocity for which his regiment was remembered in the folk history of Knoydart. The 20th had a new commander now, Lord George Sackville, a short-tempered dandy much in pain from wounds received at Fontenoy 12 months before. He was proud of the shot-holes in the scarlet coat he wore that day, and sometimes wore now in challenging pride. Perhaps his men admired his arrogant courage and his wound-shrunken leg, and when he wanted revenge for the theft of his baggage by marauding MacDonnells they obligingly gave it to him at the next township. The women were first raped, it was said, and then held to watch the bayonetting of their men. In what I can recall of from the writings left by the officers and men of this bloody army, there is no expression of compassion for the vanquished and no mercy for the terrorised. None was shown, I think, except by patrolling clansmen of the Campbell militia – which should be remembered by those who like to perpetuate an absurd and theatrical antipathy towards that name.

Sorley certainly knew of these events and agreed with Prebble that the opprobrium heaped on the name of Campbell because of the Glencoe Massacre of 1692 was ridiculous. He would argue that although the two companies of Argyll's Regiment were led by Captain Robert Campbell of Glen Lyon, only a fraction (from memory only around a tenth) of the soldiers were Campbells. They were under martial law and faced execution themselves if they disobeyed orders, yet some went to considerable lengths to warn the MacDonalds.

Sorley used to talk about how Knoydart had 'got it in the neck' after Culloden, not just from Sackville's force but also from another one led by the Lowland Scot, Captain Caroline Frederick Scott of Guise's Regiment. (His female Christian name, apparently, was an affectation of the time.) Scott also displayed his capacity for sheer cruelty when he visited Raasay in search of the prince. Sorley was convinced Scott's sadism stood out even in a time of great violence.

Even in the second half of the 20th century Knoydart was attended by despair. In 1985 Surrey property dealer Philip Rhodes bought 58,000 acres of what had once been the 80,000-acre Knoydart Estate for £1.2 million. He proceeded to sell it off in parcels and in 1993 sold the last 17,000 acres to jute company Titaghur and its chairman Reg

Brealey for £1.7 million. Mr Brealey's plan was to establish a 'Back to Basics' adventure training school for the deprived of Britain's inner cities. It was bitterly opposed by most in the 70-strong community and was refused planning permission. Titaghur's global financial problems were all too apparent in Knoydart, where the estate boat *Spanish John* was arrested regularly by creditors.

In 1997 the community-led Knoydart Foundation was established to buy the estate, but Mr Brealey decided that it should be entrusted to businessmen Stephen Hinchliffe and Christopher Harrison. Their respective roles as chairman and finance director of the Facia retail-ing empire, which collapsed in 1996 with debts of more than £100 million, were being investigated by the Serious Fraud Office and the DTI. Harrison ended up in prison in Germany for fraud involving German shoe companies. In October 1998 Knoydart Peninsula Ltd, the company that owned the estate, went into receivership with debts of £1.4 million. The following month Mr Hinchliffe was banned by the DTI from holding a company directorship for seven years and was sub-sequently sent to prison for conspiracy to defraud.

The following March the Knoydart Foundation finally bought the estate for £750,000. The buyout was financed through the founda-tion's public appeal and large amounts from its members, such as the £250,000 from the John Muir Trust and £200,000 from the Chris Brasher Trust. There were also significant amounts from public bodies such as the Highland Council and Highlands and Islands Enterprise's community land unit, as well as from the charitable foundation of West End impresario Cameron Mackintosh, whose estate is across Loch Nevis from Knoydart. An anonymous benefactor sent a further £100,000.

It had not been easy, but at the time of the 10th anniversary cele-brations the population had increased by 60 per cent and businesses had been growing. Davie Newton, a joiner who worked for the local construction company and chaired the foundation, said: 'For the last 10 years many of the choices made for this community have been made by this community. We have had to learn, and are still learning, that the mistakes, responsibilities, discussions and difficulties are all ours. Sometimes that all seems like too much hard work, other times it's as if every obstacle is in the way, but occasionally it feels just right. And for those occasions and the self-respect, we can only think that all communities should have the opportunity we have had.'

Today the population, which stood at around 70 at the time of the buyout is 115, and there are young voices in the community: five in high school, seven in primary school, four nursery age and one pre-nursery. Businesses have grown and another is on its way in the form of a brewery. Knoydart has come a long way.

There should also be recognition of the work by the local councillor at the time, Mallaig-based Charlie King, and John Hutchison, who was Lochaber area manager of Highland Council. They made Olympian efforts to help the community buyout of Knoydart and before that Eigg.

Perhaps the last word should go to John Watt, who now chairs the Scottish Land Fund. He reflected on the last two decades for this book:

> I recall one of my first cases was in Knoydart. This unique community, located on a remote peninsula with no road access, had a turbulent land ownership history and was undergoing another unsettling period with much of the original estate having been sold off and the incumbent owner of the rest in financial difficulties. The local Community Association, in partnership with Highland Council, two environmental organisations and neighbouring land owners formed the Knoydart Foundation to launch an attempt to acquire the estate. On my first visit to Knoydart I was met by Iain Robertson, who was acting manager of the estate, who ferried me across to Inverie from Mallaig. In my first meeting with the Knoydart Foundation I was asked what HIE could do to help. I said I really didn't know, but what was it that they needed? It turned out that the most urgent requirement was some financial assistance to launch a fundraising appeal, and this was what HIE was able to provide.
>
> And so started the work of the community land unit. It was to HIE's credit that it had the flexibility to utilise its resources, enhanced by modest funding offered by the Scottish Office, to tailor support packages to the needs of communities aspiring to acquire and develop land and assets. And those of us involved in these pioneering days of community land ownership in Scotland could never have envisaged what was to happen over the next 20 years. A successful buyout in Knoydart was followed by others like the island of Gigha, North (and

later West) Harris, Galson and Pairc in Lewis, South Uist, north-west Mull, along with dozens of other communities acquiring woodland, amenity areas and buildings, leading to over half a million acres in community ownership. And the political and policy environment changed out of all recognition – a Scottish Parliament, a significantly bigger CLU offering advice as well as finance, two Land Reform Acts, three Scottish Land Funds (currently amounting to £10 million annually), a Community Empowerment Act, the extension of community rights-to-buy to urban areas, and the establishment of a Scottish Land Commission. What a legacy from the struggles in Assynt and Eigg!

## Gigha

I first wrote about Gigha in 1975 as part of an article on land ownership in the Argyll islands. It had just been bought by Sir David Landale on his retirement from the renowned and somewhat controversial Hong Kong trading company Jardine Matheson, whose 19th-century foundations had been built on the profits of the opium trade. He had bought Gigha following the death of Sir James Horlick of the bedtime drink family, who had established a botanical garden on the island and had largely been viewed as a comparatively benign landlord. I wasn't a journalist at this stage and had just finished my history degree. The commission was from the ambitious arts/current affairs magazine *Calgacus*, but it folded before my piece could be published. My entry into journalism would have to wait, as would my next consideration of the fortunes of what is called God's Island.

In 2002 the residents of Gigha followed what was by then a well-worn path, and bought the island. As in most of the buyouts there had been initial uncertainty, as Catherine Czerkawska makes clear in her fine work *God's Islanders: A History of the People of Gigha* (Birlinn, 2006). When they first met to discuss the idea, only 14 out of a total population of 96 were in favour. The 14 started to proselytise, not least one Willie McSporran, who already had something of a public profile. Every so often newspapers would have articles about him and the different jobs he undertook on the island: shopkeeper, taxi driver, undertaker, fireman, ambulance driver – the list went on and was said to embrace 14 different positions at one time. This appealed to the Compton Mackenzie image of the Hebrides, so long loved by the media. Willie, however, is a highly intelligent man who doesn't suffer fools gladly. But at the same time, I know from personal experience it is hard to stay in his company for long without laughing, and laughing a great deal. I have no doubt as to the effectiveness of his powers of persuasion, as Catherine Czerkawska confirmed: 'Cometh the hour, cometh the man, and there is a sense that Willie was there at exactly the right time, to tip the balance in favour of the buyout, when fears of the huge financial responsibility involved might have seemed very daunting. I suspect that for Willie, along with other more senior residents, it was a "now or never" moment.'

Most islanders were persuaded and voted to pursue a buyout which was secured only 17 days after the ballot. Compared to some of the earlier buyouts, Gigha was comparatively straightforward, if significantly more expensive; the island was secured for its residents for £4,000,250. The lottery-backed Scottish Land Fund gave its biggest grant of £3.5 million towards the historic purchase of the island. Highlands and Islands Enterprise's community land unit contributed £500,000, double its biggest grant to date. It emerged that the island's owner, 74-year-old Derek Holt, had turned down three other offers from private parties, one of which was almost £5 million. This would not have been possible if Gigha's sale had followed bankruptcy as had happened with Assynt, Eigg and Knoydart. Simon Fraser highlighted: 'If Gigha had gone the same way, a liquidator would have been obliged to accept the highest price. The other big difference was the existence of the Scottish Land Fund and HIE's community land unit. This couldn't have been done in two weeks without them.'

The islanders, however, had to repay £1 million to the Land Fund within two years, which they did through the sale of the island's Achamore House and their own fundraising. There was criticism of the amount of public money involved, but Gigha quickly became a flagship for the buyouts, showing what could be achieved. In the 18th century around 700 had lived on the island but that had dropped to around 100. Within four years of the buyout it had increased by more than 50 per cent to 151, reversing 300 years of decline. The children attending Gigha Primary School increased from six to 21. The population is still going in the right direction and stood at 165 earlier in 2018.

Four years ago stories began to circulate that Gigha was in financial trouble. A strategic review of the Isle of Gigha Heritage Trust, the community body which owns the island, found the trust was 'in a precarious financial position, with total third-party debts of £2.7 million. The overall debt structure is unsustainable based on current revenues.' Criticism of the buyout followed. However, with an assets portfolio recently valued at around £7.5 million the position was not so pressing as it appeared, given what had been achieved.

When the community was buying the island, a housing conditions survey highlighted the scale of the task ahead. It found that of the 42 houses that came with the estate, 75 per cent were classed as 'below tolerable standard' and should not be inhabited, while 23 per cent were 'in serious disrepair'. 'If we put in a nail or a hinge, or put a slate on a roof, we will have done a bloody sight more than has been done for decades under our landlords,' Willie McSporran said at the time.

Four years ago, 30 of the properties had been renovated. In 2011 the community's efforts were recognised by the Chartered Institute of Housing in Scotland, with its prestigious Excellence in Regeneration Award. These houses alone were estimated to be worth over £4.5 million. Money was also spent adding a fourth community wind turbine to the island's 'Three Dancing Ladies' which were previously earning over £100,000 a year. So Gigha has been a story about investment. Businesses have grown on the island, selling everything from oysters to halibut and including a skin care company and a dairy, as well as those providing visitors with food, accommodation and leisure activities.

Gigha was not about to become bankrupt, but one of Scotland's headline community buyouts doing so has always been a possibility, and the response from some self-appointed guardians of the public purse would be predictable. It was something addressed by historian Jim Hunter in his study of community ownership in the Highlands and Islands. The Carnegie UK Trust commissioned him to write the story of community buyouts over the past 20 years, and *From the Low Tide of the Sea to the Highest Mountain Top*s was published in 2012. In the conclusion, he writes that maintaining the necessary commitment to such projects by local residents was a constant challenge, and continues:

> That is why it is by no means impossible that, sooner or later, one – or more than one – of the local land trusts operating in the

Highlands and Islands will get into financial difficulty, maybe even go under. If or when this happens, critics and opponents of community ownership will insist that the community ownership concept has thereby been invalidated. They will be wrong. The bankruptcy of a conventionally structured company – something which happens every day – does not of itself indicate that other companies are bound to meet the same fate.

Nor will the failure of a community ownership trust in any way signal that other such trusts are necessarily heading for the rocks. After all, if the record of private landownership in the Highlands and Islands were to be judged by the number of landlords who have gone spectacularly bust, often with very bad consequences for their tenants and dependants, then time would have been called on such ownership very many years ago.

As to those who question whether public money should be spent on the buyouts, Professor Hunter had some comparisons. The £30 million total from public and lottery sources which helped take half a million acres of land into community control over two decades was equivalent to the bill for only 600 yards of Edinburgh's tramlines. In fact it amounted to less than 7 per cent of the cost of the five-mile M74 completion stretch of motorway in Glasgow and matched the subsidy farmers and landowners receive in Britain every three or four days.

## Money well spent or what?

The most difficult of the community buyouts was Pairc on the island of Lewis, which took 13 years to complete. It was shaping up to be the first 'hostile' buyout, which meant the community sought to buy the land against the owner's wishes. The land reform legislation of 2003 had given Scotland's crofting communities this right, as long as ministers approved the purchase. With comparisons to the land grabs in Robert Mugabe's Zimbabwe being made by Tory politicians, it was bound to be tested in court. Barry Lomas, the Warwickshire-based accountant whose family had owned the 26,800-acre Pairc Estate since the 1920s, was an absentee landowner but appeared determined not to sell, and he sought recourse in Stornoway Sheriff Court and the Court of Session. Lomas claimed he was being forced to sell by the Scottish government as revenge for the Highland Clearances, but his legal challenge was founded on his human rights being infringed. However, three judges, headed by the Lord President Lord Gill, dismissed the appeal.

Shortly after the passage of the Land Reform (Scotland) Act 2003 a *Herald* investigation launched with information from Simon Fraser (Angus MacDonald of BBC Radio nan Gàidheal also did important work on this) established that the legislation did nothing to stop owners of estates setting up off-the-shelf or arms-length companies and then leasing the land and valuable assets to themselves or a third party. Mr Lomas did just that, setting up a 75-year lease with a subsidiary company which signed a deal with Scottish and Southern Energy (SSE) to erect a £200-million wind farm. Ministers went to the Scottish Land Court, but it ruled such 'interposed leases' were legal and it required legislation to close the loophole. This all took several years. In the middle of this SSE sold the energy rights to International Power.

In 2015, however, the 400-strong community, which a century earlier had numbered 4,000, managed to strike a deal with Mr Lomas and agreed a price of £500,000. As a consequence the Pairc buyout was not technically 'hostile', but it had been far from friendly.

It wasn't publicised but CLS Chairman David Cameron, from North Harris, had an important role in achieving the final settlement. Acting as a mediator in discussions between the parties, he was highly regarded by both sides. The power given to ministers to support mediation between owners and communities that was put in to the 2015 Community Empowerment Act meant that another Pairc could be avoided. The idea of the protocol over community buyouts later agreed between CLS and the landowners' organisation Scottish Land and Estates also grew out of a determination not to see Pairc repeated.

### A growing voice on the land

In 2010 Andy Wightman's *The Poor Had No Lawyers: Who Owns Scotland (And How They Got It)* was published by Birlinn. To those interested in Scottish land it was, and remains, one of the most important books yet written, and *The Herald* was proud to serialise it. In the 2013 paperback edition, Wightman, now a prominent Green Party MSP, writes: 'Community ownership has transformed the future of the Western Highlands. It has been a revolutionary movement supported by and guided by some very talented individuals, and has now formed a representative body, Community Land Scotland, to promote and expand community ownership. It will endure but the challenge is not only for it to flourish and expand, it is to become an accepted way of doing things outside its north and west heartlands. Only when it becomes as normal in Dundee or Possil as it is in Dunvegan or Pairc can it truly be said to have represented a paradigm shift.'

CLS has been growing in influence since its establishment in 2010 as the collective voice for community landowners in Scotland. Its 80-plus members own well over 500,000 acres and importantly more than half the land area of the Outer Isles archipelago. Members range from the Stòras Uibhist, which manages 93,000 acres covering almost the whole of the islands of Benbecula, Eriskay and South Uist, as well as a number of other small islands, to the Fernaig Community Trust, which bought 110 acres in 2001, and manages them for the residents of the villages of Stromeferry and Achmore and the township of Craig to the east of Plockton.

The contribution to the debate over the future of rural Scotland made by CLS has been increasing in significance and is recognised as becoming a real powerhouse of ideas. It helped persuade the Scottish government to beef up its land reform legislation of 2016 over the issue of transparency. Ministers had previously sounded a fairly embarrassing retreat over moves to establish the identity of owners of Scottish land who hide behind companies registered in an overseas tax haven. The Scottish government originally proposed that land should only be owned by an individual or a legal entity formed in accordance with the 'law of a Member State of the EU'. However, subsequently, ministers proposed instead regulations to allow only those affected by land held secretly to request information on ownership from the Keeper of the Registers of Scotland. The keeper in turn would have the power only to request information from the likes of the British Virgin Islands on companies registered there. Scottish government lawyers were nervous of forcing owners to reveal their identities in case it breached their human rights to property and privacy.

That was the position in the first week in January 2016. But the bill was amended at the committee stage by MSPs to toughen it up by insisting on owners' names being held on the land register. The Scottish government later made clear it wanted to go further still, building on that amendment by making the new register more comprehensive to 'require the public disclosure of information about persons who make decisions about the use of land in Scotland and have a controlling interest in land'. CLS had worked with the likes of Megan MacInnes, land adviser with non-governmental organisation Global Witness, and MSPs on the Rural Affairs, Climate Change and Environment Committee to persuade ministers and officials that more needed to be done. CLS also engaged with Professor Alan Miller, Chair of the Scottish Human Rights Commission, to explore how the concentrated pattern of land ownership in Scotland impacted on the human rights of those living in the local communities, which turned on its head the argument deployed by landowners that it was *their* human rights to ownership of property that were at risk from land reform. The body has highlighted the need for greater ministerial powers to protect the public interest in land ownership issues, and it has an established relationship with the majority of members of the Scottish Land Commission.

Much of this activity can be credited to the efforts of CLS's first Policy Director, Peter Peacock, who has been mentioned already in this book. He took up the part-time post after leaving front-line politics, although doubtless he had other more lucrative offers. Originally from Hawick, he had worked in the voluntary sector and arrived in the Highlands in 1980 to work for Citizens Advice Bureau and was elected an independent councillor for Ardersier to the old Highland Regional Council in 1982. He held various positions as Finance Convener, Chair of Policy and Resources Committee and Vice Convener, and was elected the first Convener of the new single-tier Highland Council in 1996. Such a pedigree speaks to his effectiveness as a politician and a wider recognition of his abilities and shrewdness. Unlike many politicians, however, he was not really egotistical at all to my mind and never displayed a need to have his name up in lights or even be given credit in the press. Impassioned oratory was not his trademark, rather it has been calm reason and analysis. He has long understood how Scotland works, how to operate behind the scenes, how to get things done.

He was elected as a Labour List MSP for the Highlands and Islands to the first Scottish Parliament in 1999 and appointed a minister. He held a number of ministerial responsibilities over the first two terms of the Parliament, including for education and children's services, local government, public services and Gaelic, culminating in holding cabinet responsibility for Education and Young People for a number of years before he retired for health reasons. He had joined the Labour Party not long before standing for election as an MSP. It was rumoured he had discussions with the Liberal Democrats, but he had always been close to Donald Dewar, whose more cerebral approach to politics appealed to him. There were some in the Labour Party in the Highlands and Islands who resented his elevation to the top of the regional list when they had spent decades 'knocking on doors'. Few however criticised him for his performance as an MSP or minister. One who closely observed his stewardship of the education brief was Neil Munro, who spent over 40 years on the *Times Educational Supplement Scotland*, for much of that time as its editor then managing editor. He told me:

> Peter was one of the most thoughtful education ministers of recent times; indeed you sometimes got the impression that he even wrote his own speeches. He was lucky in some ways, benefitting from Labour's spending largesse and exiting office before the financial crash. But he didn't rest on his laurels, driving forward an improvement agenda while engaging seriously with the teaching profession – a tricky balancing act which few, if any, education ministers managed successfully. Some critics saw Peter as a cautious minister. But he was willing to draw on policies from elsewhere and even took the politically risky step of inviting an external review of Scottish education by international experts from the OECD [Organisation for Economic Co-operation and Development], effectively a report card on his record (it was generally favourable). The high regard in which Peter was held was reflected in the expressions of shock and regret which greeted his announcement in 2006 that ill health meant he had to resign.

Peacock has never been one for tribal politics and always happily worked with those in different parties who were also pursuing a reform agenda. He was one of the founders of Barail (Gaelic for opinion), a think tank. It was originally called the Centre for Highlands & Islands Policy Studies in 1991, but its acronym, CHIPS, didn't quite strike the right chord. Jim Hunter was Chairman and Norman Gillies, Director of Sabhal Mòr Ostaig, was the driving force who, needless to say, came up with the name Barail. Others invited to attend meetings included: Angus Graham from the Western Isles Council; John Angus MacKay (Highlands and Islands Development Board, before moving on to become CEO of Comunn na Gàidhlig, and Chair of the BBC's Gaelic Advisory Committee); environmentalist Sir John Lister-Kaye; John Goodlad, Secretary of Shetland Fishermen's Association; Lochaber councillor Michael Foxley; MP Charles Kennedy; anti-nuclear campaigner Lorraine Mann; Maggie Cunningham then of Radio nan Gàidheal, who was to rise to top of BBC Radio Scotland; and my own cousin Mairi MacArthur, then secretary of the Gaelic Society of Inverness. I was also invited, but only attended one meeting, realising it might be rather difficult for me to comment on Barail's activities if I was part of it all. Some pretty good work was done by Barail, however, with papers, lectures and conferences on issues ranging from the role of women in the economy of the Highlands and Islands to the need for a university of the Highlands and Islands. One of Barail's perceived weaknesses was that it was self-appointed. I remember one local newspaper editor sounding off angrily, demanding, 'Who do they think they are?' I thought at the time this was because he was not on the invitation list.

Despite that, there is a role for such a think tank. I believe it is a role that could be performed successfully by CLS. It has the advantage over the likes of Barail of being genuinely representative and having a clear mission to promote community ownership. That in itself will ensure it retains a focus on issues truly relevant to its members.

Peter Peacock stood down as CLS's Policy Director in early 2018, but a very able replacement was found in Dr Calum Macleod. A native Gaelic speaker from Finsbay on Harris, he is on the board of the Harris Tweed Authority. He has an honours degree in Public Administration and a PhD in public policy implementation and has been teaching in universities for well over a decade. Most recently he worked at the University of Edinburgh's Institute of Geography teaching postgraduate Masters courses on Human Dimensions of Environmental Change and Sustainability and Political Ecology. But anyone who has read his articles, papers and blog knows his concern for the land is deep. Scotland will be hearing more from Calum Macleod.

# 10

# Sport

SORLEY WAS HONOURED by many bodies, but he seemed to take particular pride in being an honorary vice president of Skye Camanachd, although being made the first freeman of Skye and Lochalsh probably came a good second. I attended numerous shinty matches in Skye with him at which he would invariably end up discussing genealogy with local friend John ('The Caley') Nicolson, sometimes with his back to the pitch. But on returning to Braes for a post-match analysis over a dram at DR and Catriona's house, his contribution would suggest that he had paid closer attention than had been apparent. He would recount numerous stories surrounding shinty from the Nicolson men of the famous Kyles Athletic team in Tighnabruaich, who of course were of Skye extraction, to his own exploits playing full back for Edinburgh University in a team of notable Highlanders in the 1930s.

The highpoint for supporters of Skye Camanachd was the team's victory in the 1990 Camanachd Cup final in Fort William, beating Newtonmore 4–1. Three generations of the family attended. The victory was raised seven days later in the House of Commons by Charles Kennedy:

> May I draw the attention of the Leader of the House to early-day motion 1066, which stands in my name and that of several other Hon. Members, which congratulates the Isle of Skye Camanachd Association on its first ever victory in the Camanachd Cup at the shinty final last weekend in Fort William? [That this House warmly congratulates the Skye Camanachd Association over its victory in the final of the Camanachd Cup; notes that this is the first occasion in the history of the competition that the trophy has gone back to

the Isle of Skye; hopes that this well-publicised and popular result will lead to a continuing increase in both interest and participation in the game of shinty; and expresses appreciation to Glenmorangie whisky for their valued sponsorship of the sport.]

Would the Deputy Prime Minister care to add his congratulations to the team? But more important, will he tell the Chancellor of the Exchequer – given that the interest and participation in shinty is on the increase – that a popular move by the government, and one which would encourage the game, would be to remove the imposition of VAT on the sale of shinty sticks?

Sir Geoffrey Howe, the then deputy prime minister, replied: 'I am only sorry that the sport is not as familiar to my countrymen in Wales as it obviously is to the occupants of the Outer Isles. I am sure that the whole House will join me in congratulating Skye on its historic victory, but I do not think that those congratulations necessarily lead us to the conclusion that the entire structure of the VAT system should be transformed.' It was interesting that Sir Geoffrey thought Skye was in the Outer Isles, given his government was preparing to physically join the island to the mainland with a bridge.

Sorley was interested in different sports, such as those on display at Highland Games. He once offered to give me a demonstration of Cumberland-style wrestling which would be featured at such events. We had both been drinking, however, and Renee sent us to bed. He had gone to football matches in the past. He would often recall with great amusement going to a Hearts game at Tynecastle. The great star and top scorer of that Hearts team was the wonderfully named Barney Battles, a Scottish internationalist who had also earlier represented the USA after his family had briefly emigrated before returning to Scotland. Sorley's eyes would twinkle as he repeated the shout he heard that day of 'Sheer fucking poetry, Barney!' He just loved this unusual reference to his own literary craft.

The last conversation I ever had with him was about sport. It was in our house in Cromarty, six months after he had been diagnosed with terminal cancer. It was Saturday and he was in bed. I had gone up to tell him the half-time football scores – Rangers or Celtic must have been losing as he always enjoyed that – and then as I left the room he asked, 'Any shinty scores yet?' Not long after he went into a coma and died later that night.

As was so often the way with a range of subjects, listening to him on shinty was something of an adventure which would often start at Dun Sgathaich in Sleat in the south of Skye. It is said there is no castle in the British Isles older in legend than Dun Sgathaich. It featured in the Red Branch cycle of Celtic tales, which is supposed to go back to the first century AD. As Sorley would explain, Cu-Chulainn, the great hero of the tales, came over from Ireland to the castle to learn feats of arms from the Warrior Queen, Sgathach – in particular the *Gath-bolg*, a special sword thrust to the belly. But he found time to defeat the entire Sleat *Iomain* (shinty) team single-handedly, and to help Sgathach against the other warrior queen, Aoifa, thought also to have been living in Skye at the time. Not only did Cu-Chulainn defeat Aoifa, he proceeded to have a son with her, only to go back to Ulster. This would certainly seem to rank as one of the more significant 'away' victories in shinty history.

That Sorley never lost his passion for the game was not surprising. There is no sport which is closer to the people of Highland Scotland or more integral a part of their local heritage. Shinty games will be postponed when there has been a death in the local community, while weddings can also affect the fixture list.

Shinty is thought to have arrived in Scotland with the Irish language in the sixth century. The ruling body, the Camanachd Association, however, was only formed in 1893. The first Camanachd Cup Final was played in Inverness 1896 and, true to Highland form, the trophy was not ready for the big day. In 1924 the first full international, Scotland *vs* Ireland, was played in Dublin using compromise shinty/hurling rules. In 2005 the shinty season moved from the winter to a March–October season after a two-year trial. This year, 2018, represents 125 years of the organised version of shinty, which in itself is a remarkable fact.

What is extraordinary is that so many communities can keep a team going, never mind two or more at different age grades, and that the likes of Lochcarron has been doing it since 1884. Unlike football, the sport has long been dominated by teams from tiny communities – villages with populations of around 1,000, often less – and their surrounding areas. The final placings in 2017's Marine Harvest Premiership, the top tier of the sport, underlined this. Kinlochshiel were champions. The team draws from several small communities: Balmacara, Dornie,

Kyle of Lochalsh and Plockton. In second place was Kyles Athletic from Tighnabruaich, with a population of around 700. In third place was Lovat from Kiltarlity, with under 1,000 residents. Then came the Badenoch giants of Newtonmore and Kingussie, which have fewer than 2,500 residents between them. Oban Camanachd in sixth place was the highest placed large community with almost 9,000 residents, although they support two senior teams with Oban Celtic, the second. Glenurquhart from Drumnadrochit, with a population of around 1,000, was in seventh place. It was followed by Lochaber, who play in Spean Bridge, which has only around 600 residents. Ninth-placed Kilmallie play in the village of Caol near Fort William which is comparatively large with a population of over 3,000. But only at the bottom in 10th place was one of Scotland's major population centres represented by Glasgow Mid Argyll.

In the National Division, the second tier before the league splits into north and south, small communities again dominated: Skye were champions, followed by Caberfeidh who play in Strathpeffer (1,500). The larger Fort William (10,500) was in third place, but then came Inveraray (600) and Beauly (1,400). Oban Celtic were in sixth place. Strathglass, who play in the village of Cannich, were seventh. An outsider might have thought the team from the Highland capital of Inverness, which has a population of around 60,000 when its suburbs are included, would have done well. But it was bottom – eighteenth out of the top teams in the land. Inverness hasn't enjoyed national success since it won the Camanachd Cup in 1952 for the only time. It was a similar pattern in 2018, with small communities predominant.

New teams have started up in the south with the likes of Tayforth in Perth, most recently Aberdour in Fife, and now remarkably further afield in Cornwall, Krasnador in Russia and northern California, and the sport has always been bolstered by the university teams and the likes of Glasgow Mid Argyll. But shinty's soul remains in small Highland communities, particularly in Argyll, Lochaber, the Great Glen, Badenoch and Strathspey and north and west of Inverness.

Every Saturday afternoon the equation which relates population size to sporting success is turned on its head from Cannich to Dalmally, Glendaruel to Kincraig and Strachur to Portree. Not only that, shinty is winning increased exposure, particularly on BBC Alba. The sport's leading historian is Hugh Dan MacLennan, who wrote a doctoral thesis on its history. He was brought up in a Gaelic-speaking house in the village of Caol near Fort William by parents from Harris and played for Lochaber High School, Glasgow University, Fort William and Inverness. A friend of Sorley's, he said he wasn't surprised by Kinlochshiel's success. Its first-ever senior trophy was the MacAulay Cup in September 2016, which was followed by the historic premiership win in 2017. Hugh Dan told me for this book:

I first met Sorley as a schoolboy as a winning captain when he presented me, eventually, with the MacBean Cup when we beat Portree. He was more interested in finding out about my Harris and Scarp connections than he was in handing over the trophy – understandably, perhaps, as we had beaten the Skye team. Ten to 15 years ago Kinlochshiel were struggling, now they have got more shinty players than they know what to do with, and most of them will have come through Plockton High School. They have even started a women's team. Sorley did so much for the sport when he was headmaster there. He laid foundations, which have proved sound, and won the toughest competition in the game. If they win the Camanachd Cup, they can thank Sorley for starting it all.

I believe success goes hand in hand with the social and economic confidence of the local community. Nowhere was that more obvious than on Skye. In 1950 when they won the Sutherland Cup and in 1990 when they won the Camanachd Cup, the big one, they had all their boys playing at home. Lochcarron were at their peak when the Kishorn Fabrication yard was operating [from 1975 to 1987], when they not only had local players, but were bolstered by some from other areas. But now Skye's and Kinlochshiel's fortunes have revived. Demographics can catch up with the shinty villages. As the profile of local populations becomes more elderly, a trend often bolstered by people coming to retire, so the numbers playing shinty fall. Schools rolls have plummeted, leading to mergers and the use of mixed teams at primary level. There are normally 12 players in a team and there are five substitutes. So you need a pool of 20 at the very least for one team. How some of these places manage to keep fielding two teams is amazing.

In 2012, to Inveraray's eternal credit, they managed to get to the Camanachd Cup Final with fewer than 20 senior players. They were talented and fit, which was probably because the team's core worked for the fire service and therefore kept fit in their daily work. These are the things that matter. The move to summer shinty was not without its challenges but it has allowed the more skilled players greater opportunity to express themselves. The game is growing in the urban south, in the Central Belt, and, of course, we now have a senior team on Lewis. The women's game has also come on wonderfully well – beyond all expectations. But there is no complacency and in some traditional areas the game is in a very fragile state – usually due to lack of numbers.

At Skye Camanachd's annual dinner in 2017 the outstanding Lorna MacRae, who had captained Skye Ladies to the Marine Harvest National Division 1 title and Valerie Fraser Cup successes, rounded off a terrific season by being named Skye Camanachd Ladies Player of the Year as well as being awarded the coveted 'Caman DR'. This is presented annually to the youth player who best reflects the philosophy of the game held by my late brother-in-law, who died in 2010. DR was a native of North Uist but had attended Portree for the later years of his secondary schooling. Shinty was all but dead when he returned to Portree from Glasgow University so he began coaching it in primary schools as well as the high school, and he played for Skye himself until a serious leg break. Cup-winning school sides followed and they grew into the Skye Camanachd team who won the Camanachd Cup in 1990. The winner of his caman is chosen by DR's three sons, all shinty players of some repute.

## Ross County

The election of Ross County and Inverness Caledonian Thistle into the Scottish Football League in 1994 was an important event, and not just in a sporting context. The teams' subsequent progress through the divisions and their capturing of a national cup apiece seemed to emphasise the recovery of an area once regarded as a socio-economic basket case. Ross County already was a football club which had entered the Highland League in 1929. It had an established ground at Victoria Park in Dingwall. Its club badge incorporated the *Caberfeidh* (stag's head) from the regimental badge of the Seaforth Highlanders, a regiment which recruited in the north of Scotland. It was named after Kenneth Mackenzie, 1st Earl of Seaforth.

Inverness Caledonian Thistle was specifically created by merging two of the Highland capital's existing teams, Caledonian and Thistle. At one point it looked as though there would be a merger of all three Inverness teams. In the end, however, the wonderfully named Clachnacuddin opted to become the sole representative of the Highland capital in the Highland League. The eventual merger between Thistle, whose home ground was at Kingsmills to the south-east of Inverness, and Caledonian, based at Telford Street on the other side of the River Ness near the Caledonian Canal, was divisive. Angry and frustrated Invernessian voices levelled charges of sell-out, betrayal, even treachery, at those behind the project.

The merger was deemed necessary to apply for membership of the Scottish League. The public authorities could only provide the vital financial support for a united bid, rather than favour one. After much heated debate the merger was completed. But many Caley and Thistle fans were profoundly distressed by the merger. Some even crossed the Kessock Bridge to support Ross County in Dingwall. The day the two teams were elected to the Scottish League I made my way to Dingwall to the Ross County Supporters Club to get some local reaction. However, there was only one other person there and that was Iain MacDonald from the BBC, who had the same idea. We discussed in depth the significance of the news, then went our separate ways.

Old county loyalties die hard, and football fans in Cromarty traditionally supported the Ross-shire team in the old county town of Dingwall, sometimes as their 'wee' team, with Aberdeen, Rangers or Celtic often their big one. With senior status secured, Ross County became the main team for some, myself and son Calum included.

If anyone needs a reminder of what conditions used to be like in the Highland League there is a video on YouTube of Ross County beating St Cuthberts 11–0 in the Scottish Cup of 1993. There is one tiny stand and a covered terracing at the Jail End for home supporters, but in the rest of Dingwall's Victoria Park ground supporters are standing on grass banks with panoramic views down the Cromarty Firth and around the

Ben Wyvis massif surrounding the ground. It is unrecognisable from the all-seater stadium of today.

The two teams have enjoyed a symbiotic relationship based on passionate but largely friendly rivalry. When they were to meet in local derbies, one or other had to cross the Kessock Bridge. As a consequence the games were christened 'El Kessocko' after the Real Madrid *vs* Barcelona fixture which has long been known as El Clásico. Since 1994 Caley has led the way and won an international reputation for beating Celtic 3–1 at Parkhead in the famous 'Super Caley Go Ballistic Celtic Are Atrocious' game in 2000 when they were still in Division One. Ross County, who lived under shadow of that brilliant *Sun* headline for so long, plodded on for 10 years until they beat Celtic 2–0 at Hampden in a Scottish Cup semi-final to clinch a place in the Cup final. It inspired one fan to call a radio football programme to declare 'Ich bin ein Dingwaller'. Getting an allusion to President Kennedy's famous speech in Berlin in 1963 into a line about Ross County underlined the sophistication of the Staggies' support.

In 2017 Caley Thistle suffered relegation, and at the time of writing this book Ross County has just followed Inverness's example in being relegated. Inverness fans are entitled to gloat. Publicly, a collective schadenfreude was on display last year. When the County supporters' buses, returning from Hamilton Academicals, were passing Caley Thistle's stadium at the southern end, there was a spontaneous rendition of a version of Status Quo's 'Down Down'. Much humour was certainly enjoyed at Caley supporters' expense. After all, these were the same supporters who, when playing County the year before, after the Dingwall side's League Cup final triumph, kept singing 'Small team, small cup. Big team, big cup', referencing their winning of the Scottish Cup the previous year. But privately many Ross County supporters admitted that life wouldn't be the same without Caley Thistle. Not having the local derby – El Kessocko – to look forward to would clearly leave a gap. Not least when the next nearest Premiership team would be Aberdeen, 116 miles away.

It was more than that, however. Having both Highland teams in the top flight meant a lot to the Highland sense of identity. There was also mutual enjoyment that Central Belt teams still complained about how far away Inverness and Dingwall were, apparently convinced it is further to travel north than the Highlanders' journey south every second week. Stuart Cosgrove, on BBC Radio Scotland's *Off the Ball*, a programme whose contribution to Scottish life has not been sufficiently recognised, talked about how many football fans in Glasgow seemed to resent the Highlanders' presence, particularly that of Ross County. It is unlikely such 'Central Beltism' is just about distance. Dingwall, with a population smaller than its football ground's capacity, is deemed undeserving of top flight status by some. But this is a source of local pride. Roy MacGregor, chairman of the Global Energy Group, who also chairs Ross County's board, enjoys talking about Caley Thistle still being the 'the city club' and the County fans with some justification chant 'We are the Highlands', as they come from as far afield as Skye, Sutherland and sometimes even the Outer Isles. It is about identity. It creates a special atmosphere in the ground, where, while in the lower divisions, there used to be crowd applause when the attendance figures were read out. Great pride was taken in being better supported than many established clubs.

# 11

# Catching the Ferry

FERRIES HAVE BEEN an abiding passion, due to childhood days on Iona, and I have spent much of my time writing about Caledonian MacBrayne, known far and wide in its abbreviated form CalMac. The possibility of it being privatised has been a recurring issue. But in 1994 I persuaded *The Herald* that I should write on the smaller ferries still operating in the Highlands and Islands which, if not quite forgotten, were less well known. Nonetheless, for alliterative reasons, the series which appeared in the Weekender section of the paper was entitled 'Forgotten Ferries'. This took me from Loch Linnhe to the Sound of Mull and from Loch Nevis to the Kyle of Durness. I had planned to finish with my local ferry across the mouth of the Cromarty Firth between Nigg and Cromarty, which at that time carried just two cars and was the last vehicle ferry on the east coast of the Scottish mainland. A decision was taken in Glasgow, however, to bring the series to an end just before I got to the Cromarty Firth. In order to lay the ground, in May that year I wrote a long piece 'Who Pays Heed to the Ferryman?' on the history of ferries in Scotland. This embraced more than the Clyde and included the Western Isles, Orkney and Shetland.

It was another time, but there will still be many who can recall those vessels, once an integral part of the transport system, which departed only in the 1950s, '60s and '70s. There was the Firth of Forth crossing – just west of the world's most famous rail-bridge where over 900 years ago Queen Margaret, the second wife of Malcolm III, would have crossed on her way to Dunfermline – at the Queen's Ferry; the Tay crossing just to the east of the rail-bridge, the remnants of the 1877 bridge still discernible after its 1879 collapse; the Kessock Ferry from Inverness to the Black Isle; the Erskine Ferry which dragged itself back and forward across the Clyde on chains for more than a century. All gone, replaced by magnificently engineered bridges. Progress made; Scotland shrunk. There have been others: the Dornoch Firth, the Kyle of Lochalsh, Kylesku. But no one can doubt that such significant improvements in the infrastructure do represent genuine progress.

In my childhood and teenage years I had a burning ambition to take over one ferry, the Fionnphort Ferry which plied across the Sound of Iona. Not the metal CalMac car ferry of these past decades, but a wooden motor boat in her white and brown livery that carried passengers and freight, and occasional vehicles. To be able to stand at the stern, tiller in hand, and slip her smoothly alongside either jetty without scraping the gunwales; to know how to dodge the wind; to use the tides – these were skills worth having. I learnt them as a young volunteer apprentice to ferry men Angus and Dan MacKechnie, two brothers originally from nearby Kintra on the Ross of Mull.

In 1929 a great-uncle, John MacDonald, who had sailed the world as a sea captain, returned to his native Ross of Mull to take over the ferry. Neil Gunn mentioned him in his book *Off in a Boat: A Hebridean Voyage* (1938). Uncle Johnny died too soon for me to know him. So did my mother's father. Grandfather and Uncle Neil were contracted to load and unload, by motor boat and barge, McCallum Orme's *Dunara Castle* in the Sound of Iona, just one of the stops on her regular service to and from different island communities. These included Colonsay, Bunessan on Mull, Tiree, Soay, ports on the west of Skye, Harris and Scalpay, North Uist, South Uist and Barra, linking them all with Glasgow's Lancefield Quay.

The car ferries, however, had to come to the island sounds just as bridges had to come to the firths and the larger sea-lochs. The population was on the move, particularly in the holiday period. In the last 20 years before the Ballachulish Bridge opened in 1975, traffic on the ferry across the mouth of Loch Leven rose from 42,000 vehicles to 204,000. Anyone who regularly travelled that way in the summers of the early 1970s will recall how bad it had become, how you knew if the queue was past a certain point you were quicker to drive round by Kinlochleven. But even then the likes of the Ballachulish ferry seemed to represent something important, a reminder to urban man that 'here we play by different rules'. And it made it easier to recall the history that went with the crossing: to imagine MacIain of Glencoe in the snow of 30 December 1691, crossing on his way south to Inveraray to try to swear an oath of allegiance to William of Orange and save his people; or to look up from the southern jetty to the rock above where, on 8 November 1752, James Stewart of Acharn, Seumas a' Ghlinne (James of the Glen), was hanged from a gibbet, protesting his innocence of the murder of Colin Campbell of Glenure, featured in Robert Louis Stevenson's *Kidnapped* . James's body was left to rot for more than two years, reminding every traveller crossing the ferry that retribution and justice were often strangers. They never did capture Ailean Breac.

## Keeping CalMac together

Threats of the privatisation of CalMac have appeared regularly over the last three decades, deeply concerning the more remote and fragile communities served by the publicly owned ferry company. As is the nature of life in these outposts, it is in the Hebridean DNA to complain about lifeline ferry services provided by CalMac but at the same time defend the company against the uncertainty of the private sector. CalMac survived a serious privatisation bid in 1988. The Scottish Office dissolved the Scottish Transport Group, which had also embraced bus services, selling off its road operations while leaving the Clyde and Hebrides ferry services intact and directly responsible to the Secretary of State. In May 1993 Ian Lang, then Secretary of State for Scotland, wrote: 'I believe the time is ripe for a further study of Caledonian MacBrayne following the transfer of the company's ownership to me in 1990.' The possibility of CalMac being privatised was back on the agenda before the previous study had time to gather any Scottish Office dust. International accountants KPMG were appointed to study CalMac and ferry services in the Northern Isles where the privately-owned P&O then ran the main services with public subsidy. To illustrate the issues involved, I went to Barra to gauge the local reaction to Mr Lang's announcement. I took my car and was due to meet a photographer colleague, Paul Hackett, who was flying up from Glasgow. Paul later admitted to have had a few drinks the previous evening to celebrate his forthcoming Hebridean odyssey. He must have been one of the very few in the land unaware that planes to Barra land on the beach. Having seen the famous strand come closer and closer with no sign of a tarmac runway, he was not in great shape when he emerged from the plane.

The then Roman Catholic Priest in Castlebay, Father Donald MacKay, was one of the first we talked to, and he was clear: 'I don't think you will find many here who would support CalMac being privatised. We are very peripheral. Everything has to come in by sea from Oban. That is our one route, and already we are paying on average about 30 per cent more for food. It is a fragile economy, and it would be hard to bear a reduction on service or increase in cost.'

Not that Father MacKay would concede the generally held view that routes like Barra would suffer if the money-making Clyde routes were hived off. 'Have you seen the books? Maybe it is us that's making the money.' Whatever the internal economics of CalMac might have been, Father MacKay was right about not finding support for privatisation locally. Nobody knew quite what it would have meant, but there was a general fear that, whether as part of a privatised service or as a continuing rump of subsidised routes, the service to Barra would be considerably dearer and much reduced.

Jessie MacNeil, then the mainstay of the Barra Council of Social Service, said: 'The fact that privatisation is now back on the agenda should ring warning bells that they are really serious about it, or why bring it up again? It is possibly going to be pushed through regardless of the views being expressed by everyone. We don't know what the implications of privatisation are going to be, so we are guessing when we assume that we will be getting a reduced level of service. CalMac are no angels, and we have plenty of fights with them, but they are treated as a lifeline to the islands, and how that obligation would be honoured in a privatised service is what most concerns people here.'

KPMG's final report was delivered to the Scottish Office in the last week of May 1994. The following week, *The Herald* revealed that the consultants had advised that any planned privatisation of CalMac meant no advantage to the public purse and no benefit for services. The information came courtesy of a source concerned about what might happen to CalMac. Mr Lang refused to comment, but in September he announced: 'I am satisfied that CalMac operates economically and efficiently under the present arrangements and provides a service of high quality and reliability to the islands.' Highland and Islands MPs called repeatedly for the report to be published, but the Scottish Office resisted with the official line being: 'The KPMG report on Caledonian MacBrayne is not going to be published. It contains commercially sensitive information and was not for public consumption.'

## Europe and tendering

The CalMac story changed direction in 2000. The Scottish Parliament was less than a year old when a new threat appeared on CalMac's horizon. In April 2000 *The Herald* revealed that ministers had been advised that the organisation of CalMac's network of ferry services would have to change radically to meet European regulations requiring them to be put out to competitive tender on a five-yearly basis to justify the public subsidy paid to CalMac. The publicly owned company, which at that time had a fleet of 28 ferries linking 23 islands to the mainland, would itself have to be restructured in order for it to tender for its own routes. CalMac had to go from one company to seven in a complex and expensive restructuring process deemed necessary for tendering. As a result CalMac Ferries Ltd (CFL) would operate the ferries but pay Caledonian Maritime Assets (Cmal) for the lease of its vessels and use of its piers. If private sector operators won the tender, they too would have to lease from Cmal. The restructuring also involved plans to transfer seagoing staff to an offshore firm based in Guernsey to avoid paying National Insurance to the Treasury. *The Herald* revealed in November 2004 that if CalMac did not make this offshore move, private sector rivals would be able to submit a tender of at least £1.2 million less on staffing costs alone, because offshore companies did not pay employers' 12 per cent NI contributions.

It had been known for some time that the European Commission had been examining the payment of state aid to ferry and shipping companies in a number of member states, which had raised the spectre of privatisation. Little thought was given to the prospect of the EC demanding that CalMac's routes be tendered; this despite the Maritime Cabotage Regulation, the measure having come into force in 1992. It was a regulation and not a directive, which would have required a member state to take a particular course of action. It did not specifically say that ferry services had to be tendered to make the public subsidy CalMac received EU compliant. However, a decade or so later Labour/ Liberal Democrat Scottish Executive ministers were insistent tendering was the only way to keep Europe happy and that they had been offered no alternative. Professor Neil Kay, the economist who had become something of a specialist on the subject, opined at the time: 'It is not the commission's job to present alternatives, it is the member state's responsibility. You do not ask the umpire to formulate your strategy for you, whether the game is football or state aid.' Europe was demanding member states conform to a set of principles on public subsidy and competition, but it was up to them how they went about it. It was clear that the EC was indeed happy with tendering as a chosen route, but it was never prescriptive. There was another way.

In 2003 there was a ruling by the European Court of Justice in a case about the German bus company Altmark in respect of subsidy/state aid. CalMac received senior legal opinion that the Altmark decision allowed the Scottish Executive to stop tendering without fear of legal consequence. Brian Wilson, who had just resigned as Minister of State at the UK Department of Trade and Industry (DTI), said he believed CalMac's advice was supported by Whitehall civil servants. He said: 'I have been in touch with competition officials at the DTI who are delighted with the Altmark judgment and confirm that, as far as they can see, it means that Caledonian MacBrayne does not need to be subjected to competitive tendering under EU procurement rules. There are four criteria to be met in order to avoid the "state aid" tag and it seems very likely that the CalMac case meets all four. It is now up to the Scottish Executive, as payers of the subsidy [then almost £22 million], to satisfy themselves on these criteria in conjunction with the DTI.'

The four criteria were that: the company must have clearly defined public obligations to discharge; the basis of the subsidy should be objective and transparent; the amount paid should be only enough to cover costs and allow for a reasonable profit; and the sum paid must be determined by an analysis of costs that a typical transport company would incur. A spokeswoman for the Scottish Office quickly responded, indicating that the DTI had no role to play, saying: 'We are considering the implications of the Altmark ruling. Any final decision will be taken by the Scottish Executive in consultation with the European Commission.' This was to sow the seeds of suspicion that there were civil servants advising Scottish ministers who had been determined from the start that CalMac's routes should go out to tender.

Professor Kay was invited to give evidence to the Scottish Parliament's inquiry on the issue of tendering, and in the spring of 2005 submitted a proposal to the committee and the executive based on the Altmark ruling by the European Court. The proposal showed how basic principles outlined in the Altmark case could enable CalMac's lifeline ferry services to be made compliant with EC rules without the need for tendering. The then Transport Minister, Nicol Stephen, appeared to give an undertaking to the Transport Committee that Professor Kay would be given an opportunity to discuss his proposal with the executive. That never happened. Instead, just before the debate in the Scottish Parliament in September 2005, a briefing document appeared from the Scottish Executive which attempted to discredit the proposal on the apparently spurious grounds that Altmark was not relevant to the tendering of Scottish lifeline ferry services.

Professor Kay's argument was that the ferry routes should be treated as essential services which could be subsidised by way of Public Service Obligations (PSOs), which are recognised by the European Commission, and strengthened by the application of the European Court's Altmark ruling. With the addition of a ferry regulator similar to that operating in previously nationalised industries, the EC would be content that its regulations were being honoured. As far as we could ever gather, these ideas were never really considered seriously in Edinburgh. This was curious as two senior sources within the EC independently made clear to *The Herald* at the time that Professor Kay knew what he was talking about and that his contribution should not be dismissed. But the routes were finally put out to tender in 2006 and an offshoot of CalMac won it.

In 2007, in response to an enquiry from Alyn Smith, the SNP MEP, Jacques Barrot, the then European Transport Commissioner, said of public support for ferry services: 'If this subsidy complies with the four criteria laid down by the court of justice in its judgment in the case of Altmark Trans, then this subsidy would not constitute state aid.' He said, indeed, that the Altmark principles were not only relevant to the question of ferry services like the CalMac network, it was essential that the Altmark principles be complied with if subsidies to these services were not to be treated as illegal state aid. Professor Kay said at the time: 'The commission's response quite clearly indicates the executive was completely wrong to dismiss the Altmark criteria.'

The SNP Scottish government inherited the official thinking on this and embarked on another costly retendering of CalMac's routes.

In May 2016 the publicly owned company won again with a new £900 million contract to continue operating the Clyde and Hebrides Ferries Network for an eight-year period from October that year. The private firm Serco Caledonian Ferries Limited had also been competing for the contract to run the services, but its bid was deemed to be 'non-compliant' by the government body Transport Scotland after the firm sought changes to commercial terms aimed at striking a balance between the risks and rewards involved. The tendering process was the source of a dispute between unions which wanted the ferry services to remain in public hands.

Two months after the contract was awarded, the UK voted to leave the European Union, although Scotland voted by a significant margin to remain. Nobody knows whether CalMac's routes will ever have to be put out to tender again. Many are still of the view that they never had to be in the first place. Gordon Ross, the managing director of the highly successful Western Ferries, for one has long argued, and argued well, that there should be a role for the private sector on certain profitable routes, with CalMac focussing on those serving the more fragile communities. I can see how this might appeal, but have never been persuaded. What does happen if a private operator's vessel breaks down or is damaged? Suitable replacements are not easy to find quickly, as Serco discovered in the Pentland Firth a couple of years ago.

### Ferries come and go

There was an interesting ferry tale at the most southern end of my patch. In 1970 Campbeltown was linked to Red Bay in Northern Ireland when Western Ferries introduced a car ferry service which ran on a summer-only basis until 1973. The Northern Ireland link was re-established in 1997 with a service to Ballycastle, which cost the public purse £8 million. CalMac had wanted to run it but in 1996 the then Tory Secretary of State Michael Forsyth was determined it should be a private sector operation. So much so that he ordered CalMac to sell its ferry *Claymore* at a reasonable price to Sea Containers, a Bermuda-registered company which expanded from supplying used cargo containers to various shipping companies, diversifying into luxury hotels and even railway services including the Venice-Simplon Orient Express and the Great North Eastern Railway franchise from London to Edinburgh. This turned out to be £750,000 despite it having just gone through a £250,000 refit. It was described by Labour as 'a scandalous subsidy by the taxpayer to the private sector'. But it got worse. It transpired that the *Claymore* had been sold not to Sea Containers but to a flag of convenience company, Blue Grove, then resold to a leasing company, ING Lease, at considerable profit. ING then leased the ferry back to Sea Containers.

Sea Containers filed for bankruptcy in 2006, but nine years earlier its subsidiary, the Argyll and Antrim Steam Packet Company, began a summer service sailing on the Campbeltown to Ballycastle run. While it won plaudits for the quality of the service, the Kintyre business community was outraged when in June 1998 it was discovered that the service was being suspended for a fortnight so the *Claymore* could be used for the Isle of Man TT races. It was subsequently confirmed that the Scottish Office had not demanded any minimum level of service. There were also doubts as to how well the service was ever promoted in Ireland. Then, in September 1999, following the third summer season, Sea Containers said they were withdrawing – a major body blow for Kintyre. There is now a CalMac car ferry sailing between Campbeltown, Arran and Ardrossan and a successful fast passenger service to Northern Ireland. Kintyre, however, still dreams of Campbeltown becoming the Scottish end of a car ferry service across the North Channel to Ireland.

The ferry service at Stromeferry across the waters at the mouth of Loch Carron was restored briefly in early 2012 after a gap of 40 years. The A890 Stromeferry Bypass, which runs along the southern shore of the sea loch had been closed by a fall of about 100 tonnes of rock. The ferry had been withdrawn when the by-pass opened in 1969.The old Ballachulish ferry which runs between Glenelg and Kylerhea on Skye in the summer months was deployed while the road was cleared. When that was done, the accuracy of the wonderful road sign 'Stromeferry No Ferry' was restored.

We should also remember the boatman at Bonawe on Loch Etive, a man I knew well and admired, not least for his sense of humour. There were great stories around North Argyll about the pranks played by this man. One was that he had been asked to take a rusting wreck of a car from Bonawe to somewhere else for final disposal. He and those assisting him had considerable difficulty in getting the wreck aboard his large boat and had to resort to doing it piece by piece, aided by sledgehammers and iron crowbars. It was hard work and it wasn't helped by a crowd of tourists who had left their cars to observe and advise. Bonawe, of course, had been a ferry crossing and the old sign announcing the fact was still displayed. As the last mangled bit of the car was tossed on board, he was reputed to have immediately seen the potential humour in the old ferry signs, so turned to the assembled company, and with a summoning wave of his hand shouted: 'Next, please!'

# 12

# Hebridean Travails

MANY YEARS AGO I learnt that in the days of the Labour/Lib Dem Scottish Executive the leader of an environmental group approached a minister with the suggestion that Harris be designated as Scotland's third national park. He was bemused by the ministerial response: 'It is a good idea, indeed it is a very good idea, but that is exactly why you mustn't say anything about it.' It was the sort of advice Sir Humphrey Appleby would have given Jim Hacker in *Yes, Minister*. What the Scottish minister feared was that if environmentalists were seen to be behind such a project, it would have been immediately opposed by many islanders, who had long seen the interests of such people from outside bodies as inimical to those of the indigenous people.

I recalled this episode when I went to Harris to write a special report in the *Herald Magazine* in August 2010 about the majority of the islanders having decided that the best chance of a sustainable future for the island was that it should follow Loch Lomond and the Trossachs, and the Cairngorms in being designated a national park. I found this highly significant. It has been depressing that for much of my time as Highland correspondent environmentalists were seen by many as the enemy of development. They were caricatured as standing in the way of job-creating projects because of the threat to a rare species of bird, toad or fungus. Ordinary people, who wanted to live their lives in some of the remoter parts of the Highlands and Islands, were too often denied their chance. Suspicion of the conservation bodies was pronounced in crofting areas, the more so before 1992 when it was the Nature Conservancy Council (NCC), with its headquarters in Peterborough, which had the legal powers to seek to limit development if necessary. The creation of Scottish Natural Heritage (SNH), with the merger of NCC and the Countryside Commission for Scotland

26 years ago, helped a bit. Despite this mistrust, in 2010 the people of Harris were trying to embrace stewardship of their island based on the primacy of protection of landscape and nature.

Harris is one of the real jewels of the Outer Hebrides, which I loved visiting. These trips were always better informed by touching base with John Murdo Morrison, for many years the proprietor of the Isle of Harris Hotel in Tarbert. The island's west side boasts peerless beaches such as Luskentyre and Scarista, which have been eulogised in numerous inter-national tourism surveys. In the north its mountains fill the sky. On the east the Minch has carved one small natural harbour after another out of its rocky coast, giving the people a chance to feed themselves from the sea. This was needed, because with stone dominating the hills that roll back behind the crofting townships, little would grow, although there is evidence of attempts. Harris has dubious island credentials, being physically joined to Lewis to the north. But they have a different history. Harris came under the Macleods of Dunvegan on Skye (Siol Thormoid), quite distinct from the Macleods of Lewis (Siol Thorcuil). Until local government reorganisation in 1975 and the creation of the Western Isles Council (Comhairle nan Eilean Siar), Harris came under Inverness-shire, while Lewis was part of Ross and Cromarty with its HQ in Dingwall.

The most important consideration for any island for the last cen-tury or so has been how best to hold on to its people. Harris has not fared well on this count. Between 1951 and 2011 there was a huge decline of 52 per cent, from 3,991 to 1,916. There have been various attempts to revitalise the island's economy to stem the depopulation. Most controversial was the ill-fated plans to remove a good part of the mountain Roineabhal to establish Europe's largest coastal super-quarry at Lingerbay. Some saw Redland Aggregates' £70-million project to extract 600 million tonnes of the mineral anorthosite from the moun-tain for use in the likes of road building as salvation and a chance to reverse eight decades of chronic depopulation. Others viewed it as a prescription for environmental disaster. It was established early on that the development would be of such a scale that it would be seen easily from space. Despite that, I was told by a senior source within the then Tory-run Scottish Office that early ministerial thinking had been that it would be better just to leave it up to Western Isles Council to decide.

Officials prevailed on the politicians, and even before the council met in June 1993 to consider the planning application, Ian Lang, the Secretary of State, had officially informed the council that in the event of them supporting the project he would examine the papers to see if a public inquiry was necessary. That same month a referendum found 62.1 per cent of the islanders supported the project and 37.9 per cent opposed it. Given the local opinion and the island's demographic troubles, it was difficult not to sympathise with those backing the super-quarry. While removing part of a mountain did seem a rather drastic measure, better that than continued depopulation. A local trust fund would be established, but the real draw was the prospect of jobs, with estimates ranging from 33 to over 100. Glensanda quarry had been working on Loch Linnhe since 1986, so there was a precedent, but it was a most difficult choice for local people, and there was no doubt the development would disfigure the island forever.

The council duly supported the development. In October 1993 Mr Lang called in the planning application and in January 1994 a planning inquiry was announced. It was to be the longest inquiry in Scottish planning history. It started on 11 October 1994 and ended on 6 June 1995, during which time it sat for 100 days with over 100 witnesses appearing, ranging from conservationists to a First Nations Mi'kmaq warrior, and between 400 and 500 written representations considered. But just before the inquiry ended, the island's council performed a complete volte-face. In May 1995 the Harris Council of Social Service commissioned the Electoral Reform Society to conduct a second poll which attracted an 82.7 per cent response, with 1,013 (67.7 per cent) voting against the development and 483 (32.3 per cent) for. This marked an almost complete reversal of the position in June 1993. The overall participation two years earlier, however, had been lower, at 60.9 per cent. In October 1994, when *The Herald* and BBC's *Eorpa* programme polled 22 per cent of the island's over-16 population, it was clear that opinion had begun to slip away, with 36 per cent in favour, 36 per cent against and 27 per cent undecided.

Morag Munro, secretary of the Harris Council of Social Service, had become one of the leading critics of the project, and her dignified advocacy grew persuasive amongst her fellow islanders. At the time of the second referendum result she said: 'I think the real story here is the response to the poll. At 82.7 per cent, it must be unprecedented. The people had more information this time from the public inquiry and felt they were better able to make up their minds.' As a consequence, the night before the inquiry was due to close, the council reversed its position, voting by 21 votes to eight to oppose the quarry. The move calling for a change in the council's position had been put by Colin Campbell, a Benbecula councillor: 'How could anybody say it was unreasonable that as a result of all the information that has come out of the inquiry that people are not entitled to change their minds? All the information about dust, noise, and vibration levels, the health risks of working in that environment.'

The council's QC, Dr Robert Reed, now the Scottish judge Lord Reed, made clear in a message to the council meeting that he would have to consider his own position if the council now voted to withdraw its support for the quarry: 'If there is an adverse vote, I will certainly need clear instructions in respect of these matters. Whether I am able to accept the instructions will depend on their terms. As I have already indicated, I could not accept instructions to deliver submissions inconsistent with those I have just delivered.'

Inquiry reporter Gillian Pain indicated that she might have to delay the ending, but in the end it did close the following day in the south Harris village of Leverburgh. Pain then took four years to complete her report and retired from her job, finishing it as a paid consultant of the Scottish Office. In May 1999 the report was delivered to the then Scottish Executive, but it took till March 2000 before it finally arrived on the environment minister's desk. Four months later, the minister, Sarah Boyack, told the Scottish Parliament that before making a decision she had decided to refer to SNH the question of whether any part of the quarry site should be proposed as a candidate for a Special Area of Conservation.

Enough was enough, and Redland Aggregates went to the Court of Session where Lord Hardie described the near 10-year delay in producing a decision on the planning application as a failure of 'scandalous proportions'. He said that Ms Boyack had not only exceeded her powers but acted irrationally when she decided to ask SNH to get involved. By November 2000 Boyack had been replaced by Sam Galbraith, and one of his first actions was to reject the application. The former neurosurgeon was to tell friends, 'When you are guddling about in people's brains, you've no option but to take decisions quickly and move on.'

It came nine and a half years after the application was first lodged, seven and a half years since permission was granted by the local authority, five and a half years after the longest such inquiry in Scottish planning history closed and a year and a half since the inquiry reporter's conclusions were delivered. It is worth mentioning that Gillian Pain had actually concluded that the 200 direct and indirect jobs the quarry would bring would have been worth the undoubted environmental damage it would cause to Harris. There was a huge moral responsibility on all the opponents of the quarry who dangled alternative developments as carrots before islanders not to disappear into the woodwork. But most did, and so long had passed that few remembered.

Harris had all but exhausted itself over Lingerbay. But the focus shifted to community ownership. In 2003 there was a community-led buyout of the 55,000-acre North Harris Estate by the North Harris Trust. The 7,500-acre Seaforth Estate followed and in 2010 crofters on the west side of the island took over the 16,250-acre publicly owned crofting estates of Borve, Luskentyre and Scaristavore. All of this seemed to help focus local minds on how best to use the land. The merits of conservation as embodied in the concept of a national park grew more obvious. In a ballot 732 people voted for the idea of pursuing a national park as the way ahead, and 311 against. It was a ratio of more than two to one with a turnout of nearly 72 per cent. The vote followed a feasibility report by the Isle of Harris National Park Study Group which concluded that 10–15 full-time jobs would be created directly by a national park authority. But when indirect employment was included there could be up to 90 jobs, which would have been the equivalent to more than 1,000 in the Central Belt. It would bring significant government money and there would be access to new funding schemes from Scottish, UK and European official sources which in turn would employ islanders and attract new residents. But it would not restrict crofting activity. The feasibility study concluded: 'The most pressing needs in Harris are to reverse population decline and improve its age structure.'

The islanders had voted for a national park based on the boundaries of the parish of Harris, which included the islands of Scarp, Scalpay and Taransay, and the remote outposts of St Kilda and Rockall. Historically it had also included the old Macleod island of Berneray, but this had been physically joined to North Uist by a causeway since

1999. They wanted a park with 'call-in powers' similar to the largest in the UK, the Cairngorms National Park. This would leave most of the planning function to the local council, with the park authority only calling in applications which would affect the management of the park. The full planning powers enjoyed by Scotland's first national park, Loch Lomond and the Trossachs, were not thought appropriate by the people of Harris. The designation of Harris as a national park, I believe, could have been transformative, and may yet come. However, the timing of the move could not have been worse as regards getting funding from a Scottish government facing the biting winds of austerity blowing from Whitehall. Ministers had announced it looked likely they would spend £600 million less in 2010–11 than they had planned. But in any event members of Comhairle nan Eilean Siar helped remove any pressure on the Scottish government over a possible Harris National Park by not fully endorsing the idea. The position supported by island councillors in November 2010 was 'that the Comhairle: (a) inform Scottish Ministers that it is the view of the Comhairle that, at this stage, a convincing case has not been identified for the creation of a National Park in Harris; and (b) note that Scottish Ministers would proceed to Stage 2 if their view is that a case exists to establish a National Park in Harris and in line with the legislative process, the Comhairle would provide a final definitive view at Stage 3, when the critical components of the National Park were known'.

Councillors weren't persuaded 'at this stage'. And they had also anticipated the process towards national park designation would continue if ministers saw any merit in the Harris proposal. The Comhairle would then give a final view later. But a full three years later the Harris National Park plan was debated by MSPs for all of 34 minutes and 17 seconds in the Scottish Parliament. The then Minister for the Environment and Climate Change, Paul Wheelhouse, said he didn't want to establish more national parks for the time being. Neither did he want to set up the national strategy group to determine how a policy on national parks should develop. He explained he was concerned that at a time of such economic difficulty, communities' aspirations would be raised only to be dashed by the lack of money to establish any new parks. He elaborated: 'It is instructive to consider the experience of Harris. In 2009 the community in Harris voted in favour of pursuing national park status as a means of addressing population decline and a lack of employment. However, the then Minister for Environment [Roseanna Cunningham] made it clear that she would not consider such designation unless the local authority was supportive. In 2010, Western Isles Council conducted a thorough year-long study of all aspects of what was proposed, including for example the role of a Harris national park in relation to planning, but it concluded that a convincing case had not been made for national park status for Harris.'

It was almost an accurate description of what Comhairle nan Eilean Siar had agreed, close enough for the Scottish government to kick a national park for Harris well into the marram grass. Obviously, one of the major considerations that persuaded ministers to let the Harris park idea lie was the cost of setting one up at a time when the economic crisis was deepening. Although campaigners for more national parks have long argued that parks will pay back many times over the initial public investment. Mr Wheelhouse seemed to accept this in respect of our two existing parks – the Cairngorms and Loch Lomond and the Trossachs, set up 10 and 11 years previously. He said: 'I acknowledge that they contribute more than £260 million to local economies and attract more than 5 million visitors a year. They are positive players in our conservation and biodiversity objectives.'

Why that shouldn't also apply to Harris has never been explained properly. The idea should not be allowed to wither on the vine of spending cuts, because it seems one of the best chances Harris has of conserving not only its wildlife and landscape but also its people.

## BCCI

When the Bank of Credit and Commerce International (BCCI) crashed in July 1991, shredding the reputation of Comhairle nan Eilean Siar in the process, my family and I were in a tent in Brittany. I read in a copy of *The Guardian* that was already out of date that the local authority had suffered the largest loss in the UK, some £24 million. I couldn't remember what the council's total budget was, but this was clearly an enormous body blow. When I returned from holiday I had to catch up on what was the biggest story in my patch for a very long time.

I learned that it had been a normal, quiet July day in Stornoway. The atmosphere in the council headquarters was relaxed. Some officials had gone off on holiday. Others were winding down towards theirs. Councillors had returned to their wards to prepare for the annual influx of exiles at the Glasgow Fair. It was a good time of year. But behind the closed doors of the finance department, panic was breaking out. Explosive news had arrived that would ripple out of the building and across the whole region. BCCI had closed the doors of its branches around the world.

The council, and all connected to it, quickly became the subject of international ridicule. The risible mistake of putting all, or most of, one's eggs in one basket had been made in spectacular style. There were images of the council in chaos flashing across TV screens. The chief executive had returned, albeit at a fairly leisurely pace, from a holiday he had begun three days earlier. As he talked to reporters through his car window, he seemed unsure whether he would be resuming his holiday or not. The council convener appeared reluctant to take control. Officials were shying away from cameras or diving into their cars and speeding off as though having something to hide. Councillors tried to make the right noises, but nobody really knew what these noises should sound like. The media very quickly became the enemy. The overall impression was one of utter incompetence, reinforcing prejudices, or at least caricatures, many held regarding Hebrideans.

There were predictions that the poll tax would increase by £1,000, that the suicide rate would rise. The Presbyterian churches on Lewis and Harris held a special prayer day. It was called a 'day of humiliation'. This seemed to amuse greatly some elsewhere in the land who would never normally have considered laughing at other minorities' ways. The convener resigned and two senior officials were sacked, though one was reinstated only to retire early. The Commission for Local Authority Accounts recommended that the director of finance and his deputy be surcharged for their role, stating that they had been negligent and were involved in actions of borrowing and lending on money to BCCI which were contrary to law. The commission found that £5 million had been borrowed from Scottish Widows and on-lent to BCCI, and the sum of £11.5 million was borrowed in advance of need and deposited with BCCI. A further £6.6 million was placed on deposit with BCCI, the commission said, 'without any regard to any requirements concerning limitation to be placed on sums lent to any single institution or the need to ensure that the institution met any predetermined ranking criteria'. Not only were all the council's eggs put in one basket, it was borrowing others' eggs as well.

The council had been specifically warned against borrowing to on-lend money in 1988, but the BCCI returns looked so attractive. From the Butt of Lewis to Vatersay, islanders shook their heads in confusion and utter disbelief. 'A Hebridean farce worthy of Compton Mackenzie,' one councillor described it. For all that, the then Secretary of State Ian Lang decided against any surcharge. Perhaps that wasn't so surprising. There was incompetence elsewhere in the BCCI debacle. Serious questions had been raised internationally about the bank's activities, and there were revelations about it laundering drug money. These things were known, yet BCCI still appeared on the Bank of England's list of approved banks a matter of days before the crash.

Ten years after the crisis, the island archipelago had not sunk into the sea, but had made a remarkable recovery. There were still profound economic problems, but not because of BCCI. There were some encouraging indicators and very visible European-assisted signs of progress: a £6.4-million bridge between the islands of Harris and Scalpay; a new £4.5-million ferry service across the Sound of Harris; a £7-million causeway to the island of Berneray, and one costing £9.4 million to Eriskay. The financial recovery of the council was aided in the first place by special consent to borrow £24 million to be repaid over 30 years. Then the Western Isles were included for the first time, along with Orkney and Shetland, in the Special Islands Needs Allowance scheme. The council also recovered three dividends totalling 60 per cent of the original £24 million. This has been repaid to the Scottish Office to cover the cost of the original loan, which was paid off thereafter.

The Rev. Donald Macaulay, the Church of Scotland minister who was the council convener at the time of the BCCI crash, died in 2006. Some years earlier I asked him to look back over the events and share his thoughts. He said: 'The loss of the money at the time was not as big a blow as the reputation the council got for losing it. It discouraged councillors. I think out of fear they started writing to the press in praise of themselves and condemning others. It created a difficult situation, a difficult atmosphere within and without the council. I resigned in sympathy with the people of the Western Isles. Somebody had to stand down. I retired as a minister about the same time, but I am still preaching every Sunday. There are so many vacant churches here.'

The Western Isles Council was not alone. Ross and Cromarty District Council lost £1.8 million and there were estimated to be 250,000 creditors of the bank worldwide.

Throughout the country, councillors began to ask questions of their officials as it emerged that such borrowing and lending deals were a fact of everyday council life, from which most elected members had somehow been spared hitherto. However, it was and remains the Western Isles that comes to mind for most when BCCI is mentioned.

# 13

# Sir Humphrey in the Hebrides

THERE WAS DISAPPOINTMENT in the Highlands and Islands when, in 2007, the Scottish government turned its back on the policy of relocating public sector jobs pursued by the previous Labour/Liberal Democrat administration. That's not to make a party-political point, but to emphasise that there had been some genuine excitement in the remoter parts about job dispersal and what it might mean for them. There were doubts in the media that anything of note would ever actually happen, but it did. The policy most controversially saw the headquarters of Scottish Natural Heritage (SNH) move from Edinburgh to Inverness in 2006. Announced in 2003, it cost around £22 million. Although there were 260 SNH posts in Edinburgh, only 55 staff relocated to Inverness, with 109 opting for redundancy instead. The balance was filled through local recruitment, which was exactly the dividend sought in the Highlands. There was huge opposition to the move in Edinburgh, however, which was perfectly understandable. Most of the staff had built a life in the Scottish capital, only to be told they would be moving their families 160 miles north. The offer of a £10,000 inducement to move plus another £10,000 if they stayed in Inverness for more than two years was not enough for most to be persuaded. Staff who chose to stay in Edinburgh were to receive a civil service redundancy payment of around £40,000.

There was also known to be significant opposition amongst senior civil servants in Edinburgh, who argued in the strongest terms against the relocation in internal official reports. In the end ministers had to sign off the move, documenting an acknowledgement it was contrary to their officials' clear advice. Jack McConnell, the First Minister, had been persuaded of the need to continue to demonstrate his commitment to the dispersal of public jobs, and he endorsed the Inverness decision. Jack was of course himself an islander from Arran (I had known him from his days in the National Union of Students Scotland). It was also understood that Rachel McEwen, one of his political advisers and herself a Highlander, had been influential.

The first call for SNH to be relocated to the Highlands and Islands had been made some years earlier by Jim Hunter while he was Chairman of Skye and Lochalsh Enterprise. He initially proposed that the agency be based in Aviemore, not Inverness, but others thought Inverness would be a hard enough sell. He and Highlands and Islands Enterprise (HIE) Chair Sir Robert (Bob) Cowan, and the then Highland Council Deputy Vice Convener Peter Peacock tried to persuade SNH to locate its science function to the Highlands as part of what they saw as a start of the University of the Highlands and Islands. A dinner in Edinburgh to discuss this was a tense affair by all accounts.

Hunter was to be appointed chairman of HIE, and that body, along with Highland Council, launched a campaign in 2002 to persuade the ministers that SNH's headquarters should be closer to the natural environment, whose protection it was the agency's statutory duty to ensure. Peter Peacock, the then Deputy Minister for Finance and Local Government, was crucial to strengthening ministerial resolve in the face of much public criticism over the SNH relocation. He had been in local government in the Highlands for 17 years, ending as convener of the Highland Council before becoming a Labour MSP and Deputy Minister for Children and Education in 1999. He had been close to Hunter, despite their party-political differences (the historian being an SNP supporter) and to Dr Michael Foxley, a Scottish Liberal who was one of the most passionate advocates for radical land reform. Foxley and Peacock, along with the latter's successor as Highland Council convener, Achiltibuie-based councillor David Green, had proven themselves able campaigners in the Highland interest. Amongst their successes had been preventing the agency Nirex from establishing a nuclear waste dump at Dounreay and saving the railway sleeper services from London to Inverness and Fort William.

SNH did in the end move to a new purpose-built headquarters on the north-western periphery of Inverness. Appropriately enough it was located where the 79-mile Great Glen Way long-distance walking route to/from Fort William emerges from the nearby woodland. It is the start or finish for thousands of walkers who want to enjoy the landscape and natural environment of the Highlands. The relocation of SNH would seem now to be viewed as something of a success, with the earlier controversy rarely mentioned.

The location in Gourock of the headquarters of the publicly owned ferry company Caledonian MacBrayne was often the subject of debate. Western Isles councillors frequently argued that Stornoway should be its base or that CalMac's operation should be split between those routes on the Clyde and those going to the Hebrides. There have also been repeated claims that Oban would be an ideal base, given that it is the hub for more routes than any other port, with direct links to Islay, Colonsay, Mull, Lismore, Coll, Tiree, Barra and South Uist. It is also at the centre of the CalMac network, while Gourock is at its southern periphery and Stornoway at its northern end. Oban always made sense to me, but the argument never found favour in Edinburgh and CalMac's HQ remains on the Clyde looking out over the Tail of the Bank.

There were, however, other significant relocations of public sector activity. Highlands and Islands Enterprise were early trendsetters, sending 20 jobs across the Minch from Inverness to Benbecula to provide an administrative back-up for the entire HIE network. And in 2002 it was announced that up to 100 civil service jobs would be created in Stornoway, under the reorganisation of the Department of Work and Pensions (DWP).

But arguably the most dramatic, if not the biggest, relocation was in 2005. Eight Edinburgh-based posts administering the Crofters Building Grants and Loans Scheme (CBGLS) in the Scottish Executive's Rural Development Department were moved all the way to Tiree. In the 19th century some 5,000 people had lived on the island, but only about 14 per cent of that total remained in the early 21st century. Five of the jobs were filled by islanders and the remainder by those who had worked in Edinburgh. For decades, civil servants processing applications for the CBGLS (revamped as the Croft House Grant Scheme without the loans element) had worked in the capital, without a cheviot or blackface in sight. But after the move they just needed to lift their heads to see cattle and sheep on the machair grazings above the beach at Crossapol.

I visited Tiree in 2005 and met Morven MacInnes, at 16 the youngest recruit, and she told me: 'Last year I had been thinking of trying to go to Canada. We have relatives over there. Then I was going to go to agricultural college. But I finally realised I wanted to stay on Tiree for a few years yet. I like working on the croft and my two brothers are still here. I think my parents are quite happy.' Her grandmother, Mabel MacArthur, certainly was. She had just stood down after 11 years as chair of the community council and said: 'For young people like Morven to be getting a permanent job with a career structure on Tiree at the age of 16 is really great.' Those officials who had relocated from Edinburgh were also enthusiastic. Jackey Forbes, the office manager, had joined the civil service from school in Dalkeith 20 years earlier. Before serving in the Pensions Agency in Galashiels for three years she worked in Edinburgh in health, central services, Historic Scotland and alcohol policy. She said:

> The Tiree jobs had been circulated internally [in the Scottish civil service] before Christmas. I was interested because you never really get a chance to take something from new and develop it [in the civil service]. If you move office, everything is already set up. The procedures are there. So there is the professional challenge, and of course there was a chance to live in a completely different part of the country. I had been to Mull and to Orkney but I had never been to Tiree. In the end I had a week and a half to make up my mind. I have only been here 10 days, but I really like it – even in the rain. Everybody I have met has been really friendly and helpful. They were taking deliveries for us; they have been phoning offering to help. I haven't come across any negative reaction at all.

Her colleague Margo Forbes had previously been commuting three hours daily between Alyth in Perthshire and Victoria Quay, Edinburgh. She said: 'Now I am five minutes away from my desk and everybody I pass waves to me.' But her appointment, a promotion to managerial level, was only due to last for two years, after which she would return to Edinburgh. Borderer Mark Elsdon, 27, however, insisted he was on Tiree 'for the long haul'. The Stirling University graduate had worked for the Pensions Agency. He was confident that photography and the boat he had promised himself would sustain him, and was relishing the change.

## All change

There was to be a dramatic change of direction following the election of the SNP's minority administration in 2007 and the renaming of the Scottish Executive as the Scottish Government. John Swinney, the Cabinet Secretary for Finance and Sustainable Growth (a man I liked the few times I met him), explained the new thinking to a meeting of the Finance Committee on 29 January 2008, which is worth quoting in some length:

> The previous Administration's policy came under significant scrutiny from a range of sources – most recently from the Auditor General for Scotland, who completed a report in September 2006, and subsequently from the Finance Committee and the Audit Committee. I have studied those reports in depth and their conclusions have influenced the Government's thinking about the issue. The analysis that has been conducted suggests that the previous Administration's policy had not demonstrably achieved its intended aims of dispersal, assisting areas that are in socioeconomic need and providing cost-effective delivery solutions. Much money was spent on moving organisations, business continuity experienced a significant cost and individuals whose posts were relocated experienced disruption. In return, there was little evidence of benefit for the spend that was incurred: savings were achieved in few instances, and demonstrable benefits to communities were limited, with the exception of the small unit initiative moves.
>
> In view of those findings and our commitment to achieve efficiencies and the best use of public funds, the Administration's relocation policy will be driven forward principally by strategic estate management in the Government. The Government will implement the approach that I have set out through an estate management policy, which will be a strategic measure to ensure that the Government achieves not only the best and most efficient use of space but efficiencies in our capital and revenue spend on accommodation. It will be guided by the findings of the recent review of asset management, which I have published, and it will apply to the core Scottish Government, its non-ministerial departments, agencies and non-departmental public bodies.
>
> The Scottish Government's facilities and estates services will have a strategic overview of all accommodation moves

and commitments and will work with individual organisations to assess their needs and to identify suitable accommodation. Priority will be given to the reuse of suitable Government estate and to identifying cost-effective delivery solutions. As I said, the Government believes that the small unit initiative has delivered significant benefits and it will take forward that strand of the previous relocation policy, in recognition of the greater proportion of benefits that it achieved by delivering high-quality jobs to remote and rural areas in which even a small number of posts bring demonstrable benefits to the community . . .

I do not propose to reopen relocation decisions that the previous Administration took, unless concerns are felt about the business cases that were involved. Through the steps that we are taking on the policy, which are intended to save money, we will free up resources to devote to tested policies that will bring demonstrable benefits to communities throughout Scotland and will contribute directly to realising the Government's objectives.

It meant that while the Scottish government would not reverse any of the relocations unless there was no alternative, and while small-scale relocation of jobs might still be considered, there would be no more of the scale of SNH or of the boldness of Tiree. Henceforth the relocation of public sector jobs would be defined by what publicly owned facilities were available. Mr Swinney was only doing his job in wanting to ensure that public money was being spent wisely. It did not appear, however, that the relocations had been given very long to prove themselves. SNH had only moved into their new headquarters building about 18 months before the committee meeting, and in the case of Tiree it was just a year. The criteria against which they were to be measured should have been different to those for other public projects. The policy was about trying to get more of Scotland involved in the workings of government and the wider public sector, with the benefits of white-collar salaries being spread more widely across the country. It was about population retention in some areas. It was also about showing to remote and fragile communities that government was working for them, that they were involved in the national life of Scotland.

The banking crisis of 2008 was still a while away when Mr Swinney gave his evidence to the Finance Committee, with the critical collapse of the investment bank Lehman Brothers not happening till the middle of September. However, it had become very clear that all was not well with the world economy given the crisis in the US subprime mortgage market in the previous year. The implications of lending money to people who would struggle ever to repay their borrowings had become apparent. Government retrenchment quickly followed. Many in the Highlands, south-west Scotland and the Borders still hope the policy of relocating public sector functions might be reconsidered some time in the future. It could still help reshape a new Scotland.

Back in Tiree, former councillor Ian Gillies, who represented the island for 14 years on Argyll and Bute Council and is now secretary of its community council, reflected earlier in 2018 on the arrival of the civil service on the island:

> The relocation has had a tremendous impact on the island. I think we currently have seven or eight civil service jobs; most are occupied by local residents. They have proper standards and conditions, proper pay scales, job security and pension rights. Apart from local authority jobs, they were the first to be created on the island by an outside agency, and it has been terrific, mostly for local young people. It gave many of them a career start. Morven MacInnes, for example, now has a good job with SNH in Oban, but others followed. Most of those who came from the mainland, however, didn't really manage to build a life here for long, and there were reasons for that. Not least that about 40 per cent of houses here are holiday homes, so it was difficult for anyone moving in. The relocation, however, gave the community an important psychological boost to its self-esteem. People felt valued by the government. They keep the relocation under review, but we certainly don't want it to change.

Those who supported wider relocation of public sector jobs have been heartened by the decision of Roseanna Cunningham, Cabinet Secretary for Environment, Climate Change and Land Reform, in 2017 to base the new Scottish Land Commission in Inverness and not in the Central Belt as her officials are understood to have advised.

# 14

# For Whom the Bridge Tolled

IT WAS A protest that led to more than 100 people being convicted of refusing to pay to use the Skye Bridge, some ending up in jail, and it lasted nearly 10 years until the controversial tolls were abolished. It led to this writer giving evidence in court, being rather browbeaten by a procurator fiscal and a sheriff, and ending up being branded a liar by the Criminal Cases Review Commission.

Retired trade unionist Andy Anderson was in Porterfield Prison in Inverness for 11 nights for refusing to attend his court hearing in 1997. In his book *The Skye Bridge Story* (Argyll Publishing, 2008) he makes clear that he left an initially reluctant sheriff no choice but to keep him in custody. Six months earlier tempers were running high on Skye when renowned Gaelic singer Arthur Cormack and local councillor Drew Millar, both popular figures, were arrested and held again for non-appearance, although this seemed to be due to some administrative confusion.

*The Herald* became closely associated with the campaign led by Skye and Kyle Against Tolls (SKAT). It led to some criticism of my coverage in the paper, not least because of my association with the highly controversial figure of Robbie the Pict, a veteran constitutional campaigner who frequently appeared in court challenging the author-ities. But my editors backed my judgement, even though they must have grown weary of the story as it bounced back and forward from events on the bridge to Dingwall Sheriff Court and on occasion down to the High Court and the Court of Session in Edinburgh. Its focus was the New Roads and Streetworks Act 1991, the rather urban-sounding legislation which underpinned the toll regime on the bridge. It created the crime of refusing to pay the toll 'without reasonable excuse'. The campaigners were to argue that nobody should have to pay the toll until those collecting it demonstrated they were entitled in law to stop drivers crossing the bridge, a public highway, unless they paid it. This was their reasonable excuse. The campaign began at midnight 16/17 October 1995, the day the bridge opened and when the first tolls were charged and refused. In December 2004 tolls were finally abolished by the then Scottish Executive when the contract was bought out for £27 million from Skye Bridge Ltd (SBL), the consortium headed by Bank of America.

In the end the bridge cost both those paying the tolls, and the general taxpayer, well over £70 million, which was estimated to be 10 times more than it might have cost had the Tory-controlled Scottish Office not pushed for its creation in 1989 but instead waited until European funding was on hand to pay 50 per cent of the cost. The Scottish Office, however, had been anxious to launch the first Caledonian private finance initiative (PFI) and so the bridge was built and opened on 16 October 1995.

More than 500 arrests were made and 130 people were convicted of refusing to pay the tolls on the Skye Bridge. They were fined, but as far as is known few if any ever paid up. A year or so ago I asked the Crown Office how many of those who had failed to pay their fines had been taken to task. After doing some research an official came back to me to say that of the 130 prosecutions only five were on Crown Office records and there was no information on non-payment of fines.

The injustice felt by so many islanders had been growing for years before SKAT was formed because of work by other campaigners few now remember – in particular the Skye Bridge Appeal Group (SBAG), styled by some with an interest in Russian revolutionary history as the more moderate Mensheviks to the SKAT Bolsheviks. It had been formed in 1992 to represent all the different strands of opposition, from resident otters to the design of the bridge and, of course, the tolls. Until the bridge opened and SKAT marched into our headlines, SBAG was the voice of dissent. Without it, it is highly unlikely there would have been a SKAT.

Crucially, SBAG articulated the sense that a bridge paid for by a high-toll regime was offending against the very idea of progress as had been understood hitherto in Scotland. While other communities enjoyed the benefits of transport improvements, the people of Skye would be paying ferry fares to drive across a tiny piece of new road.

Of all the ferries I have taken over the last three decades, the image of one journey in particular remains with me – the last run of the Skye ferry from Kyle of Lochalsh to Kyleakin the day the bridge opened. People came from all over the island to be on that short trip. But they were strangely quiet. Their island would never be the same again. It was to be physically joined to the UK trunk-road network for the first time, which most warmly welcomed. But the sense of injustice was almost palpable. I don't agree with Lord Forsyth of Drumlean's view that this was just about some islanders having frequently crossed on the ferry without paying.

Since the 1970s both Labour and Tory governments built bridges to replace ferries or long road journeys to tackle remoteness in the Highlands: Ballachulish was the first to open in 1975; then the Cromarty Firth crossing four years later; Kessock at Inverness in 1982, Kylesku in north-west Sutherland in 1984; Dornoch on the other side of the county in 1991. All were free to use by drivers, who also had an option to take another, albeit less convenient, route.

During the winter months the only alternative to the ferry, then bridge, for the drivers of Skye to get to the mainland was to take a ferry to North Uist or Harris then drive to either Lochboisdale in South Uist or Stornoway in Lewis and take another ferry respectively to Oban or Ullapool. In the summer they could go by the Kylerhea to Glenelg ferry, a difficult and time-consuming journey, or Armadale to Mallaig. The Scottish Office had delayed the much-needed replacement of the Kyle car ferries which were clearly inadequate until the Highland Regional Council backed a privately financed bridge. This to me was an unacceptable use of power to further a political agenda for which there was scant support in Scotland. The people of Skye were effectively to be guinea pigs in an economic experiment, setting them apart from the rest of the country.

What SBAG successfully highlighted was that just as the final approval for the bridge was being given by the Tory government as the first PFI in Scotland, politicians were claiming success for winning Objective One status for European funding. It meant of course that the area was one of the poorest in Europe, which was a rather unusual boast, but it also meant £260 million of European money would be invested in the Highlands and Islands in the six years to 1999. It was estimated that well under £10 million of that would have built a publicly funded, toll-free bridge to Skye. But instead the people of one of the poorest areas in Europe were to pay the highest tolls in Europe, over £5 each time they crossed the bridge during the summer and a pound less during the winter. Had it been one pound or two, perhaps few would have objected.

It was SBAG members who were raising these issues over and over again, who monitored every move the government and the developers were making, who informed the public inquiry into the bridge and who spoke for the people of Skye. None more so than the late Kathleen MacRae. An occupational therapist by profession, she had been a life-long Liberal. She married an Edinburgh-based Skyeman, Ian MacRae, part of the Gaelic diaspora, whose family owned a hotel in the capital. She and Ian retired to his home territory at Breakish near Broadford. Once there Kathleen started to take an interest in local affairs and campaigned against pay-beds in the MacKinnon Memorial Hospital in Broadford and against a road that would have cut across local crofts.

Then came the bridge and SBAG, which all but consumed her life. SBAG had some influential supporters, with official patrons such as MPs Charles Kennedy, Brian Wilson, Calum MacDonald and Gaelic rock band Runrig. But none were in Kyleakin's old school on a December night in 1998. Most of the bridge campaigners were at a Scottish parliamentary election hustings in Portree. Just six people turned up for the final meeting of SBAG. Bob Danskin, who tried so hard to found the Skye Boat Company to run a ferry challenging the bridge's monopoly, was in the chair. He was flanked by Kathleen MacRae and Pam Noble, treasurer and secretary respectively. Kathy Reid was there, as were Clodagh MacKenzie and Anne Danskin. There was an air of unreality and anticlimax. They got through their agenda fairly quickly, including the memorials planned for two group members, Flo Reid and Peter Findlay, who had died since the group had been founded six years earlier 100 yards up the road in a packed village hall with all determined to fight a high-toll bridge. Now after all the letter writing, lobbying and campaigning, SBAG was calling it a day amidst a feeling of deep frustration. Just six months earlier there had been confirmation that the new Labour government was to write off at least £62 million of debts accrued by the Humber toll bridge which linked the Lincolnshire coast with Hull, the parliamentary constituency of Deputy Prime Minister John Prescott (Hull East).

That night after SBAG closed its final meeting Kathleen MacRae told *The Herald*:

> There was little point in carrying on. SKAT took the campaign on to the next stage. We have collated a great deal of information about the project over the years and it will be available to anyone who is interested. I feel very sad about it all. We had great hopes that a new [Labour] government would provide the breakthrough as far as the tolls were concerned. We did get the reductions for regular users, but you have to buy books of 20 tickets. This is of little help to the many people, particularly the elderly, who might only leave the island once or twice a year. Our biggest disappointment in the new government, however, was not that ministers believe themselves powerless to change a commercial contract, but how quickly they began to adopt the rhetoric of the Tories promoting the bridge – a bridge supposed to have been privately financed but which had millions of pounds of public money. According to the National Audit Office and the Public Accounts Committee calculations, the toll and tax payer will end up paying more than £50 million.

One of SBAG's last acts had been to donate £150 to help Robbie the Pict pursue his attempt to win an interdict in the Court of Session. Mrs MacRae explained: 'This isn't even about the tolls any more. It is about justice. From the very start this project was prosecuted at a lunatic pace and we have always been convinced that mistakes were made. But the feeling is that Scottish Office is above the law. If Robbie can show otherwise it would help restore a little faith in our institutions.'

Brian Wilson wrote a front-page editorial in the *West Highland Free Press* the week the bridge opened. He concluded: 'The people most affected should have been allowed to make the mature choice – a high-toll bridge now or a free bridge later when public finances allowed. They were denied that choice with the result that this week's events have now come to pass. But let nobody doubt that the battle for now is only beginning.'

Brian was to become critical of the SKAT campaigners and they of him, but his conclusion was correct. Two Skye councillors were among those charged with refusing to pay the tolls, less than 24 hours after Michael Forsyth, the then Secretary of State, had opened the bridge. Some 30 vehicles and around 100 people had gathered in Kyleakin shortly after midnight when the first day's free crossing concession ended. The Skye Bridge campaign had begun. People from every walk of life in Skye and Lochalsh had joined SKAT: doctors, teachers, businessmen, musicians, crofters, councillors. The local Lib Dem MSP, John Farquhar Munro, supported the campaign but did not refuse to pay the tolls because of his position as a JP. However, his wife Celia frequently refused to pay while driving his car. Some protesters travelled specifically in order to refuse to pay the bridge tolls, including Keith Brown, at the time of writing the Scottish government's Cabinet Secretary for the Economy, Jobs and Fair Work. The former general secretary of the STUC, the late Bill Speirs, also joined SKAT demonstrations against the tolls.

The campaigners were eventually to stand trial not in Portree, Skye's main settlement, but in Dingwall, 100 miles away. There were appeals for the newly refurbished Portree Sheriff Court to be used, but this was refused. The Crown's argument for hearing cases at Dingwall, the county town of the old Ross-shire, rather than Portree, which had been in Inverness-shire as was the whole of Skye, was that the alleged offences had taken place on the mainland side of the bridge, at Kyle of Lochalsh, which was in Ross-shire. The campaigners made their first of many court appearances in Dingwall in January 1996, arriving with a piper at their head and flags and placards above them.

At the time, Dingwall was the bailiwick of Sheriff James Fraser. It was on his shoulders and those of the resident procurator fiscal, David Hingston, that the bulk of the Skye Bridge legal work largely fell. It was quite a load: about 500 prosecutions started; almost 130 completed; all peppered by appeals to relevancy and competency to the High Court, not to mention appeals against conviction. Until the summer of 1997, when there was a change in prosecution policy, the Skye Bridge campaigners were effectively clogging up the judicial system in the north. It was clear from the outset that the Crown Office did not appreciate the pressure that was being put on the court in Dingwall. Neither did Sheriff Fraser nor Mr Hingston, who were hearing or prosecuting what was, in essence, the same case over and over again. Without any thought of a campaign of direct action, the government had made it a criminal offence not to pay the tolls without reasonable excuse, so all those who refused to pay had to be tried. The sheer volume of casework became ludicrous, but for more than a year there was no relief. Although other sheriffs did some of the work, it was Sheriff Fraser who became most closely associated with it in the public mind.

His reputation had gone before him. He was possessed of a notoriously short temper and would brook no mischief in his court, particularly from visiting lawyers from the south who might in any way appear to patronise. Solicitors, advocates or QCs heading up from Edinburgh were counselled by fellow professionals who had appeared in Fraser's court and sometimes felt they were not always given a chance to develop their defence. For all his awesome reputation, Sheriff Fraser could display considerable humanity, going to some lengths to give some poor wrongdoer another chance to stay out of prison. A highly intelligent man, he could also display considerable humour. What confused most, however, was his mercurial temperment.

Despite it all, Sheriff Fraser very nearly established himself as a Skye hero. On 10 June 1997 he staggered most by warning that the Skye Bridge legislation could be flawed. He upheld a legal challenge made on behalf of two of the hundreds of motorists who had refused to pay the toll and had argued that the law did not say whether the driver, passenger or owner of a vehicle should pay. Mr Hingston had argued that the tolls applied to all occupiers of tolled traffic. However, Sheriff Fraser stated: 'In my view the defence argument is sound. Legislation, and more particularly and more strictly when the provisions are penal, should say what it means and mean what it says. I go so far with the Crown argument. I agree that the approach made and the analysis indicates that the most probable implication to be taken is that all persons who are occupiers of tolled traffic are liable to pay the toll. Most probable, however, is not good enough. Legislation must be clear and its provisions must be certain. To read in or imply provisions such as are set out above makes this legislation less than certain, and, at best, no more than likely.'

The Crown announced immediately it planned to appeal. There was considerable speculation over what would happen in the event of the appeal failing. The new Labour-run Scottish Office would be put in an extremely embarrassing position over the controversy it inherited from the Tories. However, the Crown's appeal was heard in Edinburgh remarkably quickly, and three appeal court judges overturned Sheriff Fraser's ruling. The tolls would stay in place and prosecutions would continue.

As the hearings and trials progressed the defence of reasonable excuse was developed. The Scottish Office had always insisted that written permission had been given to collect the toll. In November 1997, in response to the campaigners' legal arguments, the Crown submitted a memorandum to Dingwall Sheriff Court as evidence of the toll collectors' authority. This was known as Crown Production 16. Robbie the Pict had recognised some of the pages as being from the contractual agreement documents. These were supposed to be confidential but he had managed to secure copies. *The Herald* subsequently tracked down the solicitor who was the author of the memorandum, to Greenock if memory serves. He was clear the pages in the document had nothing whatsoever to do with the right to collect tolls. I was to be called to give evidence on this matter and was given a rather tough time by Sheriff Fraser and a procurator fiscal who was standing in for Mr Hingston. The former concluded by saying: 'The only things I have understood of your evidence, Mr Ross, are your name and your address.' The fiscal meanwhile demanded a yes or no answer as to whether I had ever seen the original contract documents, and was not persuaded by the proposition that not every question could be answered in a binary manner. I had seen documents but could not swear whether they were original or copies, but had assumed the latter.

Lord Eassie was to rule in the Court of Session in March 1999 that Crown Production 16 did not give the right to collect tolls. He refused, however, Robbie the Pict's application for interdict to prevent Miller Civil Engineering from collecting the bridge tolls for the Skye Bridge Company. But in his ruling Lord Eassie found that the Secretary of State had given his written permission, but only in the pleadings lodged in response to Robbie's interdict attempt. These were lodged on April 1998, but tolls had been demanded since October 17 1995. Lord Eassie said of Crown Production 16: 'The purposes of the Memorandum were completely unrelated to the particular issue of eliciting the Secretary of State's consent to the engagement of a sub-contractor for the operation of the crossing. Accordingly . . . I have come to the view that the execution of the Memorandum does not constitute an expression of consent in writing for the purposes of Clause 1.2.3 of the Concession Agreement.'

But the state of another document was to form the basis of a much more serious challenge to the legitimacy of the tolling regime which hasn't been resolved to this day. The relevant legislation had given the Secretary of State the legal right to stop traffic and demand a toll before allowing it to proceed across the bridge. It was never imagined that any Secretary of State would be standing in the toll booth, so the rights had to be legally assigned to another party, Skye Bridge Ltd, the operator of the bridge. The official transfer of these rights had to be publicised in an Assignation Statement saying exactly to whom these rights would be assigned. The campaigners sought out this document, but were only given seven pages of typewritten sentences which carried neither a date nor a signature. They couldn't believe this could represent the official document. Robbie the Pict pursued this, and I can still remember the excitement in his voice when he phoned up to say he had just had these seven pages certified as the true and final document. In 1999 he presented this evidence to an appeal court under Lord Sutherland, who mentioned in his findings that the Assignation Statement was undated and unsigned, but made no further comment.

At the request of campaigners, Robert Black, Professor of Scots Law at Edinburgh University, studied the documentation and the legal arguments pursued by the protesters since the bridge's opening in October 1995 and their non-payment campaign began. Professor Black said of the seven pages: 'This is the most informal official document I have ever seen . . . This is not a probative document; it isn't even an authenticated document.' As a result, the people who had been collecting the tolls since 1995 did not appear to have proper authority and could be committing a criminal offence specifically created by the same legislation. Black studied the terms of the appeal court ruling from Lord Sutherland in which he acknowledged the absence of signature or date but made no further comment on it. Professor Black said this meant 'the court has not decided. I find this somewhat surprising as it is crucial to the whole scheme.'

Charles Kennedy, the Ross, Skye and Inverness West MP, wrote to the Lord Advocate Colin Boyd after Professor Black's review, but the reply he received simply referred him to Lord Sutherland's ruling. Mr Kennedy wrote back, pointing out that in Professor Black's view, Lord Sutherland had not ruled on the matter. He eventually received a reply in 2000 from the Lord Advocate. He quoted Lord Sutherland's ruling at length, and concluded: 'In these circumstances, while it is correct to say that the statement is not signed or dated, the High Court of Justiciary has taken the view that the Assignation Statement was made in accordance with statute and is valid. Consequently whether or not it is "a probative document" is not a necessary consideration.' Mr Kennedy was bemused: 'How can a flawed legal document be the basis for the widespread criminal prosecution of my constituents? The Assignation Statement transferred power from a government minister to a private company and gave it permission to charge large tolls; it must have a sound basis in law. I believe that this answer from the Lord Advocate sets a dangerous legal precedent and ignores the very real concerns of my constituents, some of whom have criminal records as a result of this suspect document. I will continue to press for a satisfactory answer to this; all those who use the Skye Bridge deserve nothing less.'

Five years later, Freedom of Information (FOI) requests I had submitted revealed that the Crown Office itself had serious concerns about the Assignation Statement. These FOI requests related to the correspondence between the Crown Office and the procurator fiscal in Dingwall following the opening of the bridge. On 6 November 1995 the Crown Office wrote to the procurator fiscal underlining how crucial the Assignation Statement would be in the prosecution of the SKAT campaigners, saying, 'It will certainly be necessary to establish the right of the Skye Bridge Ltd to collect the toll presumably as the Secretary of State's assignee.' However, in a subsequent letter dated 27 November the Crown Office conceded: 'The assignation statement does not appear to be a final document – it does not even state the date of the toll order.' These last words suggested official incredulity of the authorities that prosecutions were about to commence on such ill-prepared ground, when somebody could end up losing their liberty if they defied the court. Professor Black studied the correspondence and opined: 'I've had a look at the letters of November 6 and 27. The latter in particular seems to embody a clear recognition that the Assignation Statement is merely an uncompleted draft. And I have to say that I've never understood how any judge could think otherwise. So much for the accused having the benefit of any doubt.'

There was also doubt as to who exactly owned the company that was collecting the tolls. In January 1998 *The Herald*, following up work the campaigners had undertaken, revealed that the Scottish Office had never told the National Audit Office that the ownership of shares in Skye Bridge Ltd had changed from that published by the government in November 1991. At that time it was required by law to state which parties had more than 10 per cent of the shares. These were: Miller Civil Engineering, Dywidag Systems and Bank of America. This was also the evidence given by the Scottish Office to the Skye Bridge Public Inquiry which sat in Kyle of Lochalsh from 28 January to 7 February 1992. Companies House records confirmed that on 23 January 1992 the respective shareholding was: Miller Civil Engineering Ltd 404, Dywidag Systems (UK) Ltd 404 and Bank of America International Finance Corporation 189.

On that same day, an extraordinary general meeting of Skye Bridge Ltd was held at the bank's London headquarters when a special resolution was passed to the effect that Miller would have 405 shares which would be re-designated A shares, Dywidag's now 405 shares would be Ordinary shares and the Bank of America's now 190 shares would be re-designated C shares. According to a Scottish Office spokesman, something else happened that day: 'The shareholders of Skye Bridge Ltd granted, on January 23 1992, security over their shares in the company in favour of Bank of America International Ltd as trustee for the secured creditors. This is merely a security arrangement which in no way affects the beneficial ownership of the company. Moreover, the arrangements were concluded under terms which retained for the beneficial shareholders the power to direct the trustee in respect of the exercise of substantive rights under the shares.'

On 17 June 1995, however, the shareholding changed dramatically with Bank of America International Ltd being registered as holding 997 shares and Bank America Nominees Ltd holding three. It was understood that the Scottish Office viewed this arrangement effectively as a mortgage, whereby Bank of America would hold the shares in the company until such time as Miller and Dywidag fulfilled certain obligations. The difference, however, was that a lender does not take over ownership of a house while the mortgage is being paid off. It was also unclear why this agreement on 23 January 1992 did not reach Companies House until June 1995, the first record of the change in shareholding. A Skye Bridge Ltd spokeswoman would only say that all the relevant information was in the public domain.

A leading expert on business law, who wished to remain anonymous, advised *The Herald*: 'There is no doubt from these figures that Skye Bridge Ltd is owned by the Bank of America. If the bank is holding shares in trust, the obvious place to put them would be in Bank America Nominees Ltd, which would suggest that three shares are being held in trust. I don't understand how they can still talk about joint equity holders.' This view was supported by others. It was controversial because in 1998 Bank of America was being sued in the US for alleged misuse of public funds. The action was led by California's attorney general, who accused the bank of corruption in its role as bond trustee for the state by misappropriating funds, overcharging for services and destroying evidence of its misdeeds. Dozens of local government and public bodies joined the suit, which created potential liability for the bank of a reported $3 billion. Later in 1998 Bank of America agreed to pay $187 million to settle the case. The Skye Bridge campaigners argued that having this bank 'own' a toll bridge on a public highway in Scotland was symbolic of government failures to protect the public interest in the whole project.

In March 2003 the then First Minister Jack McConnell dropped a clear hint that the Scottish Executive was preparing to tackle the issue of the Skye Bridge tolls if Labour and the Liberal Democrats were returned to power in the election that year. However, he stopped short of a pledge to abolish the tolls. The SNP and the Lib Dems had long called for the abolition of the bridge tolls, but Labour had argued that it had done as much as it could by freezing them at the 1999 levels of £5.70 for each single car journey during the summer, which was costing the executive more than £600,000 a year. At a press conference, Mr McConnell said of the Skye Bridge tolls: 'That may be one of the issues that we have some discussions about after the election.' Jim Wallace, the Liberal Democrat leader, said at the same meeting: 'It would be on our shopping list in any coalition negotiations as it was before.'

A new coalition agreement was signed after the election in May 2003 which gave Labour and the Liberal Democrats 67 of the 129 newly elected MSPs, the necessary majority to continue in office for the next four years. However, less than 72 hours after signing a partnership agreement, the parties were in dispute over the Skye Bridge tolls. The agreement said the executive would improve access for rural communities by 'reviewing existing bridge tolls in Scotland and entering into negotiations with a view to ending the discredited toll regime for the Skye Bridge'.

The Liberal Democrats insisted that meant the tolls had to be abolished, 'otherwise we would not have agreed to the partnership agreement', while Labour played down the prospect of the tolls being removed completely, suggesting they might be reduced in line with other bridge crossings. John Farquhar Munro, Liberal Democrat MSP for Ross, Skye and Inverness West, in whose constituency the bridge was, responded angrily to what he saw as Labour's backsliding: 'That was one of the main planks to my agreement in entering the coalition agreement, that we have a commitment to abolishing the tolls. Abolishing means abolishing – not reducing or curtailing the tolls, it's abolishing.'

He would later threaten to resign unless the tolls were removed by the end of 2004. Nobody was in any doubt he would have carried out his threat. John was a man who would put constituents' interests above those of his party if they were irreconcilable. Equally, nobody doubted if he stood again as an independent in any resulting by-election he would have been returned with an even greater majority. By that time, the Scottish Executive was having to pay VAT on the tolls after a ruling by the European Court of Justice in September 2000 which had said the UK was breaching EU regulations by not applying the tax to the tolls.

In May 2004, the Highland Council decided to petition the Court of Session for a judicial review of the charges. Scottish ministers had had enough of this troublesome PFI scheme they had inherited from the Tories, and the tolls were abolished in December that year. The campaigners had done their job.

Some years later a film *An Drochaid/The Bridge Rising* was screened on BBC Alba. It revealed that the protesters actually had sympathisers among members of the forces of law and order who had to clamp down on those refusing to pay. Former police sergeant Dennis Hindman, who was based on Skye during the protest and was repeatedly called to the bridge, revealed: 'If I hadn't been a police officer, I would probably have been a member of SKAT and would probably have been down there protesting.'

There was also a moving contribution from David Hingston, procurator fiscal at Dingwall Sheriff Court. He became something of a hate figure for the campaigners, but in the film he revealed his true thoughts: 'The whole of the Skye Bridge protest was stressful on quite a number of people. I was one of them,' he said. 'PFI in my personal opinion is a fraud on the public. It is an abuse of government. This vast extra workload [prosecuting SKAT] impinged significantly on me and my own health, and probably contributed to my ultimate nervous breakdown.' But he was clear: 'It has to be said that the Skye Bridge protest succeeded. I have no doubt whatsoever that had they not made a protest, we would still be paying to cross that bridge at whatever inflated rate Miller was demanding from the public.'

Oh yes, and in the middle of it all I gave evidence to the Criminal Cases Review Commission after Robbie the Pict had not been called to enter a plea at the court diet in Dingwall. The commission decided I was telling a lie, and so was Cailean Maclean, who had said the same. We were *not* lying.

# 15

# Blowing the Whistle

SOME OF THE most important yet troubling news stories come from whistleblowers, who normally contact the press as a last resort, having exhausted all internal procedures to have their concerns taken seriously. Too often the complaints are in the first place brushed aside, and more often than not a process begins to identify then blacken the name of whoever has had the audacity to challenge those in authority. Frequently, the resulting story focuses on steps taken to cover up the failures highlighted rather than the substance of the original complaints.

One of the most difficult whistleblowing stories I had to work on was published in June 2000. It was difficult because it involved what had become the near-sacred mission to establish a University of the Highlands and Islands (UHI). The project had been widely embraced by all sections of the wider community, not least the Highland media. This was particularly true in the early days when the idea was being developed by Sir Robert Cowan, Chairman of Highlands and Islands Enterprise (HIE), who died in January 1993. He had been a truly impressive man. HIE and the Highland Council pursued the project and had as the project's academic adviser Professor Sir Graham Hills, one-time Principal of Strathclyde University.

Their vision was to gradually develop a university based on a partnership of the region's existing colleges and research institutions linked by high-capacity telecommunications networks. This then novel idea unlocked the support of local authorities and enterprise bodies from Shetland to Argyll. By 1996 the project had progressed far enough to secure the backing of an initially reluctant Scottish Office. This all changed when Michael Forsyth became Secretary of State and was followed by a grant of more than £33 million from the Millennium Commission.

It was not just to be a university in the region but of and for the region. It was to be a federation in which, as in the London University model, the colleges would, in effect, be the university and the central core would be tiny. It became known as the Polo-mint model. However, this proved difficult to achieve, and progress slowed and the target date of full university status by 2001 was becoming quite unrealistic. In June 2000 *The Herald* had learnt that the UHI project had been told officially by the Scottish Executive that it was not being designated as an institution eligible for the funding by the Scottish Higher Education Funding Council that it had been seeking as a first step. Also, that it would be 'some years before the institution will meet the criteria for a university title'.

More worrying, however, was that I was contacted by several staff within the Inverness-based management of the UHI project, complaining about their treatment at the hands of the then chief executive (I have decided not to name him here as his identity is irrelevant to my argument). What the staff were telling was deeply disturbing. I have never revealed it all, not least as my informants might have been identified. On Saturday 10 June 2000, we published a front-page story under the heading 'Staff strife amid university bid'. It began: 'The chief executive of the £100 million project to establish a university of the Highlands and Islands has been accused of mismanagement, intimidation, oppressive, autocratic and divisive leadership, resulting in a serious breakdown of staff morale.'

What my sources further described, I now realise, are common features in whistleblowing stories: particularly high levels of sickness leave and stress-related absences amongst staff; 'gagging clauses' beyond normal confidentiality constraints in contracts that many people leaving had to sign; and a complaints procedure which was totally ineffective and led in the first place to the chief executive himself or one of his close subordinates. Former colleagues of the chief executive, who had worked with him at other centres of higher education, contacted me to say that they were not surprised by the story.

An official of the Association of University Teachers Scotland confirmed he had helped to negotiate departure terms for more members at UHI than at any of the much larger, established universities in Scotland over the previous three years. The UHI project, however, was so well supported that many people simply refused to believe the story or the accompanying article by Sir Graham Hills on how the original vision of UHI was being betrayed. Those most closely involved with the appointment of the chief executive were highly critical of the story. I was 'leant on' by some powerful people who suggested I desist from further disclosures as it would damage the UHI's prospects of university designation. It was blatant moral blackmail – I had always supported the idea of a university. But the UHI senior managers by that time had already made a huge mistake in their denials, issuing a written statement (I couldn't be accused of misquotation) which said: 'UHI has not received any complaints of this nature from any member of staff and does not respond to unsubstantiated anonymous allegations. It takes these matters very seriously and has in place formal procedures for staff grievances which were agreed with the UHI staff association as well as a public interest disclosure policy and procedure to address any concerns raised through due process. No-one has taken recourse to these arrangements.'

This was repeated by an official when speaking to other Highland journalists a few days later. By this time I knew that was not true, and could prove it if necessary, but it would involve revealing the identity of my sources. We were also to learn that not only had there been complaints, but there had been a meeting to discuss them. The UHI chairman, Sir Fraser Morrison, who had been chairman of HIE, asked that agency's ombudsman, retired Scottish Officer civil servant Kenneth McKay, to investigate.

In September 2000 the board of governors of the UHI project issued a public apology over the cover-up of staff complaints against the former chief executive, who had decided to retire towards the end of August. In a statement issued on his departure he had said of his detractors: 'It is clear to me that the real agenda of this cabal has been to derail the progress of UHI towards designation.' This was nonsense.

Mr McKay's report was only ever published in redacted form, but it was still forthright. It said: 'I think it was inevitable that the UHI staff would eventually take their concerns to outside people and to the media. It is, I think, an indication of the commitment of those concerned to the UHI project that they delayed for around six months before pursuing their complaints outwith UHI. I do not think that staffing and management issues relating to any organisation should be dealt with in public, but I can fully understand why the present situation regarding UHI has occurred.'

Mr McKay was stinging in his criticism of the statement issued by UHI, denying that any complaints had been made: 'I would go further than say that the statement issued to *The Herald* was a terrible faux pas. Even noting [the chief executive's] arguments that the complaints had "not been formalised through the due process" and had not been formally recorded in any of the UHI systems, I would utterly condemn the terms of the statement for a number of reasons.'

These were that it was factually incorrect – formal complaints had been made; it gave the appearance of 'a cover-up or conspiracy'; it reinforced staff fears that their complaints were not being taken seriously; and it undermined the operation of the whistleblowing procedure. Mr McKay also found 'a strong view amongst UHI staff that they could not take their complaints to the chair of the board of governors [Sir Fraser] because of a perception he had "covered up" a previous difficulty regarding [the chief executive's] performance and was likely to continue to give him his full backing'. Mr McKay said while that perception was 'real enough', he was in no doubt it was mistaken.

The most outspoken critic of UHI's handling of the affair was Black Isle councillor Dr David Alston, a member of the UHI Foundation consultative body who is now chairman of NHS Highland. He said at the time: 'The publication of the McKay report and the statement from the board of governors of UHI are vital signs of what I hope is the board's commitment to greater openness, and the spirit of this action must be continued. They are a breath of fresh air.'

There was however never any investigation into the substance of the allegations, only the way they had been handled. Great strides were noticeably taken, however, to improve the management of the project thereafter. The appointment of Professor Alistair MacFarlane, former Principal of Heriot-Watt University, was a masterstroke. UHI eventually won full university status in February 2011, although it had been awarding degrees for three years before that.

## NHS whistleblowing

In 2017 BBC Radio 4's series *File on 4* broadcast a disturbing programme. Two years after the first independent report into the treatment of NHS whistleblowers was published, the programme investigated whether those raising concerns about patient safety were properly protected. It found that doctors who had spoken up since 'say they've faced the same catalogue of bullying and abuse by their employers' and, in some cases, the focus remained on protecting reputations rather than addressing poor care.

Six years after the UHI story, David Tierney, a senior official in NHS Western Isles, tried to blow the whistle on mismanagement and bullying and was sacked. Following representations made to him for over a year from senior staff, and in the absence of a proper whistleblowing procedure, Mr Tierney decided to write of his concerns to a non-executive board member. His professional association, the Institute of Healthcare Management, said the letter was addressed 'in strict confidence', but it was subsequently passed to the board's chairman, who was the focus of some of the concerns raised. The then Scottish Executive refused to hold an inquiry, insisting issues be dealt with locally despite a 90-page dossier with statements from 12 witnesses. Seven months later, however, a management team was sent to Stornoway by ministers to take over the running of the health board.

The Western Isles did not feature in the Radio 4 programme but Dr Jane Hamilton did. *Herald* readers would have remembered her story. We revealed how the consultant perinatal psychiatrist believed her career in Scotland had been ruined after she raised concerns about the mother and baby unit (MBU) at St John's Hospital in Livingston and warned in writing that patients could die. Two women who had been patients subsequently took their own lives. Another mother being treated there suffocated her nine-month-old daughter while suffering from severe depression. A subsequent investigation by the Mental Welfare Commission found that multiple chances to help the mother and daughter were missed.

There were other critical incidents. The first story I wrote on Dr Hamilton was in the summer of 2013. Livingston was obviously not in the Highlands and Islands, but NHS Highland did have an arrangement to send patients to the MBU there. The first story was that a doctor who had sounded the alarm over the safety of patients in the MBU had been off work for four years through suspension and stress-related illness. This was Dr Hamilton, who claimed she had been victimised as a result of her whistleblowing, and later that there had been attempts to gag her. This was denied by NHS Lothian, who sought to reassure the public of the high standards of care within the MBU.

Following that story Jim and Jan Waggitt contacted me. One of the women mentioned in the original story had been their daughter, Claire Donald, who had thrown herself off the Erskine Bridge. They had never spoken publicly before but Mr Waggitt told me: 'When we read in

*The Herald* that a doctor we had never heard of had tried to warn about the MBU, only to suffer for her trouble, it made us think long and hard. The more so after the health board tried to gloss over everything in a letter to *The Herald*, which really shocked us. That is what made us go public about Claire's death. However, we are now left with this one recurring thought – if only they had listened to Dr Hamilton.'

Claire had twice tried to commit suicide before and her parents and husband believed there was a failure to diagnose a severe psychotic illness which was far more profound than that normally described as post-natal depression. They were convinced she should never have been released from the MBU and claimed that 'Claire's last cry for help' was effectively ignored after staff were told she had suicidal thoughts but did not take her back in to the unit or even visit her. NHS Lothian insisted that Dr Hamilton's concerns had been fully investigated, but I received a phone call from a woman who was still working in the MBU who would not give me her name as she feared losing her job. She asked me not to write about what she was going to tell me as she might well be suspected of being the source. She was clearly distressed and said, 'I just want you to know that what Dr Hamilton has been saying was right and we believe she has been treated appallingly. When the so-called investigation was ongoing we tried to tell those investigating that we shared Dr Hamilton's concerns. But they just didn't want to know. They were there to write a report that everything was OK because they knew the people in charge.'

While working on the story I found some senior figures in the NHS happy to hint that I should not believe everything Dr Hamilton said; that she had 'history'. These were smears, so common in whistleblowing stories. Dr Hamilton, indeed, came to mind when I was reading Jim Hunter's great book on the Sutherland Clearances referred to earlier in which he highlighted the story of Gordon Ross, a Strathbrora schoolmaster who had complained publicly about the House of Sutherland's treatment of its tenants in so called 'improvements'. He also had the temerity to complain about his sick wife and children, including one two months old, being evicted by men who had been drinking whisky through the previous night. One daughter died three weeks later. The Duke and Duchess of Sutherland and their agents, who did not like to be the subject of public criticism, particularly in newspapers circulating in the south, saw to it his name was blackened.

Dr Hamilton settled with the health board and departed 'ungagged', convinced that a genuinely independent inquiry into the failings she identified was still desperately needed. Since then she has only able to find work south of the border, after being apparently blacklisted in Scotland. NHS Scotland chief executive Paul Gray, who subsequently met Dr Hamilton, told the BBC *File on 4* programme: 'We have asked Dr Hamilton if she would be willing to help us with advancing our understanding of the issues faced by whistleblowers and, of course, if she is willing to do that, we will be very pleased.' Whether he ever did anything about those who had demonstrably traduced her remains unknown.

What remains clear, however, is that more has to be done to protect whistleblowers. The provision of the likes of a helpline is hopeless if it just takes the complainer back to the body or eventually the individual who is the subject of the complaint. Obviously some whistleblowers may be vexatious, motivated to make mischief or to settle workplace scores. The frequent cost, professional and financial, to the genuine whistleblower, however, is unacceptable. Any journalist taking up a whistleblower's cause has to be satisfied it is justified. Corroboration, even provided off the record, is vital but not always easy to get. Whistleblowers should not have to depend on the press to get justice. It is difficult not to wonder just how many cases fall by the wayside because people are not willing to go down that route. Dr Kim Holt, the paediatrician victimised after warning of serious failings at the Great Ormond Street clinic in London which sent Peter Connelly, Baby P, home two days before he died in 2007, was supportive of Dr Hamilton, contacting the Scottish Health Minister Alex Neil. She helped me with my stories. She founded the Patients First group to make the NHS more open and accountable. Dr Hamilton was involved in setting up ASAP-NHS, an action group established to promote a safe, transparent and accountable NHS in Scotland. Both groups seek the establishment of a genuinely independent regulatory body and at the time of writing the Scottish government did seem to be moving towards appointing an independent national officer for whistleblowing, which would be effectively a branch of the ombudsman's office. This would be an important step forward, but what is really needed is a culture change. The default position should no longer be to cover up mistakes, and then do the same about the resulting complaints. What starts with a human error should not have to end badly. In 2018, an independent investigation into NHS Lothian ordered by the Scottish government found a culture of bullying and harassment.

# 16

# Dounreay

IN THE SUMMER of 1988 a newspaper carried a cartoon featuring the captain of a German freighter called *Karin B*. He was on the telephone to directory enquiries asking for the phone number for the Caithness Tourist Board. At that time the vessel was lying 20 miles off Plymouth, with her skipper at a loss to know where to sail to next. She had spent more than a month searching for a site to unload her cargo of toxic waste which was of Italian origin but had been picked up in Nigeria. She was wandering the seas after France, Britain, Spain, West Germany and the Netherlands had refused to let her land. The cartoon referred to another story. Members of Caithness Tourist Board had just given Lord Thurso a massive vote of confidence as their honorary president.

He had offended environmental opinion across the country by agreeing that the nuclear industry's waste management agency Nirex could conduct test bores on his land. This was to assess its geological suitability to host a national nuclear waste repository for intermediate level waste.

Earlier that year Caithness had been stunned by the announcement by Energy Secretary Cecil Parkinson that the Dounreay fast breeder reactor would be run down over the next nine years, reducing the workforce from 2,200 to 500. Some estimates held that 40 per cent of the population of Caithness depended on the nuclear facility which had been built in the 1950s to be at the forefront of atomic energy research, as far away from the centres of population as possible. Following the Parkinson announcement there was even talk of publicly assisted packages for people who worked at Dounreay to leave Caithness and build a life elsewhere.

It was in this atmosphere of social and economic despond that Lord Thurso had been talking to Nirex. A local fishing writer, Bruce

Sandison, had been behind a special meeting of the Caithness Tourist Board in Watten Village Hall. His argument was that if the tourist board continued to support Lord Thurso as its honorary president, it would be seen to support the idea of the county becoming a dumping ground for everyone else's nuclear waste. This could fatally damage local tourism. But Lord Thurso insisted that Mr Sandison did not represent public opinion and that the attack was part of a personal vendetta. Speaking to me in his home beside the ruins of Thurso Castle for a *Herald* profile we carried of him in September 1988, he said: 'He [Mr Sandison] has been after me because I gave him a ticking off for writing articles in fishing magazines inciting people to backpack all over the place, helping themselves to any fishing they came across. He admitted breaking into an unoccupied building of mine and spending the night there and suggesting that others should do likewise, and I took this up very strongly with the editor. That's where it all started.'

Lord Thurso won the day at Watten by 56 votes to nine, but his repository plan was to come to nothing even though he admitted his lawyers had come to an understanding with Nirex. Indeed, within a few weeks of the row the United Kingdom Atomic Energy Authority (UKAEA), which operated Dounreay, had decided that it too should alert Nirex that it was willing to have the site considered as a possible location for the proposed nuclear waste dump. In March 1989 Nirex published a short list of two possible sites, Dounreay and the Sellafield nuclear plant in Cumbria.

In response to a Freedom of Information request, Nirex confirmed in 2005 that there had been another earlier shortlist of possible sites, which had previously been considered, but not published: the small island of Fuday off Barra; the island of Sandray just to the south; Dounreay; Altnabreac on Lord Thurso's land in Caithness; and a site somewhere under the sea off Hunterston in North Ayrshire. In England there were another seven potential dump sites: two in Essex, two at the Sellafield nuclear plant in Cumbria, one in Norfolk, one in South Humberside and one under the sea off Redcar in Yorkshire. The information released by Nirex showed that this shortlist of 12 sites had been selected from a longer list of 537 potential sites, of which 159 had been in Scotland. Most of the Scottish sites were in the Highland Region (45) and Strathclyde (40), followed by the Western Isles (21), Shetland (17) and Orkney (15). It even mentioned some of our most famous islands: Iona, Islay, Jura, Canna, Eigg, Muck, Coll, Gigha, Colonsay, Tiree, Ulva, Raasay, Rum, St Kilda, Foula, Ailsa Craig, the Summer Isles and the Isle of May in the Firth of Forth. There were also military bases and training areas such as Lossiemouth, Kinloss, Leuchars, Rosyth, Machrihanish, Barry Buddon and Cape Wrath. Even Redford Barracks in Edinburgh was regarded by Nirex as a potential waste dump.

But in the end Nirex restricted its potential sites to those that were owned by the government or the nuclear industry, or where private landowners had offered their land. Dounreay became a frontrunner for the repository, which would occupy 350 acres, 1,500 feet underground. However, with news that this would entail 15 trainloads of nuclear waste arriving in Caithness every week, opinion in the north began to harden, with Highland Regional Council at the forefront. The local authority was convinced that a Nirex repository would spell economic and social disaster for the environmentally sensitive industries which underpinned the economy of the Highlands and Islands: tourism, fishing, agriculture, whisky, etc. But more important was the health risk of 90 per cent of the UK's nuclear waste coming to Dounreay. Critics could point to Inverness's rail bridge being swept away by the floodwaters of the River Ness two years earlier, a bridge over which the 15 weekly trains would have to travel. There was also a sense of injustice growing. In the spring of 1987, just months before Mrs Thatcher's third election victory, the UK government had announced that it was abandoning plans to establish a low-level nuclear waste repository in one of four rural areas of England: South Killingholme in Humberside, Fulbeck in Lincolnshire, Bradwell in Essex and Elstow in Bedfordshire. All four were in seats held by Conservatives, three of them by government ministers including Chief Whip John Wakeham.

The job losses at Dounreay and Nirex were to occupy many column inches in *The Herald* and elsewhere. The 120 miles from Cromarty to the nuclear plant became a well-worn path. But on one occasion the Highland press corps went further afield in pursuit of these stories, to Forsmark in Sweden to view the nuclear waste repository there. The Highland journalists had been flown over courtesy of the UKAEA, presumably to report back how successfully the repository had been operating. My only lasting memory of the trip was the CND logo painted on the rock at the bottom of the underground facility.

On my return I phoned Ronnie Anderson, the *Herald*'s assistant editor, who was in charge of the 'Perspective' page which carried news features. I said I just wanted to check with him when he wanted an article on Forsmark from me, as I was about to head off to my sister-in-law Ishbel's wedding on Skye. She was marrying another journalist, BBC Scotland's Alan Mackay. Scottish journalism being a relatively small world, I had known Alan for years. Ronnie asked if there was anything in the news line to report from Sweden, and when I said there wasn't, he replied: 'Write me a piece on the wedding in Skye. It sounds a bloody sight more interesting than a nuclear waste dump in Sweden.' *The Herald* could be a joy to work for!

One of the main architects of the Highland Regional Council's anti-Nirex strategy was Councillor Peter Peacock, the council's finance convener and later chairman of Policy and Resources Committee. The strategy was that the public agencies would take responsibility for nuclear waste already in the Highlands but would fight tooth and nail any moves to import more from elsewhere in the UK. He was the one who at a private meeting with ministers and officials was to remind Secretary of State for Scotland Ian Lang of the evidence he had himself given to a public inquiry a dozen years earlier into the Ministry of Defence and the nuclear industry's plans to bury highly radioactive waste deep in Mullwharchar, the 2,260-foot mountain in Mr Lang's Galloway constituency. It is entirely of granite and had been considered a suitable storage site for nuclear waste by government experts in the late 1970s. Mr Lang had opposed the development largely for similar reasons that Highland Regional Council was opposing Nirex in Caithness.

Mr Peacock spoke of the exchange for the first time during interviews for this book. He said:

I was rehearsing our arguments with Mr Lang and indicated they were somewhat the same as his at the Mullwharchar Inquiry. He smiled and said in response, 'Well you have been doing your homework.' We arrived at a discreet understanding. We would not publicly embarrass him by highlighting his previous position on nuclear dumping in Scotland, if in turn he did the right thing in government in respect of Nirex in Caithness. We stuck to our side of the bargain and apparently Mr Lang, now Lord Lang of Monkton, stuck to his.

I remember Doug Macleod of the Shellfish Growers Association being particularly helpful. He produced maps of where radioactive traces from waste emitting from Sellafield were being carried on the Gulf Stream tides right up the west coast. The danger was that, with Nirex at Dounreay, this would carry waste right around the eastern seaboard of Scotland and to Orkney and Shetland. This brought Orkney and Shetland on-board as strong supporters in opposing Nirex and I was in regular touch with the politicians there.

The campaign against Nirex coming to the Highlands was to gain national momentum, going all the way to Westminster and Whitehall. The idea that nuclear waste from across the land would be transported to the edge of the UK mainland for disposal offended many. At the height of the row I went to Dounreay to interview the managing director of Nirex, Tom McInerney. The article appeared in December 1990 under the heading 'The man they love to hate in the Highlands'. In fact I found him a rather charming, decent man, who just couldn't quite understand the row. He said: 'I find it odd that placing solid material 1,500 feet below ground can be seen as menacing when it is a benign operation. The stuff just stands there. Some of it people can handle with safety in their working day with a pair of tongs of very modest shielding and it is to be below 1,500 feet of geology. You have nuclear establishments that emit radioactive gas every second of the day; they have discharge limits on liquid effluent that discharges regularly into the waters; they have a radiation level at the fence. They are all controlled quite safely. It's odd that a nuclear dump, which doesn't do anything, is menacing, but a power station which emits something is not seen as menacing.'

But the problem was not really nuclear waste, but the fact that few outsiders trusted the nuclear industry. Even fewer trusted the government's stewardship of it. This was as difficult for Mr McInerney to understand, having spent his life in the industry, as it was for the rest of us to continue to trust official assurances about its safety. Many articulate voices were raised in opposition. None more so than that of Lorraine Mann, who was convener of a group called Scotland Against Nuclear Dumping. She was to be the leading critic of Dounreay over Nirex and later.

Growing up in the Edinburgh suburb of Corstorphine, she remembered the Cuban missile crisis and parents saying they would kill their children rather than see them die slowly from radiation sickness. She began reading about nuclear matters and never stopped. She moved to the Highlands as a primary school teacher, married and set up home near Fearn on the Easter Ross peninsula. In the mid 1980s she was at a mother and toddlers' group in Invergordon when a friend said that she had read an article about nuclear waste coming through Invergordon bound for Dounreay. This wasn't Nirex, but the proposal to establish a European Demonstration Reprocessing Plant (ERDP) at Dounreay. 'We both said somebody should do something,' Mrs Mann recalled. She was to do something a year later, appearing as a lay objector at the 94-day public inquiry in 1986 into the reprocessing plant idea. The EDRP never came, but the next thing which appeared over horizon was Nirex and its plan to establish the UK's first national nuclear waste repository at Dounreay. Mrs Mann formed a firm relationship not only with Highland Regional Council but also with Highland journalists. She used to ask us, 'Tell me when I have ever knowingly misled or lied to you and can you say the same about Dounreay?' It was not a difficult question to answer.

Away from matters nuclear, Lorraine Mann will be remembered as the person who embarrassed George Robertson, the then leader of the Scottish Labour Party and Shadow Secretary of State of Scotland, in the 'Great Debate' in the old Royal High School building in Edinburgh in February 1995. It was criticised over the absence of Ian Lang to defend the status quo. Alex Salmond was appearing as spokesman for the cause of Scottish independence and Mr Robertson as the advocate of devolution. This was two years before Labour was to win power and another two years before a referendum endorsed the establishment of a Scottish parliament. Mrs Mann was in the audience and said: 'I'd like to ask a question to both of the gentlemen, really, and I think it should be a fairly straightforward and simple one to answer. What is your second choice? We know what your first choice is. We have independence, devolution or the status quo. What is your second choice?'

The *Herald* editorial observed the next day: 'Mr Salmond was able to say devolution without much difficulty. Mr Robertson found several visibly uncomfortable ways not to answer, allowing Mr Salmond to invite the audience to make the obvious deduction . . . This task was made all the easier for them by Mr Robertson's earlier observation that if he thought devolution would lead to independence he would not be arguing for it. That is something which Mr Salmond persuasively predicted (and can be relied upon to ensure) will haunt Mr Robertson for some time to come.' But some in the Labour Party compounded their party's difficulties over the episode by dismissing Mrs Mann as an SNP stooge. She was a member of no party and nobody's stooge. Three years later she was to help found the short-lived party called Cairdeas – the Highlands and Islands Alliance. But 'the Lorraine Mann Question' went down in Scottish political folklore.

In July 1991, after geological surveys, Nirex recommended to ministers that Sellafield and not Dounreay should be the site for the national nuclear waste repository. The campaign against Nirex had proved successful. It was a significant moment for Highland Regional Council, which had provided the democratic will needed. It showed that the days of the landowner-dominated council were over. Henceforth people in the Highlands could expect their local authority to tackle more important issues than trying to keep the rates down. Figures such as Peter Peacock, Michael Foxley and David Green were moving the council's agenda, and Nirex had whetted the appetite of others.

## Dounreay's demise

Neither Dounreay nor Lorraine Mann were to disappear from the headlines. Following the Cecil Parkinson announcement ending the fast breeder research in the spring of 1988, the UKAEA had been looking to establish a continuing role for Dounreay, not least after Nirex's departure. Its focus was increasingly on winning contracts to reprocess nuclear fuel from elsewhere. The 15,000 spent nuclear fuel rods stored at more than 30 research reactors across Europe were of particular interest. The US Department of Energy was opposed to the nuclear fuel rods (which it had been supplying to European reactors over a 20-year period until 1978) being sent to Dounreay for reprocessing. This was seen as inconsistent with its non-proliferation policy because reprocessing left radioactive waste plus weapons-grade material which could be used again. In 1993, for example, the US Department of Energy offered the Belgian research reactor operators SCK-CEN some $500,000 not to proceed with a reprocessing contract at Dounreay.

Official American attitudes to reprocessing at Dounreay were to undergo a fairly radical change, partly because of continued domestic resistance to the waste coming into America, not least from Carroll Campbell, the governor of South Carolina, where the military nuclear complex of Savannah River was located. In addition, the UK Department of Trade and Industry (DTI) had been lobbying American counterparts to send Highly Enriched Uranium (HEU) to Dounreay for reprocessing. The DTI had always denied this but *The Herald* obtained a letter dated 19 May 1994 to the head of the atomic energy division at the DTI which refers to telephone conversations with two scientists who were working in this area. The letter said: 'I was somewhat surprised to find out that neither . . . knew anything about your suggesting to the US DoE that it made sense for the British at Dounreay to deal with spent European MTR [Material Testing Reactor] fuel, leaving the Americans to handle fuel where there was a real proliferation threat.' It also made clear that the previous year the Americans had 'not seriously considered the Dounreay option at all'. US authorities began to see Dounreay as a more attractive option, but from the mid 1990s mishaps and disclosures were to seriously damage the Caithness plant's reputation for competence and safety. It was to end in 1998 with the new Labour government announcing its final decommissioning.

## Things get worse

My first visit to Dounreay was in August 1988 when staff associations and trade unions were holding a meeting to develop a strategy to offset the impact of the Cecil Parkinson's announcement of the run-down of the fast breeder reactor, which really had been Dounreay's *raison d'être*. My first port of call was the UKAEA's press office in the nuclear plant, where conversation started with my being challenged by the chief press officer as to which side I was on: 'Are you for or against Dounreay and nuclear power?' This was intended to establish whether I was an 'anti-nuke'. I hadn't really been involved in the nuclear debate hitherto, although I could recall the campaign against the building of the Torness nuclear power station in south-east Scotland. But it was hardly something that my then employer, the *Times Educational Supplement Scotland*, was interested in covering.

Being questioned at Dounreay was an early indication of just how embattled that part of Caithness felt at that point. Thurso was a company town. Its population had risen from 3,203 to 8,037 between the census of 1951 and that of 1961. This was directly due to the decision in 1954 to create the centre of the UK's fast reactor research and development programme at Dounreay, with people coming from all over Britain to work there – the 'atomics' as they became known. Between 1954 and 1964 over 1,800 new houses were built in Thurso. Meanwhile the number of schoolchildren in the whole of Caithness climbed from 3,926 to 6,010 between 1954 and 1977. There were apprenticeships (Dennis MacLeod, an engineer from Sutherland who made his fortune in gold and diamond mining in South Africa and Canada and came back to endow various projects in the Highlands including the UHI Centre for History in Dornoch, started as a Dounreay apprentice) and a new technical college for school leavers, leading to jobs at Dounreay. All that was apparently being threatened in 1988, when it was hard to find many local critics of the plant. That was slowly to change with revelations of what had been going on there over the years. The work at the plant had come under the Official Secrets Act, which had protected the UKAEA's reputation. The role of Dounreay's regulators, the UK Nuclear Installations Inspectorate, and their apparently close relationship with the UKAEA down the years also came under scrutiny

*The Herald* was closely involved with some important stories which by their nature were often rather complex and difficult to fully understand, never mind report. One for which *The Herald* won praise had nothing to do with what I had written. On April Fool's Day in 1993, Highland Regional Council's planning committee visited Dounreay to consider an application from the UKAEA to extend one of the plant's low-level waste pits. What they saw helped change the public perception of the plant forever. Until then, many councillors and many more members of the public had been happy to accept that Dounreay knew what it was doing and it could be trusted not to pollute the environment. But those visiting the plant that day saw thousands of drums and bags of nuclear waste scattered on the surface of the waste pits. Some of the drums had been lying rusting since 1985. Some were half-submerged in wet concrete. Others were stacked on top of an existing waste pit and covered only by tarpaulins.

The next day *The Herald* was the only paper to publish a photograph of what the councillors had seen. It hadn't been taken by a *Herald* photographer – I didn't have one with me that day. It was member of the UKAEA staff who had offered to organise the photograph. He had been concerned by his employers' stewardship of the site. We never mentioned this in the *Herald* coverage then or since to protect his identity but, given that the plant is being decommissioned, it is safe to do so now.

When the closure was announced, Lorraine Mann said she was convinced the publication of the photograph had been a highly significant development: 'Although the TV cameras were there, it was the fact that people could sit with their *Herald* the next day and study the photograph which made such an impact. They could see the expressions on the councillors' faces. They began to realise how Dounreay had abused the secrecy it had enjoyed. After that, people would not be so willing to take Dounreay's word.'

### From Georgia with love

At the end of October 1997 it was announced that the government had banned fishing within two kilometres of Dounreay, following the discovery of 34 fragments of irradiated nuclear fuel on the seabed that summer which were feared could enter the food chain. Estimates of the number of particles were to grow to many thousands. In 2011 the Scottish Environment Protection Agency (SEPA) announced that the seabed surrounding the Dounreay plant may never be returned to its original pre-nuclear natural state.

In June 1998, however, the government announced that it was approving a transfer of 5kg of highly enriched uranium from Georgia to Dounreay, to keep it out of terrorists' hands in what was then an unstable country. But I was informed by an inside source that the total amount of nuclear material sent to Dounreay from Georgia was 14kg, not just the 5 kg of highly enriched uranium (HEU) publicly stated by the government and the UKAEA. The additional 9kg was low-enriched uranium (LEU). *The Herald* established that the first Scottish Secretary, Donald Dewar, or UK Energy Minister John Battle knew of the true size of the cargo was six weeks after the two lorries carrying the Georgian fuel had arrived in Dounreay.

SEPA, which the government insisted had been fully consulted over the consignment and agreed to it coming, learned about the extra material only when officials read the *Herald*'s story. A SEPA spokeswoman said: 'That was the first we knew about it.' We had also learned that before the Georgian cargo arrived, SEPA had specifically asked the government for its exact configuration. When asked why the information about the extra LEU had not been made public, Dounreay insisted all questions had been answered faithfully, but all questions had related to the HEU. Lorraine Mann supported the HEU being taken out of Georgia to Dounreay, but thought the lack of candour from officialdom was deeply worrying: 'Low-enriched uranium is not a proliferation threat; it can be used for medical purposes, but is no use in weapons construction. This begs the question why it is here at all. It could have safely stayed in Georgia, unless of course there was some commercial quid pro quo in all of this for Dounreay. More important is the issue of honesty and candour. Dounreay says that nobody asked about LEU, but that is quite disingenuous, given the wording of the statement it issued. But we also have the spectre of civil servants lying to Ministers or at least withholding information. It is profoundly damaging to democracy.'

The episode confirmed to many that despite publicly adopting a policy of being open and honest about Dounreay, old habits were dying hard within the UKAEA.

## MUF

That same month (June 1998) another episode further proved that secrecy remained the default position. This was when it was revealed that enough enriched uranium to make more than ten nuclear bombs had gone missing from Dounreay between 1965 and 1968. A report into the contents of the controversial Dounreay waste shaft was published by the UKAEA's own waste management group. It concluded that 170kg of HEU had been unaccounted for and estimated that at least 22kg would have been put in the shaft.

It predicted: 'Unaccountable losses are likely to be spread over various facilities, and are likely to be recovered during their decommissioning.' This led to speculation that the missing material had been 'covertly transferred' into the military programme for bomb making at a time when the Cold War was at its height. Yet it had been denied for 40 years that Dounreay had ever been involved with the development of nuclear weapons.

Just 24 hours after the publication of the report, Dr John McKeown, UKAEA's chief executive, had an explanation for the missing uranium:

'The calculation that was done assumed that there was more material going into the plant to the extent of 1 per cent. It is not a case of the material having been hidden, it is not a case of the material being lost, quite simply it is a case of the material never having existed.' It was a line embraced by Tony Blair in an answer to Alex Salmond on the same day which resulted in the then Prime Minister possibly misleading Parliament. Mr Blair said: 'The allegations about the supposedly missing highly enriched uranium were based on a misrepresentation of 30-year-old records which are far from complete by any modern standards.'

In a withering put-down of Alex Salmond who had raised the issue at Prime Minister's Questions, Mr Blair continued: 'I can confirm that no such material has ever been sent from Dounreay for use for United Kingdom weapons purposes, and I suggest that the Honourable Gentleman reads carefully what has already been said by the chief executive [of UKAEA] and others on the issue. For the Honourable Gentleman to alarm the public in this way is irresponsible in the extreme, but entirely typical of him.'

In the following month, however, the President of the Board of Trade, Margaret Beckett, said the missing material had indeed existed but some had been burnt in the fast reactor and some had been discharged. In a written answer on 27 July 1998, Mrs Beckett insisted that the missing material had not gone into weapons programmes, but continued to confirm that some from Dounreay could have.

> As a result of an audit of the records requested by this Government, however, it is clear that there were in the past documented transfers from Dounreay which related to UK military programmes. Prior to 1973 when AWRE [the Atomic Weapons Research Establishment] at Aldermaston and Dounreay were both part of the UKAEA, it is probable that some of the material transferred from Dounreay to Aldermaston will have been used in the UK weapons programme. This is not the case for any transfers which occurred between 1973 and 1987, when all such transfers ceased, since these involved fuel for uses in reactors only.

In January 1999 a report on the 'material unaccounted for', or MUF, published by the DTI safeguards office said the original report of 170kg having been lost had been a worst-case scenario and 'the material unaccounted for would have been significantly less than 86kg of U-235'. But it had existed. So was it the Prime Minister or the President of the Board of Trade who had misled parliament? It seemed one of them had, but we never knew which.

## TRIGA

In 2000, as Dounreay looked forward to a new green destiny of decommissioning, its past came back to haunt it again with calls for a public inquiry into a £2-million contract to reprocess 17kg of contaminated radioactive fuel from ICI's plant at Billingham in Teesside. Campaigners claimed the contract was a public scandal surrounded by 'intrigue and secrecy' worthy of a Jeffrey Archer novel.

The first anyone heard about the contract was in October 1997, when Dounreay issued a press statement saying it had won the contract to 'process' fuel from Billingham. The work would be done in Dounreay's D2670 plant, which few people seemed to know existed. It was not until February 1998 that a parliamentary question elicited the information that the contract would cover 17kg of something called TRIGA (Training, Research, Isotope, General Atomic) fuel and that it was not for 'processing' but 'reprocessing', which was controversial as it results in significantly greater waste and discharge, all to recover plutonium and uranium. What UKAEA did not mention at the time was that Dounreay had never dealt with TRIGA fuel before and that the US authorities, who regarded TRIGA as high-level waste, had supplied it to Billingham in the first place and were willing to take it back. SEPA, one of Dounreay's two official regulators, confirmed that they had no knowledge of UKAEA's proposal to reprocess TRIGA and that an application to increase discharges had made no mention of it. Lorraine Mann accused UKAEA of trying to set up a new line in commercial reprocessing without official permission.

While the Billingham contract was small, the potential was there for bigger contracts for Dounreay, with 5,000 rods of spent TRIGA fuel lying at reactors in 19 countries across the world, including Bangladesh, Indonesia and Mexico. But by then Dounreay's fate had been sealed.

## The shaft

The Dounreay shaft gained notoriety. There had been an explosion in it in 1977, but little was known about it until the 1990s. It had been sunk through fractured flagstone in 1956 to provide access while a liquid waste pipeline was being built. It was largely unlined and filled with water. This has to be continually pumped to maintain its water levels below sea level to prevent wholesale leakage into the Pentland Firth. Low and intermediate nuclear and chemical waste had been dumped in it as well as other debris from 1958 until 10 May 1977, when a hydrogen explosion blew the concrete cover off the shaft and blasted debris up to 40 metres away. The shaft was then sealed.

There had been a brief mention of an explosion during the Dounreay Inquiry in 1986. Consultants were later called in to advise the government because Dounreay did not want to bear, forever, the extra expense of pumping the shaft. The consultants produced a report in 1990 which was technically in the public domain, but in fact was in the depths of the House of Commons Library. 'You would have had to know about the shaft to ask for the report on it,' one source told *The Herald*. In March 1993 we brought the shaft to the public's attention, highlighting the deep concerns about it held by a respected independent consultant who had just visited the plant.

Dr Peter Kayes, of Environmental Dynamic, had been hired by Highland Regional Council to report on Dounreay's planning application to extend a waste pit. He was 'puzzled' why Dounreay hadn't mentioned the shaft when he had requested full information of radioactive waste disposal in all its forms. He feared that little was known of its contents. He believed that the shaft contained material far more radioactive than that stored in the nearby low-level waste pits, which had been the main subject of his investigations. He said: 'In addition, the strontium 90 levels are some 60 times greater, caesium 137 levels are some 35 times greater, the plutonium 239 levels are 25 times greater, and the plutonium 240 are about four times greater.'

His comments on the pits were even more damning and a month later Highland Council's planning committee made their visit and *The Herald* got its front-page photograph of the rusting drums floating half-submerged in the waste pits. What was equally stunning was the fact that the regulatory authorities, Her Majesty's inspectorates of pollution and nuclear installations, had not seen fit to act on what apparently had been an accepted part of Dounreay life. The question became: just how close an eye had the regulators been keeping on things? They certainly didn't appear to be concerned that for 19 years after 1958 Dounreay had not kept proper documentation of what was being put down the shaft despite the demands of the Radioactive Substances Act 1960, and despite nuclear waste being taken to Dounreay from government research centres hundreds of miles away in England for dumping in the shaft.

The 1990 consultants' report even found that five of 23 drums of strontium titanate brought from Harwell in 1974 were leaking and were a possible source of strontium 90 found on the foreshore. No records had been kept about containers used to dump other wastes but it was 'probable' that some material had been dumped in cardboard drums. The regulatory authorities, however, did not at that time license the Dounreay site, so presumably did not monitor the shaft between 1958 and 1977. One might have thought that they would have been involved in 1977, when there was an explosion serious enough for the shaft to be sealed. The investigation into that explosion, however, was not carried out by the inspectorates or any other independent body, but by UKAEA itself. It stated publicly at the time that surface contamination had been cleared up, prepared a report which satisfied the Industrial Pollution Inspectorate, and that was that. No copy of the report had been published.

But in 1998 an inventory of the shaft's contents recorded 16,348 disposals between June 1959 and May 1977, from rubber gloves and vacuum cleaners to lathes and other machinery. There was also 20 years' worth of nuclear and chemical waste. Drums containing sodium were dumped there in 1959 but nobody knew whether they were intact or not. There was unsupervised fly-tipping and workers fired rifles into the shaft to sink polythene bags which had begun floating on the water. Some experts suggested this could have set off a chain reaction.

At the time it was perhaps strange to think that no UKAEA employee sought to publicise what happened at the shaft, or indeed the later dumping at the pits. But not only were they economically dependent on the plant, since Dounreay's establishment in the mid-1950s the workforce had been subject to the Official Secrets Act and would have faced the very real prospect of prosecution, and indeed imprisonment, for any breach. For so long the nuclear industry had been an integral part of the greater governmental machine, of its defence system, whose traditions of all-pervading secrecy were handed down from the Second World War, and throughout the Cold War. A Dounreay manager was no more likely to blow the whistle on the plant's activities than a nuclear inspector. They were on the same side. Which side the British public was seen to be on was less clear. But the public's trust in the nuclear industry and the government's stewardship of it had been weakening over the previous decade in the face of continued fears about childhood leukaemia and other health risks.

The stark evidence presented by the shaft, the waste pits and the growing number of radioactive particles being found on the foreshore showed that the tradition of secrecy had been badly abused down the years. The plant's most loyal supporters began asking questions, as the *Caithness Courier* reported: 'There is an instinctive reluctance among people in Caithness to criticise a facility which created prosperity and stability in many shops and homes for four decades. As the prosperity and stability begins to subside and the "shock horror" stories begin to occur almost weekly, the signs of unease, worry and suspicion are there to see.'

But the final blow to the Dounreay management's credibility had probably been when we learnt that the main electricity supply and the back-up supply to the Fuel Cycle Area, where the most dangerous nuclear work was undertaken, were both disrupted. This happened at 9 p.m. one evening in May 1998 and they were not restored until 1 p.m. the following day. A contractor working on a digger, digging out ducts for BT, had cut through the main cable, disrupting the power supply. The ventilation system ceased operating and all 300 non-essential personnel were evacuated. The area included the facility where the controversial cargo of nuclear fuel from Georgia was being stored and plant D1203, where the bulk of the fuel was due to be processed at the end of that month. It also embraced the near-40-year-old D1204 plant where 1,200 rods of spent nuclear fuel from Australia would be reprocessed under a contract Dounreay had been hoping to sign. A major safety audit was announced with 10 inspectors from the Nuclear Installations Inspectorate and SEPA going in. A month later the government announced an end to commercial reprocessing. The plant was to be decommissioned, which would take many years and create employment. It was billed as being an exciting new chapter, but the Dounreay management needed help to convince press and public that change really would be delivered.

Lynne Staples-Scott arrived from the Moray Council and started to turn public perceptions round, but when she left to go to work for BP, John Ross – the other member of 'the Ross Bros' – and I were asked by a senior figure in the plant's management what it would take to convince the press that the old Dounreay had gone for good. We said the first thing they should do was appoint Colin Punler as communications manager. Colin had covered Dounreay for the *Caithness Courier* and *John O' Groat Journal* from the papers' Thurso office for many years. No journalist had followed events at the plant more closely than Colin, and he had been prepared to criticise. In 2001, much to our surprise, his appointment was announced. I am sure it wasn't as a result of our influence, but just maybe we started some people thinking. Colin, who had spent so long trying to make the plant accountable, was the right man to help write its new greener chapter. He had a talented team including the likes of Tina Wrighton, who is still there. Journalists accepted that Dounreay's public commitment to being open, honest and transparent had become more than just words.

# 17

# Cromarty Rising

Cromarty boasts one of Scotland's youngest standing stones. The Emigration Stone is 13 feet of Caithness flagstone erected to mark the 200th anniversary of the birth of the town's most famous son, the polymath Hugh Miller. It is a memorial to the scores of emigrant ships which left the Cromarty Firth in the 19th century. Sixty-two were documented to have set sail with passengers from Sutherland, Caithness, Ross-shire and parts of Inverness-shire, virtually all bound for Canada. As they left, crowds would gather on Cromarty Links to wave their farewells. One who witnessed the departures was Miller himself. He was to make his name as a stonemason, writer, geologist and journalist, not to mention as the leading lay figure of the Disruption of 1843 and the establishment of the Free Church. However, in 1831 he was in Cromarty and wrote an article for the *Inverness Courier* about watching one ship leave, laden with Highland humanity, and the mixed emotions of those on board: 'The *Cleopatra*, as she swept past the town of Cromarty, was greeted with three cheers by crowds of the inhabitants and the emigrants returned the salute, but, mingled with the dash of the waves and the murmurs of the breeze, their faint huzzas seemed rather sounds of wailing and lamentation, than of a congratulatory farewell.'

These words now appear on Cromarty's standing stone, courtesy of Richard Kindersley, a stone carver with an international reputation, whose other work includes the memorial in Dunblane Cathedral to the children of Dunblane Primary School killed in the 1996 massacre. Around the edges of the stone appear the names of the other ships which left the firth: the *Brilliant*, the *Canada*, the *Tweed*, the *Triton*, the *Zephyr* – all sailing ships.

In October 2002 Dr Margaret Mackay, the Canadian-born director of the School of Scottish Studies archives at Edinburgh University, stood at the Cromarty shore dedicating the stone. Her great-great-grandparents had been on board one of the ships, the same *Cleopatra* Hugh Miller wrote about for the *Inverness Courier*. She said: 'I am thrilled by this because it was so much part of my family's history. Their long voyage has been passed down in my family over the years. I remember being taken here [Cromarty] when I first visited Scotland in the 1960s. John Mackay was from Torroble, near Lairg, and his wife was Christina Munro, from Balbair, by Bonar Bridge. They were living at Culrain, near Ardgay. There is nothing to suggest that they didn't leave of their own volition. Indeed they were actually able to take extra provisions with them, which was fortunate because the *Cleopatra* took over 13 weeks to cross the Atlantic to Quebec. Normally it took about six weeks.'

Maggie told me earlier in 2018: 'They also took an axle and two wheels with them when they sailed on the *Cleopatra* in 1831. It may be that neighbours or relatives who had gone out before wrote and advised them to bring the makings of a cart, but they bought an ox on their arrival and their descendants were known as the "Ox Mackays" to distinguish them from the many other Mackays in the settlement. They ended up in an area in Oxford County, Ontario, near a place called Thamesford, in townships called Nissouri and Zorra.'

## The fisherfolk's last voice

The East Church in Cromarty on the Black Isle was packed for the funeral of Bobby Hogg in October 2012, who had died aged 92. He lived just up the road from us and had been a good friend of mine, right to the end. His death gave me what was probably my only truly global scoop. Bobby had been the last fluent native speaker of the Cromarty fisher dialect. *The Herald* had broken the news that his passing had ended a linguistic tradition that had stretched back centuries. According to the minister at his funeral, the news of Bobby's death subsequently reached 191 countries. Bobby's grandson, Iain, said that the family had received messages from Holland, Italy, Mexico, the USA, Brazil and Jamaica. David Alston, then local councillor and deputy leader of the Highland Council, was in Poland at a conference where people were talking about it. He said the idea of knowing who the last speaker was and being able to record the death of the dialect so exactly had fascinated several there.

Bobby's younger brother Gordon had been the other surviving tradition bearer, but he had died in April the previous year, aged 86. He was the last person to immediately understand that when his brother was saying, 'At wid be scekan tiln ken?' he was asking: 'What do you want to know?' Professor Robert Millar of Aberdeen University's Linguistics department, and author of *Northern and Insular Scots*, said Bobby Hogg's death was highly significant:

> It is the first time that an actual Scots dialect has so dramatically died with the passing of the last native speaker. This was always going to be the danger of the Black Isle as there were so few speakers even when it was healthy, when the fishing was still good, so Bobby Hogg's passing is a very sad day. It was a very interesting dialect, and was unlike any of the others. There are one or two who still have some facility in the Cromarty fisher dialect, but most of the time they speak Highland English. Bobby was the last fluent native speaker who spoke no other tongue from a child. He was what we term a 'dense' speaker. So all we have now are the recordings. Most of the other Scots dialects still have thousands of speakers with varying degrees of proficiency, although it has to be noted that most of these are healthiest in rural heartlands such as Shetland, the North-east and the upper valleys of the Borders. It is difficult to say what will happen with the other dialects of Scots in the future. It is possible some of these at least will blend into colloquial English.

Bobby Hogg had worked across Britain, from Leicester to Dounreay, but kept coming back to Cromarty. His wife Helen was also from Cromarty and was a direct descendent of Hugh Miller. But the Hoggs were from the separate fishing community. In the 1861 census there were no fewer than 96 living in Cromarty and its environs, and there are still some today. In February 2007 *The Herald* interviewed Bobby Hogg when he and Gordon were about to be recorded by Am Baile, the Highland Council-funded project which has created a digital archive of the history and culture of the Scottish Highlands and Islands. He said then:

Our father was a fisherman and all his folk had been fishermen stretching way back. It was the same on our mother's side, too. When we were young we talked differently in the fishertown to the rest of Cromarty. It wasn't written down. It was an oral culture. We had this sort of patois, which I think had both Doric and Gaelic in it. There were words, a lot to do with the fishing, which nobody else could understand. But there were a lot of other differences in the way we spoke. We would always say 'thee' and 'thine'. The older ones were very biblical in their speech and would always be saying things like 'O Blessed Jesus' or 'O Holy one of Israel'. It wasn't blasphemy. It was just the way they spoke. When we went out in the morning we were always told to 'Put the Lord afore you'. And you would never hear the fisherfolk swear.

He thought the dialect's decline had matched that of fishing in Cromarty. Bobby had watched how the community had changed. When he was young in the fishertown every house along its two streets and all its lanes and vennels had a connection to the sea through fishing or the Royal or Merchant Navy. He would lament: 'Now there is not one person there who goes to sea.'

He recalled there were six people with the name James Watson, so nicknames or bynames had to be used all the time. He himself was called 'Bolt'. He didn't know why but knew it had Shetland origins. His son was called 'Koka', after his great-great-granny. Bobby had been fond of saying: 'Our folk have been fishermen all the way back to Galilee.' But he himself had begun work as a mechanic in a garage in Dingwall, had served in the RAF as a fitter during the Second World War and then went on to be become an engineer working all over Britain. There was a tale for every turn his life took. The Hoggs' home in Cromarty was a place where anyone could drop in for a cup of tea or a dram, but most importantly for the craic, as I can testify. It was the first port of call for many who wanted to learn about Cromarty and its people. According to the records, there were Hoggs in Cromarty in the 16th century when they were boatmen and fishermen. Bobby's daughter returned to live in Cromarty, as does his son and, yes, he has a boat.

## Pouring oil on local waters

Just before Christmas 2015 I was alerted to plans by the Cromarty Firth Port Authority (CFPA) to transfer up to 8,640,000 tonnes of crude oil between tankers lying at anchor just outside the mouth of the Cromarty Firth. Cromarty was the closest community to the proposed transfer site, but neither its community council nor its Highland councillors had been told of the plan. There had been no public consultation apart from a modest announcement appearing in a local paper saying the port authority was applying to the Maritime and Coastguard Agency (MCA) for a licence to conduct the transfers. A local resident happened to notice it. *The Herald* carried an exclusive story on Christmas Eve that year under the headline 'Concern for dolphins in Cromarty oil transfers'. It was the start of a campaign, which at the time of writing is still being waged. The group Cromarty Rising was formed locally and took the fight to the Highland Council, the Scottish Parliament, Westminster, the European Commission and the General Assembly of the Church of Scotland. It was to bring into question Scottish civil servants' actions in handling the issue. It was to reveal the absence of any real public accountability of trust ports such as the CFPA, whose board appoints its own members without any outside scrutiny. This despite being charged with the management of a public asset in the naturally-formed waterway.

The fear was and remains that an oil spill would herald environmental catastrophe and damage the local economy. Cromarty has never experienced tourist numbers in the same numbers as nearby Inverness and Loch Ness, never mind Oban, Skye and Fort William on the west coast. However, in recent years Cromarty has been increasingly identified as a 'green tourism' destination centred on the wildlife and dolphin watching boat trips run by EcoVentures.

Public meetings were held, the largest seen in Cromarty for many a year. At the first, local residents were asked to exit one door and those from elsewhere another. On leaving, the former group had to vote whether or not they backed the port authority's plan, and 100 per cent voted against it. This was not a case of the 'nimbyism' (Not In My Back Yard) which greets so many development proposals. At one of the other meetings the chair of the Cromarty and District Community Council, Jacquie Ross, a deputy headteacher at the local secondary school, put up a photograph of the Cromarty Firth full of oil rigs all the way up to Invergordon and said, 'This is Cromarty's backyard and has been for many years. We have lived with the oil industry for generations and have benefitted from it. Nobody should accuse us of nimbyism.'

What had really annoyed the community was that the port authority had defended its position by saying that ship-to-ship oil transfers had been conducted safely in the Cromarty Firth for 30 years without any local objections. This was entirely true, but seen as disingenuous as these earlier transfers had involved one tanker tying up to the long jetty over at Nigg and a second tanker coming alongside and securing itself to the first. One did not have to be a master mariner to know that was clearly a safer operation than two tankers conducting the operation in an area of open water which itself was environmentally precious. One of the first to sound a warning was Dr Greg Fullarton, a Cromarty-based environmental consultant whose specialism was marine biology. He said:

> This could be disastrous to conservation interests. The main protected area is the Moray Firth Special Area of Conservation, designated for the bottlenose dolphin population. We have the Rosemarkie to Shandwick Coast Site of Special Scientific Interest [SSSI]; the Cromarty Firth Special Protection Area; the Cromarty Firth SSSI; and the Cromarty Firth Ramsar site all within a few miles. They have been designated by government here and in Europe precisely because they need protection. The emergency coastguard tug is based in Orkney, so if something goes wrong there is potential to wipe out dolphin, seal and salmon populations not to mention the birds for which the firth is renowned. The port authority's environmental modelling seemed to be based on one tonne of oil escaping; however these tankers will transfer up to 180,000 tonnes at a time. Neither does the modelling take any account of the fact that the wind can blow from the east for several weeks a year, and that the tide goes in as well as out. So any spillage could be blown or swept right up the firth, and not just away from it as has been assumed.

He wasn't alone in his concerns. Professor Paul Thompson had been leading dolphin research at Aberdeen University's Lighthouse Field

Station in Cromarty for over a quarter of a century and said: 'If you were trying to find a place in Europe that posed the maximum risk to a protected dolphin population, this would probably be it. It is one of the most predictable places bottlenose dolphins will visit in Europe, and they occur here throughout the year. Most of the North Sea's bottlenose dolphins occur on the east coast of Scotland, and there are days when 25 per cent of this population could be within a few miles of that site.'

Professor Thompson said that in the event of an oil spill, it could not be assumed that dolphins, seals, porpoises or any other marine mammals or wildlife would simply swim away. There was no recognised research evidence to suggest that they would. 'So it would be incredibly challenging for anyone to produce a risk assessment which didn't recognise that there was a residual risk of a catastrophic oil spill that could have a major impact on the dolphin population. My argument is that at least at a Scottish level, ideally a UK level, we should be doing a strategic assessment to determine whether we need to do ship-to-ship transfers. If we do, then we should establish where on balance these should occur. Ironically, this comes at a time when Scotland is involved in major work on marine spatial planning with Marine Conservation Areas [MCA].'

Thompson said dolphins were protected under the European Habitats Directive, and many people assumed that oil transfers could not be permitted within this Special Area of Conservation. But that wasn't necessarily the case, he argued: 'For many years now we have worked to reduce arguably much lesser threats, developing codes of practice for wildlife cruises and controlling disturbance from recreational boat users. However, this application to transfer millions of tonnes of crude oil every year in the most sensitive part of this protected area is now receiving serious consideration by the MCA.'

The campaign gained momentum. Well over 100,000 signed a petition against the port authority's plan and 27 local community councils around the wider Moray Firth objected or expressed their concern. It highlighted the dysfunctionality of the current devolution arrangements, whereby the UK Department for Transport, through the MCA, was responsible for deciding whether the oil transfer plan posed an acceptable risk to the environment, when it was the Scottish government which was charged with protecting that same marine environment under European law. But there was also impatience with the Scottish government's apparent reticence to become involved, in marked contrast to ministers' approach some years earlier. In 2007 the Scottish government had asked the harbour authority Forth Ports to freeze plans for ship-to-ship oil transfers in the Firth of Forth by SPT Marine Services, who wanted to pump about 7.8 million tonnes of Russian crude oil a year between tankers anchored four miles off the coast. Local authorities on both sides of the estuary voiced opposition to the scheme. In the face of such opposition Forth Ports announced in February 2008 the plan would go no further.

The Scottish government claimed that it had not been consulted over the Cromarty Firth plan. Documents released under Freedom of Information to the Cromarty Rising group, however, revealed that Marine Scotland, the government body responsible for the country's seas, had been approached directly by the MCA, which was considering the application. Departments in Edinburgh also consulted internally on the plans with discussions about what position ministers should take in response to the serious environmental concerns that were raised. Officials prepared four drafts of a response to the MCA's consultation only for it to be blocked by a senior civil servant. The documents also revealed that ministers were not being briefed initially by their officials, whose default position appeared to be supportive of the port authority. Local campaigners feared that if they weren't winning the battle in Edinburgh, they had little chance of persuading the Southampton-based MCA.

In 2017, however, the MCA issued a statement: 'The MCA has directed Cromarty Firth Port Authority to withdraw the application made in 2015 and submit a new application. On behalf of the MCA, CFPA will undertake a public consultation on this new application, and the full involvement of the Scottish government, environmental agencies and wildlife organisations will be sought. The MCA will be contacting organisations and individuals who contributed to the first consultation to inform them of the new consultation.'

*The Herald* subsequently asked the MCA to release the internal briefing papers behind its decision. The agency did so without hesitation. The documents showed that Cromarty Rising's concerns and criticism of the CFPA's application had been well founded. Crucially, the MCA said the purpose of wanting to carry out the oil transfers at all 'is not explained'. It pointed out ship-to-ship operations were already carried between tankers lying alongside the nearby Nigg Oil terminal jetty, 'and no reason has been given why these cannot continue'.

'These have considerably less risk than STS [ship-to-ship] at anchor, both as regards the probability of an incident and as a consequence from the oil spills,' the MCA said. Further, it did not accept, as the application suggested, that the worst case scenario was that only one metric tonne would be released in an oil spill. It questioned whether the appropriate equipment was available in the Cromarty Firth and said the Oil Spill Contingency Plan showed the necessary response would be operational in four hours: 'This timing is unacceptable due to the proximity of land and the need to contain and recover any spill very quickly,' the MCA said. Meanwhile, the importance of the area for the dolphins was not fully recognised 'and needs significantly more detailed assessment', the MCA insisted. 'The physical risk to marine mammals from the proposed STS operations does not appear to have been considered at all.' The MCA calculated the port authority's plan would have involved 576 vessel movements a year.

John Finnie, Scottish Green Party MSP for the Highlands and Islands, said: 'This complacency from the CFPA shows local communities were right to raise serious concerns over the proposals. No consideration was given to the potential consequences of a spill. CFPA's failure to even acknowledge the potential scale of any leak is seriously concerning, as is the complete absence of any contingency measures.' But a spokeswoman for the port authority, which has always insisted it takes its environmental responsibilities very seriously, said: 'We will be submitting a revised application addressing the points raised by the MCA.'

As of August 2018, when I finished editing this book, no new application has been submitted by the Cromarty Firth Port Authority. But the campaigners had not been resting on their laurels. In January they complained to the European Commission over Scottish ministers' failure to intervene to stop the port authority proceeding on important nature conservation grounds. Lawyers advised Cromarty Rising that for the oil transfers to proceed, a separate licence must be obtained from the Scottish government's agency Marine Scotland under Article 12 of the European Protected Species Directive because of the impact on bottlenose dolphins.

The Scottish government issued a statement:

> We have made our position on this matter clear – powers over the licensing of ship-to-ship oil transfers are reserved to the UK government and must be devolved for applications in Scottish waters. The waters of the Cromarty Firth are a haven for seals and dolphins, and Scottish Ministers are far from convinced oil transfers could take place there without an unacceptable risk to the marine environment. We are not aware of any current application to the UK Government for a new ship-to-ship oil transfer licence either in the Cromarty and Moray Firths, or in any of Scotland's waters, but we would expect the UK Government to invite Scottish ministers and local communities to respond to any future applications.

It didn't go far enough for the campaigners. It seemed, however, to be a far remove from the Edinburgh administration's initial position to support the port authority on the quiet, while saying as little as possible publicly, all under the technical camouflage that only Marine Scotland had been directly consulted by the MCA. The contrast with the official response to the earlier plans for the Firth of Forth has never been properly explained.

There has been speculation since then that Scottish ministers had taken the issue more seriously and behind the scenes had been putting pressure on the port authority not to submit a second application.

## Trust ports

There was another important issue raised by Cromarty Rising. It brought to the attention of MSPs on the Scottish Parliament's Petitions Committee the absence of any mechanism to scrutinise decisions taken by a trust port such as the Cromarty Firth Port Authority. It was created by an act of parliament in 1973, but was devolved along with other such ports in Scotland. Since 2003 it has appointed its own board members without the ministerial scrutiny they were subject to before devolution.

In 2012 the Scottish government's agency Transport Scotland produced guidance for the good management of trust ports. It said: 'Trust ports are independent statutory bodies, governed by their own local legislation and run by independent boards who manage the assets of the trust for the benefit of stakeholders.' It listed these stakeholders, including 'local and regional businesses' and 'the local community'. Campaigners said 27 community councils around the Cromarty, Moray and Dornoch Firths were such stakeholders and had opposed the port authority's application. Local businesses had also raised concerns. But Transport Scotland confirmed to *The Herald* that it could not interfere in the port authority's business, and nor could Scottish ministers. The only course for redress, if 'stakeholders' believed the port was acting against local interests, was to go to court. It remains a mystery how, in the 21st century, a body created by an act of parliament to manage a marine waterway shaped by natural forces is above any official democratic scrutiny. There is a glaring public interest deficit in this, which MSPs should address.

Whatever the final outcome of the Cromarty Firth ship-to-ship controversy, the Cromarty Rising group has served its community well. No new jobs have been associated with the port authority's plan. Its justification is to earn more money for reinvestment in port facilities at Invergordon. This of course is what a trust port should be doing but, as far as anyone could establish, the amounts it stood to earn were modest – £577,000 a year. Internal accounting aside, the port authority's approach to the project and lack of meaningful public engagement are seen by many as an object lesson on how a quasi-public body should not behave.

Cromarty Rising is another example of how, when threatened, communities so often throw up the right people to lead them. In Cromarty's case there was the scientific authority of Greg Fullarton and Paul Thompson; there was the expertise of Duncan Bowers on the oil industry, having spent much of his working life in it; there was the local councillor Craig Fraser, who was happy to badger his colleagues higher up the SNP chain of command; and there was Jacquie Ross, whose chairing of large protest meetings was a tour de force, displaying control doubtless necessary to take school assemblies. It has been one of the joys of my jobs to observe how communities come together in such a way when necessary.

## Our wonderful eccentric

Cromarty has boasted many people of significance and some great characters, but none is more fascinating that the 17th-century laird Sir Thomas Urquhart. He was one of the great eccentric geniuses of Scottish history and claimed to have traced his forebears back to Adam and Eve. I had heard of him from Sorley, who had long been intrigued by him and the report that Urquhart had died in exile in the Netherlands, in 'an immoderate fit of laughter' brought on by hearing news of the restoration of Charles II to the throne in 1660. Urquhart was possessed of an extraordinary mind which was recognised by Sorley's friend the poet Hugh MacDiarmid in his 1936 book *Scottish Eccentrics*.

Urquhart was no ordinary laird. He was also a writer, translator, philosopher, traveller and soldier. He published a treatise on mathematics that few could understand, pondered the mysteries of natural philosophy and wrestled with the reasons for the existence of so many colours. He translated the works of François Rabelais, the French Renaissance writer and humanist who specialised in rude fantasy, satire, the grotesque and bawdy jokes and songs. This corpus of work includes the likes of 'Gargantua's Discourse on Bum Wiping'. Urquhart's translation was hailed by some as 'more Rabelaisian than Rabelais' and a work of lasting genius. He opposed the hysteria of witch hunts but claimed to have 'openly purged' many who had been communicating with 'foul spirits'.

He denounced Scottish bankers who went off to London to make their fortunes and indeed invented a word to describe city bankers – quodomodocunquizingclusterfists, which should perhaps come back into use. He was no kinder to lawyers, Presbyterian ministers or his creditors. It was said that he and his brother imprisoned their father in Cromarty Castle to prevent him from running up more debt, whereas Sir Thomas himself tended to run away from debt, usually to continental Europe. An Episcopalian, he fought on the Royalist side in the Covenanting Wars of the 17th century and in support of Charles II against Oliver Cromwell's army. He fought at the Battle of Worcester in 1651 where he was taken prisoner but successfully bargained for his freedom by offering Cromwell his plans for a universal language. Cromwell never got the plans, but did get unexpected support from Urquhart when he co-wrote a pamphlet defending Cromwell's dissolution of Parliament in 1653. Scotland should make more of Sir Thomas.

I was going to end with our wonderful eccentric, but decided to leave you with some thoughts on Cromarty which did not appear in *The Herald*. I was asked by members of the Cromarty & District Community Council to write an introduction to *Cromarty: An Illustrated Guide*, which they were publishing in 2001 in conjunction with the Cromarty Courthouse Museum. Here it is:

As you turn the corner at Davidston and begin the long descent of the A832 into Cromarty, the physical features of the Cromarty Firth play a trick on your eyes. To the north are the waters of the firth but as you look eastwards past Cromarty you see the Sutors, the two hills which guard the entrance to this famous natural harbour. They appear to squeeze the water up towards the sky, creating a split-level sea. A distant oil tanker seems to be permanently on top of the far horizon, too nervous to move, balancing precariously for all the world as though one big wave could tip her over the edge. The illusion should serve to warn visitors that they are approaching somewhere a bit different, where images can confuse. The view of the Sutors' sea has certainly stayed with this writer since first visiting Cromarty in 1988, little knowing this place was to be home from that year. It took just one visit to realise that this village, which is not a village (officially) but a town which used to be a royal burgh was like nowhere else in the land. Every community is unique but, with apologies to George Orwell, some are more unique than others. Certainly, that was the first impression which these last years have done nothing to change.

There are plenty of fishing villages with their quaint fisher-towns, right up and down the east coast of Scotland, but here there were huge elegant 18th- and 19th-century merchants' houses rising within a creel's throw of the cottages. In between them there were lanes and vennels which were almost Parisian or Provençal in their feel, which made no sense whatsoever. There was 17th-, 18th-, 19th- and 20th-century architecture with families living in examples of each. There was a brewery, brewing no beer and huge stables sheltering no horses. There were three buildings called 'The Factory' which were houses, a restaurant and a pub. There were tennis courts unused and covered with weeds, but across the fence bowlers were in serious competition on a green lovingly kept. Even the Sutors, the hills mythology held were two guardian shoemakers, were different viewed from Cromarty. They didn't seem to be Scottish in character at all. They appeared to belong more in a calendar from New Zealand, probably the North Island.

There were children, boys and girls, playing football on the area of grass between the primary school and the shore, with none looking up as three throbbing tugs passed close by, pulling a reluctant rig back out to sea to earn her keep – just one part of the young footballers' landscape, nothing remarkable at all. After all, sometimes there would be oil rigs all the way up the firth, lighting the winter darkness like Christmas trees. There was a statue of Hugh Miller with a seagull on his head next to a chapel with no roof. This place would be hard to leave. That remains as true today as it did then. Perhaps the more so, having learnt a little more of the place. Learnt from those who can still close their eyes and see Cromarty as she was between the wars; when there were over 20 shops in Church Street alone; when there was little room on the pavements on Saturday afternoons as families from the 'farm touns' around the Black Isle came down to do their shopping for the week; when there was a daily ferry service to Invergordon as well as Nigg; when the Royal Navy still thought of the firth as home from home for its fleets.

Like everywhere else Cromarty changed and changes still, as the oil rigs in the firth bear witness. They symbolise a very specific period in our economic history. Their fabrication across the water at Nigg, their maintenance in the firth and their operations in the North Sea, have yielded wage packets for many Cromarty homes. Yet the rigs represented something more, an unimaginable departure from what had gone before. If all the sailors buried round the firth were to rise one day to look across their familiar waters, they would recognise the cruise liners on their way to Invergordon, the

North Sea supply boats, the tugs, the *Cromarty Rose* ferry, as all being variations on a very ancient theme, but what could they make of these castles in the sea? They would, however, probably recognise the dolphins as old friends, still making their tours of inspection apparently untroubled by all the late 20th-century development and certainly appearing to enjoy their new celebrity. Killer whales have also paid a visit recently, coming within 100 metres of Cromarty harbour. This visit, by all accounts, is unprecedented in living memory. So will they return? Perhaps they will. Most do once they understand that the Sutors don't really push the sea up to the sky. It just seems that way.

Now I am off to learn Gaelic.

# Index